CliffsNotes®

EMT-Basic Exam

CRAM PLAN™

Northeast Editing, Inc.

WILEY

Wiley Publishing, Inc.

About the Author

Northeast Editing, Inc. has been developing electronic and print products for educational publishers since 1992. Founded by Tracey Vasil Biscontini, the company works with clients to create high-quality, socially sensitive test-preparation and library-reference products, textbooks, teacher guides, and trade books for students of all ages.

Located in a former rectory in Jenkins Township, nestled between Wilkes-Barre and Scranton in northeastern Pennsylvania, the company employs ten full-time editors, several part-time employees, and a large pool of local freelance authors and editors. The staff enjoys a relaxed work environment that feels like a home away from home.

When they're not hard at work, the editors and writers at Northeast Editing, Inc. enjoy breaks in a large backyard and take time to scratch the bellies of the three rescued cats that live at the office.

Editorial

Acquisitions Editor: Greg Tubach

Project Editor: Lynn Northrup

Technical Editors: Julia Diane R. Fox, Nick Montelauro

Composition

Wiley Publishing, Inc. Composition Services

CliffsNotes® EMT-Basic Exam Cram Plan™

Published by:
Wiley Publishing, Inc.
111 River Street
Hoboken, NJ 07030-5774
www.wiley.com

Copyright © 2011 Wiley Publishing, Inc.

Published by Wiley, Hoboken, NJ
Published simultaneously in Canada

Library of Congress Control Number: 2011922787
ISBN 978-0-470-87813-2 (pbk)
ISBN 978-1-118-01760-9 (ebk)

Printed in the United States of America
10 9 8 7 6 5 4 3 2 1

Table of Contents

Introduction

In every city and town across the country, emergency medical personnel are standing by to deliver life-saving care in the event of a medical emergency or accident. Emergency medical service (EMS) professionals, including EMT-Basics, are dedicated to not only preserving life, but also to improving the quality of life for their patients.

The life of an EMS professional is extremely rewarding, but it can also be very challenging and stressful. EMS professionals must have the ability to remain calm in dangerous situations and think quickly to resolve problems. These abilities are critical to your success as an EMS professional.

In addition, every EMS professional must be dedicated to a life of learning. The world of emergency medicine is always changing, requiring EMS professionals to learn new skills and hone the skills they already possess to provide patients with the best care.

Of course, before you ever set foot in the field, you must take and pass a state-approved EMT-Basic course modeled after the National Standard Curriculum developed by the National Highway Traffic Safety Administration (NHTSA). In most states, you're required to complete between 110 and 150 hours of training in the classroom. After completing the course, you'll be eligible to take the EMT-Basic exam, and upon successful completion you will receive your certification.

Levels of Certification

If you're holding this book, then you've already taken the first steps to starting your career as an EMT-Basic. The EMT-Basic is just one of several levels of EMS certification. The basic levels of certification, which may vary from state to state, include the following:

- **Certified first responder.** Some cities and states provide training programs for first responders. As the name suggests, first responders are often the first emergency personnel to arrive on the scene of an accident or medical emergency. These individuals are trained in basic lifesaving procedures, such as oxygen administration and basic airway maneuvers. Some first responders are also trained in the use of an automated external defibrillator (AED), which is often used in cardiac emergencies.
- **Emergency Medical Technician-Basic.** EMT-Basics must complete a state-approved course modeled after the national guidelines developed by the NHTSA. During this training, candidates learn how to respond to medical and trauma emergencies. EMT-Basic candidates are trained in airway management, respiratory and cardiac emergencies, and patient assessment. In addition, they learn the basics of scene assessment and technical operations. Most EMT-Basics are trained in assisted medication administration, which requires a basic understanding of pharmacology, anatomy, and physiology. Additional training is sometimes required depending on state guidelines.
- **Emergency Medical Technician-Intermediate.** The training that EMT-Intermediates receive is similar to the training that EMT-Basics receive, with a few additional courses of study. In addition to the core curriculum, EMT-Intermediates receive training in advanced airway maneuvers, intravenous fluid administration, and medication administration.

- **Emergency Medical Technician-Paramedic.** Paramedics are the most highly trained EMS professionals. Like EMT-Basics and EMT-Intermediates, paramedics must take an NHTSA-approved course. However, paramedics must complete about 1,400 hours of clinical training and a field internship before they can receive certification. Their training includes comprehensive knowledge of advanced airway techniques, medication administration, and trauma emergencies. Many paramedics complete additional training in specialized fields, such as critical-care transport or pediatrics.

EMS Agencies

There are many types of EMS agencies that you can contact for information about employment once you receive your certification. The different types of EMS agencies that may be available in your region include the following:

- **Volunteer agencies.** Volunteer agencies are generally made up of concerned citizens who devote their time and skills to serving their communities. In most cases, volunteers do not get paid for their services. However, these agencies will sometimes sponsor people in their EMS training. Many EMTs start their careers at a volunteer agency because it's a great place to receive hands-on training and gain experience.

- **Municipal agencies.** Municipal agencies are often organized and supported by a state, city, or town. Often, you'll need to take a written exam in order to gain employment with one of these agencies. Unlike volunteer agencies, these organizations have the ability to provide EMTs with salaries and certain benefits. There is also the opportunity for career advancement at these agencies.

- **Hospital-based agencies.** In some cities and towns, hospitals have their own ambulance services that cover specific areas. These agencies are very similar to municipal agencies in terms of the level of care they are able to provide to patients and the various benefits they can offer to employees.

- **Proprietary agencies.** Proprietary agencies are private EMS agencies that are assigned to a specific hospital or area. These agencies are often contracted by hospitals or municipalities that do not have their own EMS transport systems. Proprietary agencies may also provide specialized services, such as air medical transport.

- **Other agencies.** Other EMS agencies include first-responder units, air medical transports, and specialty EMS agencies. First-responder units provide first-responder services to emergency calls in various regions. Air medical transport is often called on during trauma emergencies that require rapid transport to a hospital or specialized facility. Specialty EMS agencies sometimes work on movie and TV sets or provide services for special occasions, such as sporting events.

About the Test

Before you can start your career in emergency medicine, you must pass the EMT-Basic exam. Most of the state exams are based on the national exam developed by the National Registry of Emergency Medical Technicians (NREMT). This standardized test is designed to measure your competence in a number of important subject areas.

It costs around $70 to take the EMT-Basic exam. This nonrefundable fee is charged every time you attempt to take the test. Candidates have six opportunities to pass the EMT-Basic exam. After failing the first three attempts, the candidate must complete 24 hours of remedial training before taking the test again. The candidate will then have three additional attempts to pass the exam. If the candidate fails to pass the exam during these final three attempts, he or she will be required to take the entire EMT-Basic training course again.

The test has between 70 and 120 questions. You will have two hours to complete the exam. The following chart provides a breakdown of the types of questions that you will most likely see on the EMT-Basic exam:

EMT-Basic Exam Topics	Percentage of Questions on NREMT-Basic Cognitive Exam
Airway and Breathing	18%
Cardiology	17.3%
Trauma	16.7%
Medical	15.3%
Obstetrics and Pediatrics	16%
Operations	16.7%
Total	**100%**

It is important to remember that your state exam may contain questions that are not included on the NREMT cognitive exam. In addition to reading this book, you should review the notes from your class and the objectives of the National Standard Curriculum to ensure that you're prepared for any question that may come up on the exam.

In January 2007 the NREMT changed the format of their test to a computer-based test (CBT). Candidates now take the exam at a computer within a testing facility. The NREMT uses a computer adaptive testing (CAT) method that tailors the exam to each individual.

The system delivers one multiple-choice question at a time. The first few questions help the computer measure the candidate's abilities. When the candidate answers a question correctly, the computer will select a slightly more difficult follow-up question. When the candidate answers a question incorrectly, the computer will choose a slightly easier question. As the candidate continues to answer questions, the computer determines whether the candidate's ability meets the passing standard.

Your state may not adhere to the NREMT's testing guidelines, so it is important to contact your local testing facility for more information. To find out more about certification testing in your area, turn to the appendix, "Resources for EMT Candidates," to find the contact information for your state EMS agency.

Your exam results are usually available within a week or two. Candidates taking the NREMT exam can often access their results within 24 to 48 hours of taking the exam on the NREMT Web site. An overall score of 70 is often considered passing. If you don't meet the passing standard, you can retake the exam. Your local testing facility will provide more information on when you'll be eligible to retake the test.

Certain state licensing agencies may utilize a scoring system that differs from the one employed by the NREMT. Contact your state's division of emergency medical services to learn more about the scoring guidelines for certification in your area. Again, you can locate the contact information for your state EMS agency by turning to the appendix.

About This Book

The first step in preparing for the EMT-Basic exam is to determine how much time you have to study for the test and select the appropriate Cram Plan: the two-month plan, the one-month plan, or the one-week plan. Each plan has a schedule for you to follow, along with estimates of how much time you'll need to complete each task.

Start by taking the diagnostic test, which will pinpoint your strengths and weaknesses. The answer explanations will indicate the areas of study in which you need the most practice. Each chapter includes practice exercises that will help strengthen your skills in various subject areas. At the end of the book, you'll find a full-length practice test, which will give you an idea of how you might perform on the EMT-Basic exam.

I. Diagnostic Test

The purpose of the Diagnostic Test is to identify the areas that require further study as you prepare to take the EMT-Basic exam. This Diagnostic Test includes questions that you may see on the National Registry of Emergency Medical Technicians (NREMT) cognitive exam. However, it is important to remember that some of you will be taking state or municipal exams that differ from the NREMT exam. Therefore, this Diagnostic Test includes questions that may not be included on the NREMT cognitive exam. This is done to ensure that you're exposed to a variety of subjects that may appear on other EMT-Basic exams.

The number of items on the NREMT cognitive exam can range from 70 to 100. Candidates have two hours to complete this exam. Again, it is important to remember that not every EMT-Basic candidate takes the NREMT exam. Therefore, the number of items you see on a state or municipal exam and the amount of time you have to complete the test may differ.

The Diagnostic Test includes 100 questions that cover the following subject areas:

- Airway techniques
- Patient assessment
- Medical emergencies
- Trauma
- Treatment of infants and children
- Operations
- Advanced airway maneuvers
- Anatomy and physiology

Although the NREMT exam uses a computer-based testing model that chooses questions at random based on the candidate's answers, the questions on this test are grouped by subject to help you identify target areas for your study sessions. Note the questions you answer incorrectly so you can review the subject areas that continue to present problems.

Answer Sheet

1 Ⓐ Ⓑ Ⓒ Ⓓ	36 Ⓐ Ⓑ Ⓒ Ⓓ	71 Ⓐ Ⓑ Ⓒ Ⓓ
2 Ⓐ Ⓑ Ⓒ Ⓓ	37 Ⓐ Ⓑ Ⓒ Ⓓ	72 Ⓐ Ⓑ Ⓒ Ⓓ
3 Ⓐ Ⓑ Ⓒ Ⓓ	38 Ⓐ Ⓑ Ⓒ Ⓓ	73 Ⓐ Ⓑ Ⓒ Ⓓ
4 Ⓐ Ⓑ Ⓒ Ⓓ	39 Ⓐ Ⓑ Ⓒ Ⓓ	74 Ⓐ Ⓑ Ⓒ Ⓓ
5 Ⓐ Ⓑ Ⓒ Ⓓ	40 Ⓐ Ⓑ Ⓒ Ⓓ	75 Ⓐ Ⓑ Ⓒ Ⓓ
6 Ⓐ Ⓑ Ⓒ Ⓓ	41 Ⓐ Ⓑ Ⓒ Ⓓ	76 Ⓐ Ⓑ Ⓒ Ⓓ
7 Ⓐ Ⓑ Ⓒ Ⓓ	42 Ⓐ Ⓑ Ⓒ Ⓓ	77 Ⓐ Ⓑ Ⓒ Ⓓ
8 Ⓐ Ⓑ Ⓒ Ⓓ	43 Ⓐ Ⓑ Ⓒ Ⓓ	78 Ⓐ Ⓑ Ⓒ Ⓓ
9 Ⓐ Ⓑ Ⓒ Ⓓ	44 Ⓐ Ⓑ Ⓒ Ⓓ	79 Ⓐ Ⓑ Ⓒ Ⓓ
10 Ⓐ Ⓑ Ⓒ Ⓓ	45 Ⓐ Ⓑ Ⓒ Ⓓ	80 Ⓐ Ⓑ Ⓒ Ⓓ
11 Ⓐ Ⓑ Ⓒ Ⓓ	46 Ⓐ Ⓑ Ⓒ Ⓓ	81 Ⓐ Ⓑ Ⓒ Ⓓ
12 Ⓐ Ⓑ Ⓒ Ⓓ	47 Ⓐ Ⓑ Ⓒ Ⓓ	82 Ⓐ Ⓑ Ⓒ Ⓓ
13 Ⓐ Ⓑ Ⓒ Ⓓ	48 Ⓐ Ⓑ Ⓒ Ⓓ	83 Ⓐ Ⓑ Ⓒ Ⓓ
14 Ⓐ Ⓑ Ⓒ Ⓓ	49 Ⓐ Ⓑ Ⓒ Ⓓ	84 Ⓐ Ⓑ Ⓒ Ⓓ
15 Ⓐ Ⓑ Ⓒ Ⓓ	50 Ⓐ Ⓑ Ⓒ Ⓓ	85 Ⓐ Ⓑ Ⓒ Ⓓ
16 Ⓐ Ⓑ Ⓒ Ⓓ	51 Ⓐ Ⓑ Ⓒ Ⓓ	86 Ⓐ Ⓑ Ⓒ Ⓓ
17 Ⓐ Ⓑ Ⓒ Ⓓ	52 Ⓐ Ⓑ Ⓒ Ⓓ	87 Ⓐ Ⓑ Ⓒ Ⓓ
18 Ⓐ Ⓑ Ⓒ Ⓓ	53 Ⓐ Ⓑ Ⓒ Ⓓ	88 Ⓐ Ⓑ Ⓒ Ⓓ
19 Ⓐ Ⓑ Ⓒ Ⓓ	54 Ⓐ Ⓑ Ⓒ Ⓓ	89 Ⓐ Ⓑ Ⓒ Ⓓ
20 Ⓐ Ⓑ Ⓒ Ⓓ	55 Ⓐ Ⓑ Ⓒ Ⓓ	90 Ⓐ Ⓑ Ⓒ Ⓓ
21 Ⓐ Ⓑ Ⓒ Ⓓ	56 Ⓐ Ⓑ Ⓒ Ⓓ	91 Ⓐ Ⓑ Ⓒ Ⓓ
22 Ⓐ Ⓑ Ⓒ Ⓓ	57 Ⓐ Ⓑ Ⓒ Ⓓ	92 Ⓐ Ⓑ Ⓒ Ⓓ
23 Ⓐ Ⓑ Ⓒ Ⓓ	58 Ⓐ Ⓑ Ⓒ Ⓓ	93 Ⓐ Ⓑ Ⓒ Ⓓ
24 Ⓐ Ⓑ Ⓒ Ⓓ	59 Ⓐ Ⓑ Ⓒ Ⓓ	94 Ⓐ Ⓑ Ⓒ Ⓓ
25 Ⓐ Ⓑ Ⓒ Ⓓ	60 Ⓐ Ⓑ Ⓒ Ⓓ	95 Ⓐ Ⓑ Ⓒ Ⓓ
26 Ⓐ Ⓑ Ⓒ Ⓓ	61 Ⓐ Ⓑ Ⓒ Ⓓ	96 Ⓐ Ⓑ Ⓒ Ⓓ
27 Ⓐ Ⓑ Ⓒ Ⓓ	62 Ⓐ Ⓑ Ⓒ Ⓓ	97 Ⓐ Ⓑ Ⓒ Ⓓ
28 Ⓐ Ⓑ Ⓒ Ⓓ	63 Ⓐ Ⓑ Ⓒ Ⓓ	98 Ⓐ Ⓑ Ⓒ Ⓓ
29 Ⓐ Ⓑ Ⓒ Ⓓ	64 Ⓐ Ⓑ Ⓒ Ⓓ	99 Ⓐ Ⓑ Ⓒ Ⓓ
30 Ⓐ Ⓑ Ⓒ Ⓓ	65 Ⓐ Ⓑ Ⓒ Ⓓ	100 Ⓐ Ⓑ Ⓒ Ⓓ
31 Ⓐ Ⓑ Ⓒ Ⓓ	66 Ⓐ Ⓑ Ⓒ Ⓓ	
32 Ⓐ Ⓑ Ⓒ Ⓓ	67 Ⓐ Ⓑ Ⓒ Ⓓ	
33 Ⓐ Ⓑ Ⓒ Ⓓ	68 Ⓐ Ⓑ Ⓒ Ⓓ	
34 Ⓐ Ⓑ Ⓒ Ⓓ	69 Ⓐ Ⓑ Ⓒ Ⓓ	
35 Ⓐ Ⓑ Ⓒ Ⓓ	70 Ⓐ Ⓑ Ⓒ Ⓓ	

CUT HERE

Directions (1–100): Select the best answer for each question or incomplete statement.

1. While treating a patient, you call your supervising hospital on your cell phone and speak to the on-duty medical director regarding treatment of a patient with chest pain. The medical director authorizes an additional dose of nitroglycerine, outside of normal protocol. This is an example of

   A. standing orders.
   B. off-line medical control.
   C. on-line medical control.
   D. consent.

2. Your patient is experiencing uncontrollable vomiting. Upon arriving at the patient's residence, you notice a trash can containing approximately 400–500 cc of bright red blood. You find that the patient is not currently vomiting. Appropriate body substance isolation (BSI) precautions would include

   A. gloves only.
   B. gloves, goggles, and mask.
   C. gloves, goggles, mask, and gown.
   D. no BSI precautions are required for this patient.

3. Guidelines for proper lifting technique include all of the following EXCEPT

   A. keeping the weight close to your body.
   B. keeping your stance as wide as possible.
   C. lifting with the muscles of your legs, not your back.
   D. avoiding twisting your body while lifting.

4. You respond to a call for a "man down." On the scene, you find two police officers and a man lying on a sidewalk. The man is not responding to vocal stimuli. As you begin your assessment, the patient begins moving spontaneously, but he doesn't seem to understand what you're telling him, and he can't answer any of your questions. You may treat this patient

   A. only after obtaining consent from a family member.
   B. only if the patient can verbalize his full consent.
   C. after receiving permission from medical direction.
   D. without obtaining anyone else's consent.

5. An urgent move should be used

   A. when the patient is in immediate danger on the scene of an accident.
   B. when the patient must be moved quickly to treat life-threatening problems.
   C. for patients who require rapid transport but with spinal immobilization maintained.
   D. without regard for spinal immobilization.

6. Nasopharyngeal airways should not be used in patients suspected of having

   A. skull or facial fractures.
   B. jaw fractures.
   C. cervical fractures.
   D. hemorrhagic shock.

7. The preferred method of providing artificial ventilation is the

   A. one rescuer bag-valve mask technique.
   B. two rescuer mouth-to-mask technique.
   C. two rescuer bag-valve mask technique.
   D. two rescuer mouth-to-mouth technique.

8. You respond with your partner to a 911 call for a "man down." Upon arriving at the scene, you find the patient lying face down between two cars in a parking lot. As you begin your assessment of the patient, you notice noisy breathing. You know that to open this patient's airway, you should first use

   A. a head-tilt chin-lift maneuver.
   B. an oropharyngeal airway.
   C. a nonvisualized airway such as the Combitube.
   D. a jaw thrust maneuver.

9. The most common cause of airway obstruction is

   A. food.
   B. vomitus.
   C. the tongue.
   D. airway swelling.

10. You can assume that a patient has a patent airway without further assessment if the patient

    A. has a pulse.
    B. is conscious.
    C. does not complain of dyspnea.
    D. can speak without difficulty.

11. You are ventilating an apneic patient with a bag-valve mask. To ensure the proper volume for each breath, you should

    A. terminate each breath when you see the chest begin to rise.
    B. completely empty the bag with each breath.
    C. deliver each ventilation quickly to maximize chest pressure.
    D. deliver at least 20 breaths per minute.

12. A disadvantage of the oropharyngeal airway is it

    A. can't be used on patients who have a gag reflex.
    B. doesn't allow the airway to be suctioned while in place.
    C. can't be used on infants or children.
    D. is often difficult to position the airway properly.

13. After opening the patient's airway using a head-tilt chin-lift maneuver, the EMT-Basic should

    A. move on to other assessment steps because the airway has been successfully managed.
    B. ask a bystander or family member to maintain the patient's airway.
    C. remain in place to maintain the airway position and assess breathing.
    D. none of the above

14. You are treating an unconscious patient with gurgling, agonal respirations. After performing a jaw thrust to open the airway manually, your first treatment priority is to

    A. begin ventilations with a bag-valve mask.
    B. complete the initial assessment.
    C. place a nonvisualized airway.
    D. suction the oropharynx.

15. You find an unresponsive patient in the supine position on the floor of a restaurant. The patient has cyanosis of the face, neck, and hands. When he attempts to breathe, you see very little chest rise and hear a harsh, high-pitched squeaking coming from the patient's mouth. The patient's companion says that the patient had not complained of any illness until he abruptly stood up and was unable to speak. You suspect

   A. acute asthma attack.
   B. pneumonia.
   C. foreign-body airway obstruction.
   D. anaphylaxis.

16. Which of the following patients should have a nasopharyngeal airway placed?

   A. a patient who has had difficulty breathing for the past three hours
   B. a patient with snoring respirations after being hit in the face with a baseball bat
   C. a patient with a bloody nose after a rollover motor vehicle collision (MVC)
   D. none of the above

17. Your patient complains of shortness of breath and shows signs of respiratory distress, including cyanosis, tachypnea, and accessory muscle use. The patient's chest rise and fall appears to be adequate. The best device to deliver oxygen to this patient is the

   A. nasal cannula.
   B. nonvisualized airway.
   C. nonrebreather mask.
   D. partial rebreather mask.

18. You are transporting a major trauma patient who you believe to be in hypovolemic shock. During the transport, the patient's ventilations become ineffective, and you begin assisting ventilations with a bag-valve mask. On reassessment, you expect to see

   A. bradycardia.
   B. decreasing pulse oximetry reading.
   C. decreasing blood pressure.
   D. cyanosis.

19. You respond to a nursing home for a call about a patient with a history of COPD. You are told that the patient complained of difficulty breathing, so oxygen was applied at 2 liters per minute by a simple face mask. After several minutes, the patient became drowsy and then unconscious. As you assess the patient, you find him barely breathing and begin assisted ventilations with a bag-valve mask. After a few minutes, the patient improves and begins waking up. Why did the patient rapidly deteriorate after oxygen was applied?

   A. The patient was given too much oxygen.
   B. The patient was allowed to rebreathe carbon dioxide.
   C. The patient could not tolerate the face mask.
   D. none of the above

20. Ideally, patients on oxygen for long periods of time should receive oxygen that is

   A. warmed and humidified.
   B. warmed and dehumidified.
   C. cooled and humidified.
   D. cooled and dehumidified.

21. Which assessment is performed at least once for every patient?

   A. initial assessment
   B. rapid trauma assessment
   C. detailed physical exam
   D. focused history and physical exam

22. The scene size-up begins _____ and is complete_____.

    A. when you arrive at the patient's side; after you have considered all possible hazards
    B. when you arrive at the scene; when the call is complete
    C. when the ambulance is moving toward the call; after you have considered all possible hazards
    D. when the call is dispatched; when the call is complete

23. The purpose for performing the steps of the rapid trauma assessment in the same order each time is to

    A. minimize patient anxiety.
    B. ensure no steps are omitted.
    C. prioritize sources of hemorrhage.
    D. complete the general impression quickly.

24. Patients who should receive a rapid trauma assessment include all of the following EXCEPT

    A. a patient with a single gunshot wound to the leg.
    B. a patient involved in a motor vehicle accident with rollover.
    C. a patient involved in a low-speed, rear-impact MVC who is unresponsive.
    D. a patient who fell from a second-story window.

25. Details about the patient's complaint, such as the duration, severity, or activity at onset, are part of the _____. The mnemonic used to remember these components is_____.

    A. past medical history; SAMPLE
    B. past medical history; DCAP-BTLS
    C. history of the present illness; OPQRST
    D. physical exam; SAMPLE

26. An appropriate interval between reassessments of your unconscious patient might be

    A. 3 minutes.
    B. 6 minutes.
    C. 9 minutes.
    D. 11 minutes.

27. You are called to a residence where a 6-year-old seems to be experiencing an asthma attack. The child's mother meets you at the front door and leads you into the kitchen. Before you even reach the patient, you immediately begin assessing the child's level of consciousness and obvious level of distress. You also search for any visible life threats. This "at a glance" or "doorway" assessment is known as the

    A. initial assessment.
    B. focused assessment.
    C. chief complaint.
    D. general impression.

28. Before beginning treatment of any single patient at an MVC involving multiple vehicles, you should complete all of the following EXCEPT

    A. estimate the number of patients.
    B. assess for scene hazards.
    C. request additional resources from dispatch.
    D. determine which patient you will be transporting.

29. You respond to the home of a 48-year-old male complaining of chest pain. Following the scene size-up and initial exam, what is the proper order of assessments?

    A. rapid head-to-toe exam, detailed physical exam, and focused history and exam
    B. detailed physical exam, ongoing assessment, and detailed physical exam
    C. focused history and exam, ongoing assessment, detailed physical exam, and ongoing assessment
    D. rapid head-to-toe exam, detailed physical exam, ongoing assessment, and focused history and exam

30. After questioning your patient about the details of his chest pain, you ask if he also has shortness of breath, nausea, or dizziness. These symptoms commonly accompany cardiac-related chest pain and are known as

    A. pertinent details.
    B. associated complaints.
    C. signs.
    D. interventions.

31. In which order should the EMT-Basic perform the following steps when assessing the chest?

    A. inspection, palpation, and auscultation
    B. auscultation, inspection, and palpation
    C. palpation, percussion, and auscultation
    D. inspection, auscultation, and percussion

32. The least reliable method of assessing circulation in the adult patient is to assess

    A. blood pressure.
    B. pulse quality.
    C. capillary refill.
    D. skin color.

33. You are caring for a patient who is unresponsive after falling from a roof. After managing all life threats and assessing airway, breathing, and circulation, your next action is to

    A. perform a rapid trauma assessment.
    B. obtain vital signs.
    C. determine the patient's priority.
    D. perform an ongoing assessment.

34. Pulse oximetry is useful for

    A. determining how much oxygen your patient requires.
    B. determining whether ALS is needed.
    C. trending a patient's respiratory status.
    D. assessing a patient's ventilation effort.

35. The detailed physical exam may be omitted for certain patients for all of the following reasons, EXCEPT:

    A. It often leads to little relevant information for patients with localized, nontraumatic complaints.
    B. There may not be time during short transports.
    C. There may not be enough resources if the patient requires critical interventions.
    D. It may yield a diagnosis that the EMT-Basic is incapable of treating.

36. Edema is a common exam finding in patients with congestive heart failure. This can be seen in the patient's

    A. lower extremities.
    B. hips.
    C. neck.
    D. A and B

37. Any positive or negative effect of a medication other than its intended action is known as a

    A. complication.
    B. side effect.
    C. dosage.
    D. indication.

38. You are treating a 34-year-old roofer who has been working outside for more than six hours in high heat and humidity. You determine the patient is suffering from heat stroke. The characteristic of this illness that distinguishes it from other heat-related illnesses is the presence of

A. muscle cramps.
B. dry skin.
C. moist skin.
D. vomiting.

39. Activated charcoal works by

A. acting as an antidote to common poisons.
B. inducing vomiting to eliminate poisons.
C. allowing safe excretion of poisons.
D. preventing additional clot formation.

40. Anaphylaxis is defined as the presence of signs of an allergic reaction combined with

A. airway compromise.
B. respiratory distress.
C. shock.
D. A or C

41. When examining the abdomen, the EMT-Basic should assess for all of the following EXCEPT

A. crepitus.
B. rigidity.
C. rebound tenderness.
D. guarding.

42. You are treating a patient who complains of increasing shortness of breath, swelling of the ankles, and nonproductive cough over the past week. She states that she has been treated for various cardiac problems in the past but has been unable to afford her medications for the last month. As you assess the patient, you find rales in all lung fields. During transport, this patient would be most comfortable in the _____ position.

A. supine
B. prone
C. Fowler's
D. lateral recumbent

43. The Cincinnati Prehospital Stroke Scale evaluates all of the following EXCEPT

A. facial droop.
B. grip strength.
C. arm drift.
D. speech.

44. Patients assumed to be experiencing behavioral emergencies are sometimes actually having a medical emergency causing a change in behavior. Conditions that may mimic behavioral emergencies include

A. hypoglycemia.
B. stroke.
C. heat exposure.
D. all of the above

45. Your ambulance is called to a home for a patient with generalized weakness. When you arrive, you are brought to the bedroom of an elderly patient lying in a hospital bed. The patient is responsive only to loud verbal stimuli and complains only of feeling tired. As your partner begins an assessment, you gather more history and find out that the patient has felt increasingly weak for the past three days and has had little appetite. She denies she has had a fever. The family also tells you that they have noticed the patient passing large amounts of dark, tarry stool during this time period. Your partner reports the patient's abdomen is slightly distended and firm to the touch. You suspect

A. ruptured abdominal aortic aneurysm (AAA).
B. hepatitis.
C. gastrointestinal hemorrhage.
D. appendicitis.

46. Before administering oral glucose to your diabetic patient, you should ensure that the patient

A. has a blood glucose level (BGL) of less than 80.
B. has a blood glucose level (BGL) of less than 60.
C. is conscious and can swallow.
D. is completely unresponsive.

47. While treating a patient complaining of severe difficulty breathing, the patient asks for your help taking his inhaler. You search through his plastic bag of medications, looking for an inhaler marked with any of the following medication names EXCEPT

A. albuterol.
B. Advair.
C. Ventolin.
D. Alupent.

48. In adults, the most common cause of a single, generalized seizure without complications is

A. fever.
B. trauma.
C. infection.
D. none of the above

49. Drug names you may find on medication packaging include all of the following EXCEPT

A. chemical name.
B. trade name.
C. generic name.
D. all of the above may be found on medication bottles

50. The most reliable indicator of the severity of an allergic reaction is

A. amount of antigen to which the patient was exposed.
B. amount of time from exposure to onset of symptoms.
C. route of exposure.
D. body surface area affected by rash.

51. A condition in which the heart is unable to pump efficiently and fluids accumulate in the lungs, neck veins, or extremities is called

A. myocardial infarction.
B. cardiogenic shock.
C. congestive heart failure.
D. pulmonary embolus.

52. Patients who are treated for cardiac arrest and experience a return of spontaneous circulation should

A. have a Combitube or other nonvisualized airway inserted.
B. be monitored closely to ensure that they do not go back into arrest.
C. be allowed to remain at home if pain free.
D. continue receiving chest compressions until they are conscious.

53. Risk factors for thromboembolism events include all of the following EXCEPT

   A. pregnancy.
   B. prolonged travel.
   C. smoking.
   D. Viagra use.

54. A condition in which blood supply to an area of the heart is interrupted or insufficient causing injury to the tissue is called

   A. cardiac arrest.
   B. cardiac tamponade.
   C. myocardial infarction.
   D. arrhythmia.

55. When taking over care of a patient in cardiac arrest from first responders or bystanders who have been performing CPR, you should confirm that the patient is all of the following EXCEPT

   A. pulseless.
   B. apneic.
   C. conscious.
   D. unresponsive.

56. You respond to a call for an MVC and find your patient unconscious with obvious signs of shock but no obvious external injuries. You know that the most common type of shock encountered in the trauma patient is

   A. neurogenic shock.
   B. cardiogenic shock.
   C. hypovolemic shock.
   D. anaphylactic shock.

57. Your patient was stabbed with an unknown weapon in the left upper chest. First responders applied an occlusive dressing and secured it with tape on all four sides. Upon your arrival, the patient is now unconscious with bulging neck veins, tracheal deviation to the right, poor chest rise on the left, and barely palpable pulses. You recognize this injury as _____, and your first action should be to_____.

   A. cardiac tamponade; begin CPR
   B. simple pneumothorax; apply oxygen via nonrebreather
   C. cardiac tamponade; begin artificial ventilation with a bag-valve mask
   D. tension pneumothorax; remove or loosen one side of the occlusive dressing

58. You respond to a call about a stabbing and find your male patient sitting on a bar stool with a broken beer bottle impaled in his anterior thigh. This is your patient's only injury, and the bleeding appears minimal. You should

   A. remove the object, apply pressure, and dress and bandage the wound.
   B. stabilize the object in place with bulky dressings.
   C. apply direct pressure until bleeding stops, and then remove the object.
   D. none of the above

59. Your patient was burned over the entire surface of both anterior legs when she spilled boiling water while cooking. The burns appear as large, red areas that are intensely painful and have already started to form large, fluid-filled blisters. You classify these burns as

   A. third-degree burns, covering 18% of the body.
   B. superficial burns, covering 24% of the body.
   C. full-thickness burns, covering 24% of the body.
   D. partial-thickness burns, covering 18% of the body.

60. Patients with penetrating neck trauma are at greater risk for all of the following life threats EXCEPT

    A. air embolism.
    B. cervical spine injury.
    C. cardiac tamponade.
    D. hemorrhagic shock.

61. While assessing your patient who has a painful, angulated injury to his left lower leg after a skateboarding accident, you notice that the foot is cool, pale, and has no pulses. You should

    A. pull gentle traction until the limb is completely realigned.
    B. splint in the position found and transport rapidly.
    C. pull gentle traction until the limb's pulses and color improve.
    D. none of the above

62. You are assessing the victim of a motorcycle accident who complains of severe pain when either hip is flexed. You notice the patient's feet are both rotated externally. You feel crepitus and the patient screams in pain when you perform a pelvic rock. You should

    A. reassess pelvic rock every 5 minutes to monitor for changes.
    B. apply bilateral traction splints.
    C. apply a pelvic wrap or binder and treat for shock.
    D. all of the above

63. Your patient is a 44-year-old male who was attempting to fix a machine at work when both arms became entangled in the machine. Both arms are now pressed between large pieces of metal. He doesn't appear to be in significant pain, but the factory's mechanics and the rescue team tell you it will be at least 2 hours before they can disassemble enough of the machine to free him. You should expect to treat the patient for

    A. neurogenic shock.
    B. bilateral amputations.
    C. crush syndrome.
    D. minor soft tissue trauma.

64. You respond to a call for a male who put his hand through a window. First responders report a large amount of bright red blood. When you arrive, they are applying direct pressure with three hands and blood is still flowing freely from the patient's upper arm. He appears pale, disoriented, and frightened. After assessing his ABCs, your first treatment should be to

    A. apply pressure to an appropriate pressure point.
    B. elevate the extremity.
    C. apply a tourniquet.
    D. apply high-flow oxygen.

65. You respond to a call about a patient with multiple soft tissue injuries after a domestic disturbance. As you enter the scene, you see that the patient has wounds on each of her arms. One arm is spurting bright red blood. The other arm slowly oozes dark blood from a very shallow wound. You identify these as _____ and _____ hemorrhages, respectively.

    A. venous; arterial
    B. arterial; venous
    C. venous; capillary
    D. arterial, capillary

66. Your patient is a 24-year-old male who lost control of his ATV and struck several trees. On assessment, you find your patient responsive only to painful stimuli with rapid breathing, tachycardia, and diaphoresis. You direct your partner to begin packaging the patient as you continue your assessment and note several small puncture wounds around the left chest and flank, bulging neck veins, and a blood pressure of 70/52. Your patient's breath sounds are clear and equal bilaterally. The patient's most likely injury is

   A. tension pneumothorax.
   B. hemothorax.
   C. cardiac tamponade.
   D. ruptured spleen.

67. When treating trauma patients with suspected head, neck, or back injuries, it is important not to release manual immobilization until the patient is fully immobilized with an appropriately sized cervical collar and

   A. a long spine board with towel rolls or head blocks.
   B. a vest-type short back device.
   C. A or B, but not both
   D. both A and B

68. Of the following, the injury at highest risk for infection is

   A. an animal bite.
   B. a human bite.
   C. a spider bite.
   D. a superficial burn.

69. Your patient is a 19-year-old football player who was "speared" while being tackled approximately 20 minutes prior to your arrival. He complains of left shoulder pain and looks pale. His radial pulse is 130 and weak. You suspect

   A. internal bleeding.
   B. shoulder dislocation.
   C. heat exhaustion.
   D. pneumothorax.

70. Your initial method of external hemorrhage control should almost always be to

   A. use a tourniquet.
   B. locate a pressure point.
   C. attach a splint.
   D. apply direct pressure.

71. The most common cause of uncomplicated seizures in the pediatric patient is

   A. failure to take prescribed medications.
   B. trauma to the patient's head or neck.
   C. fever.
   D. aneurysm.

72. Pediatric patients are at higher risk for airway obstruction for all of the following reasons EXCEPT:

   A. Their necks are longer and less flexible than adults' necks.
   B. They often place foreign objects in their mouths.
   C. Their airways are smaller and more easily obstructed.
   D. Their tongues are proportionally larger than adults' tongues.

73. Pediatric patients who are struck by moving cars commonly

   A. turn to run away and are struck in the back.
   B. turn toward the vehicle and are struck in the chest or head.
   C. fall onto their outstretched arms.
   D. roll up and over the hood and windshield.

74. You are called to a home in the early morning hours for a baby who is not breathing. Upon your arrival, you find several distraught family members. First responders on scene state the 10-month-old patient was found in the supine position in his crib when the mother checked on him in the morning. She found the baby to be cold and limp. First responders verified the patient to be apneic and pulseless. The parents state that the patient had not been ill except for a very minor runny nose and deny any possibility of trauma. After a thorough autopsy, the coroner is unable to determine a cause of death. He is likely to diagnose

    A. abuse.
    B. febrile seizure.
    C. SIDS.
    D. airway obstruction.

75. An important sign of respiratory distress that is common in infants but less common in adults is

    A. suprasternal retractions.
    B. accessory muscle use.
    C. nasal flaring.
    D. pursed lip breathing.

76. To assess the hydration status of a 12-month-old patient, a key question to ask caretakers would be

    A. what the patient's normal heart rate is.
    B. whether the patient appears pale or flushed.
    C. the number of wet diapers the caregivers changed today.
    D. if the patient wet the bed last night.

77. The structure of the pediatric airway is more susceptible to obstruction because it

    A. is more rigid than an adult airway.
    B. is less rigid than an adult airway.
    C. has a smaller epiglottis than an adult airway.
    D. has more cartilage than an adult airway.

78. When treating an infant with a foreign-body airway obstruction, you should alternate _____ until the obstruction is relieved.

    A. five back slaps and five finger sweeps
    B. ten back slaps and thirty chest thrusts
    C. three finger sweeps and five back slaps
    D. five back slaps and five chest thrusts

79. Perfusion is usually gauged in the pediatric patient by assessing

    A. blood pressure.
    B. radial pulse.
    C. carotid pulse.
    D. capillary refill.

80. Of the following, the LEAST suspicious injury when assessing for signs of child abuse is

    A. multiple bruises in different stages of healing.
    B. injuries that don't fit the mechanism of injury.
    C. bruises to the shins and knees.
    D. circumferential burns.

81. When driving in emergency mode with lights and siren operating, ambulance operators in most states are permitted to do all of the following EXCEPT

    A. exceed the posted speed limit.
    B. park wherever needed.
    C. assume that other drivers will see them and yield.
    D. drive the ambulance the "wrong" way on a one-way street.

82. Responders should never approach an operational helicopter unless they

   A. have prior training in proper approach angles.
   B. crouch or duck to avoid the rotor blades.
   C. are signaled to approach by the pilot in command.
   D. are asked to retrieve a piece of equipment by the flight crew.

83. Principles of proper incident command or incident management should be used on

   A. the scene of every emergency response.
   B. any scene with more than one responding unit.
   C. any scene with more than one patient.
   D. a scene where hazards are identified.

84. Basic theory of extrication states that when performing disentanglement at an MVC, the objective is to remove the

   A. patient from the vehicle.
   B. hazards from the extrication scene.
   C. vehicle from around the patient.
   D. patient from the hazardous area.

85. You respond with your partner to a call for a two-vehicle MVC. You are the first on the scene and determine from a distance that a small passenger van with a single occupant was struck by a pickup truck with at least two occupants. A bystander tells you that the pickup truck is carrying a large liquid tank and pump in the truck bed. The tank appears to be leaking, but the driver is unable to tell you what it contains. This scene should be treated as

   A. a hazardous materials scene.
   B. a multiple casualty incident.
   C. too dangerous to enter without assistance.
   D. all of the above

86. The written or electronic run report should be finished

   A. before transferring care to the emergency department.
   B. after the patient's diagnosis is known.
   C. within 24 hours of completing the run.
   D. as soon as possible after the run.

87. What is the first thing you must do when you arrive on the scene of a medical emergency or accident?

   A. Locate the patient.
   B. Identify potential hazards.
   C. Notify dispatch of your arrival.
   D. Perform an initial assessment.

88. Which term describes how ambulance operators must act in regard to other drivers when responding to an emergency?

   A. negligence
   B. compliance
   C. duty to act
   D. due regard

89. When operating at a hazardous materials incident, responders and equipment assigned solely to EMT-Basics should stage in the

   A. hot zone.
   B. transport area.
   C. treatment area.
   D. cold zone.

90. You respond to a call about a sudden out-break illness at a packed gymnasium. Dispatch informs you that dozens of people are sick. You quickly glance at your watch to start a mental timeline and recognize the date as the anniversary of a major foreign invasion five years ago. Immediately you begin to suspect the cause of the illness to be

   A. bird flu.
   B. carbon monoxide poisoning.
   C. a terrorist attack.
   D. none of the above

91. Radio systems that receive, amplify, and rebroadcast radio transmissions are known as

   A. cell systems.
   B. 800 MHz radios.
   C. repeaters.
   D. MDTs.

92. The simplest effective disinfectant solution is prepared by mixing

   A. one part bleach to ten parts water.
   B. two parts bleach to ten parts water.
   C. ten parts bleach to one part water.
   B. ten parts bleach to five parts water.

93. The only position that must be assigned any time incident management is implemented is the position of

   A. transportation leader.
   B. safety officer.
   C. triage sector officer.
   D. incident commander.

94. Oxygen tanks may be identified by all of the following EXCEPT

   A. their blue color.
   B. the two-pin index system.
   C. the USP label.
   D. their medical regulators.

95. Occupants and crew of an emergency response vehicle should wear all available safety restraints

   A. only when traveling long distances or at high speeds.
   B. only when no patient care is being performed.
   C. any time the vehicle is in motion.
   D. whenever there are more than two passengers in the vehicle.

96. Sellick's maneuver involves applying pressure over the

   A. cricoid cartilage.
   B. thyroid cartilage.
   C. carina.
   D. epiglottis.

97. After placing the endotracheal tube and inflating the cuff, you ask your partner to begin bag-valve mask ventilations while you confirm placement. You see unequal chest rise and fall and auscultate clear breath sounds on the right, but no sounds over the left side of the chest or the epigastrum. Your next action should be to

   A. deflate the cuff, withdraw the tube 1–2 cm, and reinflate the cuff.
   B. ventilate through the esophageal lumen and attempt to confirm placement.
   C. remove the ETT and reintubate with a larger tube.
   D. inflate the cuff with an additional 5–10 cc of air to ensure a tight seal.

98. Endotracheal tubes should be secured with tape or a commercial device

   A. before the patient is moved to a carrying device.
   B. as soon as they are placed.
   C. as soon as proper placement is confirmed.
   D. before the ambulance begins moving.

99. Of the following patients, who should be treated immediately with an advanced airway?

   A. a patient with snoring respirations immediately after having a seizure
   B. a patient responsive only to painful stimuli who coughs when suctioned
   C. a trauma patient whose GCS is 13
   D. none of the above

100. When using a _____ blade, the intubator should place the blade _____.

   A. MacIntosh; into the vallecula.
   B. Miller; into the vallecula.
   C. Wisconsin; into the vallecula.
   D. Macintosh; under the epiglottis.

IF YOU FINISH BEFORE TIME IS CALLED, CHECK YOUR WORK ON THIS SECTION ONLY. DO NOT WORK ON ANY OTHER SECTION IN THE TEST.

Answer Key

1. C		31. A	
2. C		32. C	
3. B		33. C	
4. D		34. C	
5. C		35. D	
6. A		36. D	
7. C		37. B	
8. D		38. B	
9. C		39. C	
10. D		40. D	
11. A		41. A	
12. A		42. C	
13. C		43. B	
14. D		44. D	
15. C		45. C	
16. D		46. C	
17. C		47. B	
18. C		48. D	
19. B		49. A	
20. A		50. B	
21. A		51. C	
22. D		52. B	
23. B		53. D	
24. A		54. C	
25. C		55. C	
26. A		56. C	
27. D		57. D	
28. D		58. B	
29. C		59. D	
30. B		60. C	

61.	C	81.	C
62.	C	82.	C
63.	C	83.	A
64.	C	84.	C
65.	D	85.	D
66.	C	86.	D
67.	A	87.	C
68.	B	88.	D
69.	A	89.	D
70.	D	90.	C
71.	C	91.	C
72.	A	92.	A
73.	B	93.	D
74.	C	94.	A
75.	C	95.	C
76.	C	96.	B
77.	B	97.	A
78.	D	98.	C
79.	D	99.	D
80.	C	100.	A

Answer Explanations

1. **C.** *On-line medical control* involves communication between you and a member of medical direction regarding a patient you are currently treating. Off-line medical control involves creation of standing orders, protocols, and quality assurance programs to improve and monitor the overall treatment regimens of all patients. *(Chapter V: Section A.5)*

2. **C.** Because there is a high likelihood of splashing body fluids due to the patient's vomiting, the entire body should be protected from contamination. This means you will need to wear *gloves, goggles, mask, and gown.* You should always choose a level of protection based on the anticipated risk, not the patient's current condition. *(Chapter V: Section A.1)*

3. **B.** When lifting, you should *keep your stance as wide as possible* with your feet approximately shoulder-width apart. You should also keep your back straight, use your leg muscles to lift, keep the weight close to your body, and avoid twisting or reaching while you lift. *(Chapter V: Section A.3)*

4. **D.** This patient is showing signs of having an altered level of consciousness and is unable to make his own decisions regarding consent or refusal of treatment. The patient may be treated under implied consent, which assumes that if the patient were able to make a decision, he would want to be treated for his medical condition. Therefore, the EMT-Basic may treat the patient *without obtaining anyone else's consent.* *(Chapter V: Section C.1)*

5. **C.** An urgent move should be used *for patients who require rapid transport but with spinal immobilization maintained.* This move, however, can only be made when the spine is immobilized. A rapid extrication technique would be a good example. Choices A and B describe indications for performing an emergency move, in which the patient is removed immediately and without consideration of maintaining immobilization. A non-urgent move is the preferred technique when a patient has no apparent significant injuries. In this case, the greatest care is taken to move the patient with as little risk to the spine as possible. *(Chapter V: Section A.4)*

6. **A.** *Skull or facial fractures* increase the risk of the nasopharyngeal airway traveling into the cranium. For this reason, other airways should be employed in cases involving these injuries. *(Chapter VI: Section B.2)*

7. **C.** The bag-valve mask device allows for more precise control over delivered volumes and also allows for delivery of a higher percentage of supplemental oxygen. However, to ensure proper tidal volumes, two hands should be used to maintain a mask seal, necessitating a second rescuer to deliver the breaths. Therefore, Choice C is the best answer. *(Chapter VI: Section C.3)*

8. **D.** Because it's unknown if the patient has sustained any trauma, you must assume a head or spinal injury and, therefore, a head-tilt chin-lift maneuver is your best option. Airway devices such as the oropharyngeal airway or Combitube may be appropriate, but should not be employed before simple maneuvers. Therefore, the *jaw thrust maneuver*, Choice D, is the most appropriate choice. *(Chapter VI: Section B.1)*

9. **C.** Although Choices A, B, and D are common sources of airway blockage, *the tongue* is the most common cause of airway obstruction. All unconscious patients are at risk for this kind of airway obstruction. *(Chapter VI: Section B.1)*

10. **D.** To produce speech, a patient must have an open airway and sufficient control over it to pronounce words. Therefore, you can assume that a patient has a patent airway without further assessment *if the patient can speak without difficulty*. Patients with airway obstructions will not complain of dyspnea because they often will not be able to speak. They may, however, still have a pulse and be conscious for several minutes after the obstruction has occurred. *(Chapter VI; Chapter XII)*

11. **A.** The EMT-Basic should deliver air until *the chest begins to rise*. This ensures adequate tidal volume. The EMT-Basic should then terminate the breath before delivering any more pressure into the chest. Ventilations should be delivered slowly and at a rate of 10–12 breaths per minute to avoid high pressures, which will diminish cardiac output and are more likely to cause gastric distention. *(Chapter VI: Section C)*

12. **A.** The oropharyngeal airway is among the simplest, quickest, and most effective airway adjuncts available to the EMT-Basic. They are produced in sizes appropriate for almost all patients, including infants and children, and they allow the passage of a soft suction catheter either through the lumen of the airway or through grooves on the outside of the adjunct. *It cannot, however, be used on patients who have or may have a gag reflex* because it may stimulate vomiting, which could compromise the airway. *(Chapter VI: Section B.2)*

13. **C.** Any patient whose airway requires manual maneuvers to open must be closely monitored to ensure that the airway remains patent. Assigning that function to another EMT-Basic or higher-trained provider would be appropriate, but assigning it to an untrained bystander would be negligent. Therefore, Choice C is the best option. *(Chapter VI: Section B.1)*

14. **D.** The presence of gurgling noises indicates a liquid airway obstruction. A manual maneuver should be employed, and then you should immediately *suction the oropharynx*. Once the liquid obstruction is cleared, ventilations may be delivered and the initial assessment should be completed. Nonvisualized airways are time-consuming and, therefore, should only be placed after all other assessments are complete unless simple airway adjuncts fail to produce effective ventilation. *(Chapter VI: Section B.3)*

15. **C.** The abrupt onset of the patient's distress and immediate inability to speak should lead you to suspect a *foreign-body airway obstruction*. Other clues include the patient's activity at onset (eating a meal) and the high-pitched sounds made during inspiration, known as stridor. *(Chapter VI; Chapter X: Section C.1)*

16. **D.** Nasopharyngeal airways are contraindicated in patients with signs of facial injury or a mechanism of injury that suggests facial or skull fractures. A patient who is able to speak well enough to communicate a chief complaint most likely doesn't require airway intervention. Therefore, Choice D is the best answer. *(Chapter VI: Section B.2)*

17. **C.** The *nonrebreather mask* is the most appropriate choice from this list. Nasal cannulas and partial rebreather masks are low-flow devices that deliver lower concentrations of supplemental oxygen than the nonrebreather mask. While it may be argued that the patient may need or may soon need assisted ventilation, the patient is conscious, so the nonvisualized airway would be contraindicated at this time. *(Chapter VI: Section C.5)*

18. **C.** After initiating positive pressure ventilation, the patient's tidal volume and pulse oximetry should improve. Pulse rate may decrease, but a patient in hypovolemic shock will most likely remain tachycardic. However, the higher pressures generated in the chest by forced ventilations will reduce the venous return to the heart, especially in a hypovolemic patient. Therefore, the patient's cardiac output will deteriorate and *the blood pressure will likely decrease rapidly*. *(Chapter VI: Section C.3; Chapter IX: Section A.2; Chapter XIV: Section A)*

19. B. Although many providers are told that COPD patients should not receive more oxygen than what they are on continuously at home, it's unlikely that an increased amount of supplemental oxygen will significantly affect the COPD patient in the short time that the EMT-Basic is in contact with the patient (less than several hours). However, the scenario indicates that the patient was given only 2 liters of oxygen per minute. This is less than the 6 liters per minute required to "wash out" the carbon dioxide the patient exhales into the mask. Therefore, *the patient was allowed to rebreathe carbon dioxide*, which led to unconsciousness. *(Chapter VI: Section C.5; Chapter VIII: Section B.2)*

20. A. Gas cools as it is released from a compressed cylinder. Medical oxygen is stored with as much moisture removed as possible to avoid corrosion of storage and delivery devices. Because of this, oxygen delivered over long periods of time can be irritating to the delicate mucous membranes. Systems that can *warm and humidify* the gas before it's delivered to the patient are much more comfortable and can help prevent injuries to mucous membranes. *(Chapter VI: Section C.5)*

21. A. Depending on the patient's mechanism of injury or chief complaint/apparent life threats, he may or may not require a rapid trauma assessment, focused exam, or detailed physical exam. However, an *initial assessment*, sometimes called a primary assessment, must be performed during every patient encounter to ensure that life threats aren't overlooked. *(Chapter VII: Section B)*

22. D. The scene size-up is a continuous process of assessing the scene for hazards and changing conditions. The EMT-Basic should begin this process as soon as information is received about the call. For example, if a call is dispatched about a laceration at a drinking establishment in the early hours of the morning, the EMT-Basic should immediately begin considering what hazards may be present (bleeding, crowds, intoxicated patients and/or bystanders), and start formulating plans to deal with those hazards. This process should continue with constant reassessment of the potential hazards until the call is complete and the ambulance and crew are ready for another emergency. Therefore, Choice D is the best answer. *(Chapter VII: Section A)*

23. B. All steps of each assessment should be performed in a familiar, practiced order. This is to *ensure that no steps are omitted*, which could lead to an oversight of a significant finding or injury. *(Chapter VII: Section B)*

24. A. Although gunshots are a common mechanism for serious or fatal injuries, *a single wound to the leg* may be adequately assessed with a focused exam as it's unlikely to produce injuries in other body parts. However, if there is question as to the number of wounds, the travel path of the bullet, or if the patient shows unexplained signs of shock, a rapid trauma assessment would be indicated. *(Chapter VII: Section C)*

25. C. The past medical history involves the patient's prior diagnoses, treatments and surgeries, and daily medication regimen. The details of the current illness, in comparison, are called the *history of the present illness*. The mnemonic device *OPQRST* (onset, provocation, quality, radiation, severity, and time) will help the EMT-Basic remember the important details to be gathered. *(Chapter VII: Section C.1)*

26. A. The accepted standard for reassessing an unstable, critical, or otherwise concerning patient is no less than every 5 minutes, although more frequent reassessments are encouraged. Choice A is the only interval that meets this standard. *(Chapter VII: Section D)*

27. D. The *general impression* is formed upon first seeing the patient. It can often be accomplished from across the room—hence the nicknames given in the question. The chief complaint can sometimes be ascertained from this assessment, but generally is given by the patient once you approach him. The initial assessment and focused assessment require the EMT-Basic to be in direct contact with the patient. *(Chapter VII: Section B.1)*

28. **D.** Multiple casualty incidents (MCIs) are challenging, especially to the medical unit that arrives first. EMT-Basics must be careful not to immediately begin treatment of any single patient, no matter how critical his condition may appear, until appropriate resources have been called and triage has been completed or established by other responders. If you immediately begin treatment, you could delay care and transport to other, possibly more critical or more salvageable patients. Therefore, after consideration of scene hazards, at least one member of the first crew to arrive on the scene must estimate the number of patients, determine the resources needed, and immediately transmit this information to the dispatch center. Therefore, Choice D is the best answer. *(Chapter VII: Section A.4)*

29. **C.** After the initial exam, assessment of the responsive medical patient should always begin by obtaining the patient's history. In this case, a focused history and physical exam are appropriate. Ongoing assessments should be assessed at least every 15 minutes for a stable patient or at least every 5 minutes for an unstable patient. A detailed physical exam may be omitted on some patients, but should be performed if time allows. Therefore, Choice C provides the best course of assessment. *(Chapter VII: Section D)*

30. **B.** Questioning a patient about *associated complaints* is an important part of obtaining the medical history. The complaints serve to help narrow down the differential diagnosis and often give the EMT-Basic important direction in applying treatments. *(Chapter VII: Section C)*

31. **A.** Examination of the chest should be performed in the order given to ensure a quality examination. Percussion isn't often useful in the field as it requires large amounts of experience and practice to be able to interpret correctly, and the field environment isn't conducive to using percussion because of its noisy surroundings. Therefore, Choice A is the best answer. *(Chapter VII: Section B.3)*

32. **C.** While a useful tool for the pediatric patient, *capillary refill* time is often unreliable in adults, especially in patients with peripheral artery disease, patients who have been exposed to cold environments, and patients who have had surgery in the assessed limb. Pulse quality, skin signs, and blood pressure are the measures of choice. *(Chapter VII; Chapter X: Section B)*

33. **C.** After controlling life threats, it's important for the EMT-Basic to *determine the patient's priority*. This not only determines the tactics of "load and go" or "stay and play," but also determines the course of the rest of the patient assessment. *(Chapter VII: Section B.6)*

34. **C.** Pulse oximetry is a valuable tool when *trending a patient's respiratory status*, but should not be used to determine treatments alone. EMT-Basics should base their treatment on objective assessment of the patient's respiratory status, including chest rise and fall, presence or absence of cyanosis, presence or absence of accessory muscle use, and similar signs. However, the pulse oximeter is useful in documenting improvement or deterioration of the patient's condition during treatment and transport. *(Chapter VII: Section B.4)*

35. **D.** Although the EMT-Basic may feel confident in the patient's field diagnosis after previous exams, the detailed exam should be performed if time and resources allow, as *it may yield further information not previously seen*. Even if the information does not change the EMT-Basic's treatment plan, it may be vitally important to ALS providers or ER staff. *(Chapter VII: Section C)*

36. **D.** Edema is an abnormal collection of fluid between the cells in an area of tissue. This is usually the result of fluid overload and/or cardiovascular disease. Edema can commonly be seen in the feet, ankles, and lower legs of patients who spend most of their time sitting or standing. However, in patients who are bedridden or who have spent most of their time in bed while ill, it's common to find edema in the hip and upper leg areas. It's also important to examine the neck to look for the presence

of jugular venous distention, but because this fluid is still within the blood vessels, it's not considered edema. Therefore, Choice D is the best answer. *(Chapter VIII; Chapter XIV: Section A)*

37. **B.** An action is the desired result of administering a medication. While a *side effect* is associated with a negative connotation, a medication can have positive side effects as well. *(Chapter VIII: Section A.8)*

38. **B.** The correct answer is Choice B, *dry skin*. Heat stroke is the most serious of the heat emergencies and is characterized by a failure of the body's normal temperature regulation mechanisms, the most obvious of which is perspiration. When the body fails to produce sweat, the body temperature can rise rapidly. Without treatment, the patient will quickly progress to unconsciousness and death. Aggressive treatment is required if your patient presents without the ability to perspire. *(Chapter VIII: Section D.3)*

39. **C.** Activated charcoal binds to many common poisons in the body, *allowing safe excretion of poisons* from the body. This prevents the poison from being absorbed by the gastrointestinal tract. *(Chapter VIII: Section A)*

40. **D.** The correct answer is Choice D. Anaphylaxis is a life-threatening allergic reaction that causes swelling of the upper and lower airway or peripheral vasodilation leading to shock. Not every anaphylactic reaction will have all of these symptoms, but presentation of a patient with either is a life threat that must be quickly addressed. *(Chapter IX: Section A.2)*

41. **A.** When assessing the abdomen, the EMT-Basic should watch for pain upon applying pressure (tenderness), pain upon releasing pressure (rebound tenderness), tensing of the abdominal muscles to prevent deep palpation (guarding), and the presence and character of any masses felt. *Crepitus* would be an unusual finding because there are no bones within the abdominal cavity. *(Chapter VIII)*

42. **C.** This patient is most likely suffering from pulmonary edema, a buildup of fluid in the lungs. These patients often prefer to sit upright, which maximizes the amount of lung tissue available for gas exchange and minimizes the work of breathing. *Fowler's position* is best for optimal diaphragm excursion, which will assist in breathing. *(Chapter VIII)*

43. **B.** While commonly assessed, *grip strength* is unreliable in some patients and is not part of the Cincinnati Prehospital Stroke Scale. A patient who tests positive for facial droop, arm drift, or abnormal speech has a 70% likelihood of suffering from a stroke. *(Chapter VIII)*

44. **D.** *All of the above* may produce symptoms that are often initially assumed to be a behavioral problem. The EMT-Basic must be careful to assess for and attempt to rule out any medical cause for the patient's behavior before treating him for a behavioral emergency. *(Chapter VIII: Section H)*

45. **C.** The correct answer is Choice C. The patient's history of dark, tarry stools indicates that blood is entering the GI tract and is being partially digested before it's passed. This may indicate a *gastrointestinal hemorrhage*. Although aneurysm may be present, a ruptured aneurysm would have caused intense pain and led to shock within minutes. Hepatitis can be a source of firmness in the abdomen but is not associated with blood in the stool. Appendicitis is characterized by right lower quadrant tenderness, fever, and vomiting. *(Chapter VIII)*

46. **C.** When administering oral glucose, you must always ensure that the patient *is conscious and can swallow*. By ensuring that the patient can adequately swallow, you can avoid making a bad situation worse. It is not necessary to know the patient's blood glucose level because hypoglycemia can usually be suspected based on history and physical exam alone. In addition, giving oral glucose to a patient who is already hyperglycemic is not likely to be harmful because the glucose is rapidly metabolized by the body. However, to a patient who may be hypoglycemic, oral glucose may be a lifesaving treatment.

Therefore, it should be administered to any patient with altered mental status and suspicion of either hypoglycemia or hyperglycemia. *(Chapter VIII: Section D.1)*

47. **B.** While of great benefit to many patients, *Advair* is a medication used to treat long-term causes of respiratory problems and is of little use in an emergency setting. Albuterol, which goes by the trade names Ventolin and Proventil, and metaproterenol, also known as Alupent, are short-acting beta agonists that dilate the bronchioles within a few minutes. *(Chapter VIII)*

48. **D.** The correct answer is Choice D, *none of the above*. In children, fever is the most common cause of a seizure. Trauma and infection are also occasional causes of seizures in adults. However, the most common cause of a single, generalized seizure in an adult is failure to take prescribed medications. *(Chapter VIII: Section D.1)*

49. **A.** Medications are labeled by generic name (such as acetaminophen, albuterol, or hydrocodone), or by trade name (Tylenol, Proventil, or Vicodin, respectively). *Chemical names* are difficult to pronounce and remember. For this reason, they are not generally found on medication packaging. *(Chapter VIII: Section A)*

50. **B.** The correct answer is Choice B. In this case, you must consider the *amount of time from exposure to onset of symptoms*. Patients who experience serious allergic reactions or anaphylaxis generally experience symptoms within a few minutes of exposure, sometimes in as little as 30–60 seconds. Patients whose onset of symptoms is delayed by many minutes or hours generally experience less severe reactions that don't usually require lifesaving care. *(Chapter VIII: Section E)*

51. **C.** *Congestive heart failure* is the result of impaired function of the heart. This can be due to a variety of causes, and results in fluid "backing up" behind the inefficient pump. This blood backs up in the great veins and causes fluid to "leak" into the lungs and tissues of the distal extremities. *(Chapter VIII)*

52. **B.** Patients who have been successfully resuscitated are at high risk of going back into arrest. For this reason, they should be *monitored closely, with pulse checks every 30 seconds, to ensure that they do not go back into arrest. (Chapter VIII)*

53. **D.** Choice D is correct. Thromboembolic events such as CVA, myocardial infarction, or pulmonary embolism may be caused by a blood clot that forms in the distal veins and then enters the bloodstream. Eventually the clot lodges in an artery, causing ischemia and tissue death to whichever tissues are supplied by that artery. Pregnancy, prolonged travel, and smoking are all risk factors for embolus formation. *(Chapter VIII)*

54. **C.** *Myocardial infarction*, most commonly called a heart attack, results when blood flow is not sufficient to support the functioning of the heart's muscle cells. While this can sometimes lead to a cardiac arrest, the two are not always related. Cardiac tamponade results from blood or fluid accumulating around the heart. Arrhythmia is an irregular heartbeat resulting in extra or skipped beats. *(Chapter VIII: Section C.1)*

55. **C.** Choice C is the correct answer. It is important to ensure that the patient is pulseless, apneic, and unresponsive prior to resuming CPR or applying the AED. Therefore, CPR or AED use would not be indicated for a patient who is *conscious. (Chapter VIII: Section C.5)*

56. **C.** The correct answer is Choice C. *Hypovolemic shock* is commonly encountered in trauma patients as a result of internal or external hemorrhage. If a trauma patient is found to be in shock without other cause and no external bleeding can be identified, internal hemorrhage should be assumed. *(Chapter IX: Section A.2)*

57. D. This patient is experiencing a *tension pneumothorax* as evidenced by his jugular venous distention, tracheal deviation, and rapidly deteriorating circulatory status. The most important and immediate remedy is to *loosen the occlusive dressing* to attempt to allow any trapped air to escape. This may depressurize the chest and allow resumption of normal breathing and circulation. *(Chapter IX)*

58. B. The correct answer is Choice B. Impaled objects should only be removed if they interfere with airway procedures, assisted ventilations, or CPR. Because this patient's injury is to his thigh, the object should be stabilized in place and removal should be deferred to hospital staff. *(Chapter IX: Section B.4)*

59. D. Partial-thickness burns involve the outer two layers of skin but are not deep enough to destroy nerve endings underneath, making them extremely painful. Partial-thickness burns are easily identified by the presence of blisters. Using the Rule of Nines, this patient's burns can be estimated at 9% for each anterior leg. Therefore, Choice D is correct. *(Chapter IX: Section B.5)*

60. C. The neck contains large vessels including the carotid arteries and jugular veins. Damage to any of these may result in profuse bleeding or air embolism due to large amounts of air entering the central circulation. Cervical spine injury is also possible because any penetrating injury is likely to be close to the spinal column. However, penetrating injury to the neck doesn't present any increased risk for *cardiac tamponade. (Chapter IX: Section D)*

61. C. Injuries that impair circulation can quickly become limb-threatening. Although the general rule is to splint injuries in the position you find them in, in this case, it becomes more important to restore blood flow. Therefore, you should *pull gentle traction until the limb's pulses and color improve*, and no further. The limb should be immobilized in that position and rechecked frequently for circulation. *(Chapter IX: Section C)*

62. C. This patient exhibits classic signs of a pelvic fracture, which is not only painful but can also result in significant internal hemorrhage without external signs. In this case, *you should apply a pelvic wrap or binder and treat for shock*. The patient must then be transported to a trauma center without delay. *(Chapter IX: Section C)*

63. C. The correct answer is Choice C. *Crush syndrome* is a result of even modest pressure applied to the soft tissues over time. It can be a devastating injury even without large amounts of force. Not only does crush syndrome result in large amounts of damaged tissue, but it also predisposes the patient to cardiac dysrhythmias and other systemic complications due to the long period of impaired circulation followed by rapid washout when the patient is freed. Often these patients will be conscious and appear very stable until the crushing force is removed, then will quickly deteriorate once they are free. Advanced life support and early treatment for shock are essential. *(Chapter IX: Section B)*

64. C. This patient is suffering from what is likely a life-threatening hemorrhage and already has advanced signs of shock. With less severe hemorrhage, attempting control with pressure points or elevation may be appropriate, and oxygen is appropriate for any significant hemorrhage. However, the lifesaving treatment in this case is to immediately *apply a tourniquet. (Chapter IX: Section A.3)*

65. D. The correct answer is Choice D, *arterial* and *capillary* hemorrhages. The "spurting" of blood from the first wound, combined with its bright red color, indicates that the hemorrhage is from an artery, a high-pressure vessel carrying blood saturated with high concentrations of blood. The second wound's very slow rate of hemorrhage and superficial depth indicate that only capillaries are involved. While all sources of hemorrhage require treatment, it is important for the EMT-Basic to be able to distinguish them and prioritize their care. *(Chapter IX: Section A)*

66. **C.** All of these injuries are possibilities. In fact, all may be present on the same patient with this mechanism of injury. However, the most likely injury is *cardiac tamponade* because a tension pneumothorax would result in decreased or absent breath sounds on the injured side. Cardiac tamponade is characterized by the pericardium filling with blood from a cardiac injury, reducing the heart's ability to pump effectively. As this progresses, the patient will display jugular venous distention, muffled heart sounds, and narrowing pulse pressure—the trio known as Beck's triad. *(Chapter IX)*

67. **A.** Patients must be immobilized on *a long spine board with towel rolls or head blocks* before they can be considered fully immobilized. Vest-type devices such as the Kendrick Extrication Device supply additional immobilization in situations where a long spine board can't immediately be applied, but once the patient is freed or access is gained, the patient should then be secured to a long spine board. However, when doing this, the short back device is often left in place because removing it is likely to cause excess manipulation to the patient's spine. *(Chapter IX: Section D.2)*

68. **B.** *A human bite* causes less tissue damage than a bite inflicted by an animal, but it is a source of exposure to numerous bacteria that can cause problematic infections. The risk is often amplified because most patients in this situation wait to seek treatment, whereas patients who receive an animal bite seek treatment immediately because of the commonly known risks of diseases like rabies. *(Chapter IX: Section B)*

69. **A.** This patient is displaying a classic mechanism and signs of a ruptured spleen. Patients with this type of injury often complain of referred pain in the left shoulder, while the pale skin and tachycardia indicate the patient is most likely in shock. Any trauma patient in shock should be suspected of having *internal bleeding* until proven otherwise. *(Chapter IX: Section A.4)*

70. **D.** *Applying direct pressure* will resolve up to 95% of external hemorrhage. Although the other methods are helpful, direct pressure should usually be implemented first. In rare cases of disfiguring injuries or when massive hemorrhage is present, a tourniquet may be the initial method of control as a lifesaving measure. Outside of the military arena, injuries of this severity are rare. *(Chapter IX: Section A.3)*

71. **C.** In children, a sudden *fever* can often precipitate seizures. These febrile seizures are often "outgrown" and do not indicate the presence of a seizure or other neurological condition. However, any new onset of seizures always warrants physician evaluation. It should also be emphasized that seizures are not always the result of an exceptionally high fever—some have theorized that the likelihood of seizure is more closely related to the rapid onset of fever experienced by some children. *(Chapter X: Section C.3)*

72. **A.** The airways of pediatric patients are smaller, more flexible, and, therefore, more easily obstructed. Pediatric patients are also at higher risk for airway obstruction as a result of the tongue falling back into the oropharynx because their tongues are larger in proportion to the size of their mouth. Therefore, Choice A is the best answer. *(Chapter X: Section C.1; Chapter XII: Section B)*

73. **B.** While adults commonly turn away from the vehicle as they attempt to flee, younger patients commonly turn to face the perceived danger. Because of this, children usually *fall onto their outstretched arms* and sustain injuries to the face and chest. *(Chapter X)*

74. **C.** Without a definite cause of death, this patient is likely to be considered a victim of *Sudden Infant Death Syndrome (SIDS)*. While no cause of death has been identified, common characteristics of SIDS deaths include prone position in the crib, blankets or other soft objects near the child's face, and recent mild upper-respiratory symptoms. It's important for the EMT-Basic to realize that these deaths are not the result of any mistreatment or abuse. *(Chapter X: Section C.9)*

75. **C.** Because infants breathe primarily through their nose, their nostrils often "flare" or expand in an effort to take in more air. This is a subtle but important sign for the EMT-Basic to notice. The other

signs may be seen in children, but are also common in adults. Therefore, Choice C is the best answer. *(Chapter X: Section B)*

76. **C.** *The number of wet diapers changed in the past several hours* can be an important assessment finding. Infants and small children are difficult to assess because they're unable to verbalize complaints. Therefore, subjective symptoms of dehydration such as weakness or thirst can't assist with the assessment. A patient who has gone an unusually long time without a wet diaper is often dehydrated. *(Chapter X: Section B)*

77. **B.** The pediatric airway is smaller, thinner, and *less rigid* the adult airway because the cartilage rings that protect the adult airway have not yet fully formed. This creates an increased risk of airway obstruction due to flexion of the neck or any pressure on the anterior neck. *(Chapter XII: Section B)*

78. **D.** In infants, abdominal compressions are dangerous and ineffective. Therefore, they're replaced with back slaps and chest thrusts. Finger sweeps shouldn't be performed in pediatric patients unless an object is visualized because of the increased likelihood that an unseen small object may be pushed further into the oropharynx. Therefore, Choice D is correct. *(Chapter XII: Section C.1)*

79. **D.** In pediatric patients, blood pressure becomes difficult to measure accurately, as do radial and carotid pulses due to the relative small pulse points and relatively large collections of fatty tissue. Therefore, *capillary refill* becomes the measure of choice. *(Chapter X: Section C.1)*

80. **C.** Children often sustain bruises to the anterior aspect of the lower legs. These alone shouldn't normally arouse suspicion unless they are unusually severe, unusually numerous, or combined with other findings such as inconsistent history or other suspicious injuries. Therefore, *bruises to the shins and knees* would be the least suspicious injury when assessing for signs of child abuse. *(Chapter X: Section A)*

81. **C.** Although drivers are asked or required to yield to emergency vehicles, *it's never permissible for the ambulance operator to assume they will.* Doing so places the crew and other motorists at great risk. Emergency vehicles should always be driven defensively. *(Chapter XI: Section A.1)*

82. **C.** Although the flight crew may rarely require the assistance of additional EMT-Basics, people should not approach the helicopter without ensuring that the pilot is aware of their presence and *gives permission for their approach.* All personnel should remain outside the rotor disc until the pilot indicates that the approach is safe. *(Chapter XI: Section A.2)*

83. **A.** While most responders think of incident management as only being applicable to multiple casualty incidents or those requiring a large number of resources or units, the principles can be applied to every emergency scene. Using the tenets of incident management will allow better coordination—even among a small number of responders—and allows the command structure to be quickly scaled or expanded if an incident escalates after the initial response. Therefore, Choice A is the best answer. *(Chapter XI: Section C.2)*

84. **C.** When disentangling a patient from a vehicle or other mechanism of entrapment, the idea is to *move or cut the object*, so the patient may be freed. It's dangerous to manipulate a patient within the object, as additional injury may result. Hazards should be removed or mitigated and certainly the patient will eventually be removed from the scene, but these are separate phases of the extrication process and aren't included in disentanglement. *(Chapter XI: Section B.1)*

85. **D.** The leaking liquid should clearly be treated as hazardous until it can be identified. It may be fuel, pesticides, or other potentially harmful substances. Until it's identified, the scene must be considered unsafe. Also, the scenario states that you have identified that there are no fewer than three patients, but your partner and you are the only two EMS providers available to provide care initially. Therefore, you must perform triage and create a plan for requesting and integrating more resources.

The presence of more patients or needs than can be adequately handled with current resources is an essential definition of a multiple casualty incident and requires use of incident management principles for a successful operation. Therefore, the correct answer is *all of the above*. *(Chapter XI: Section C.3)*

86. **D.** All documentation should be completed *as soon as possible* after placing the ambulance back in service. This ensures that the finer details can be recorded while they are fresh in the documenter's mind and that the record is quickly available for hospital personnel and/or operational functions. *(Chapter VII: Section E.1; Chapter XI: Section A.1)*

87. **C.** The first thing you must do after arriving at the scene of a medical emergency or accident is *notify dispatch of your arrival*. Although the other steps are important, notifying dispatch of your arrival and recording the time of your arrival should be your first priority. *(Chapter VII: Section E.1; Chapter XI: Section A.1)*

88. **D.** *Due regard* describes the way that reasonable individuals would act in a similar situation to ensure the safety of those around them. It is vitally important for the ambulance operator to always show due regard for other drivers when responding to an emergency. *(Chapter XI: Section A.1)*

89. **D.** The hot zone is the area of operation for hazmat technicians and other fully protected responders. To prevent contamination of transport units and potential contamination of hospitals, EMT-Basics should be positioned in the *cold zone.* They should not treat any patient who hasn't been fully decontaminated. *(Chapter XI: Section D.2)*

90. **C.** The timing of the event and the sudden illnesses experienced by numerous persons may indicate a *terrorist attack*. While illnesses such as bird flu can cause widespread illness, it would be unusual for those types of illnesses to spread so quickly. Carbon monoxide poisoning is a possibility, but it would be difficult to create a toxic level of CO in such a large space without at least some patients developing symptoms earlier and more gradually. *(Chapter XI: Section E.1)*

91. **C.** *Repeaters* are devices that extend the range of smaller radios by receiving a weak signal and rebroadcasting it at a higher power, either on the same frequency or another frequency. Use of these systems allows providers to communicate over great distances with even the smallest handheld radios. *(Chapter VII: Section E)*

92. **A.** The correct mixture of *one part bleach to ten parts water* allows most surfaces to be completely disinfected in several minutes. The EMT-Basic should be careful when preparing this solution, as too little bleach will result in poor disinfection. Too much bleach can cause harsh vapors or smells that will be irritating to some patients or can cause damage to the skin of the person using the solution if proper protection isn't worn. *(Chapter XI: Section C.1)*

93. **D.** On smaller incidents, an *incident commander* may fill all of these roles. However, a basic principle of incident management states that all personnel have one boss and that all authority is delegated by and from the incident commander. An incident commander must be appointed or designated before any other position can be filled. *(Chapter XI: Section C.2)*

94. **A.** Oxygen cylinders are denoted by green coloring. They also are marked with a U.S. Pharmacopeia (USP) label because it's considered a medication. They also may be identified by a properly fitting medical regulator that fits the bottle through the pin-index system, which includes two index pins for oxygen cylinders and regulators. Oxygen cylinders do not have a *blue color*. *(Chapter XI: Section C.1)*

95. **C.** Regardless of speed or distance, any movement of the emergency response unit presents a risk to crew and other occupants. Therefore, restraints should be used *any time the vehicle is in motion* unless lifesaving care is necessary, in which case, the crew should consider stopping the ambulance until the providers can be restrained again. *(Chapter XI: Section A.1)*

96. **B.** Sellick's maneuver is performed by applying pressure to the anterior neck with two fingers directly over the *thyroid cartilage*. This causes the trachea to be displaced posteriorly, improving the intubator's view and, ideally, occluding the much more flexible esophagus to prevent gastric insufflations and/or regurgitation. *(Chapter XII)*

97. **A.** Because of the angles at which the left and right mainstem bronchi form the carina, an endotracheal tube that is advanced too deeply will often result in a right mainstem intubation. Intubators should be aware of this and be ready to withdraw the tube 1–2 cm at a time until breath sounds are heard bilaterally or the tube is removed and another intubation attempt can be performed. Therefore, Choice A is correct. *(Chapter XII: Section A.1)*

98. **C.** After the endotracheal tube is placed, *the most immediate need is to confirm placement* by evaluating breath sounds, chest rise and fall, skin signs, and any other confirmation methods available and recommended by medical direction. Delaying the confirmation process to secure the tube first may lead to delayed recognition of a misplaced tube and/or gastric insufflations, hypoxia, and other complications. As soon as the tube is confirmed to be properly placed, it should be securely fastened, tied, or taped in place to avoid dislodgement. *(Chapter XII: Section A.1)*

99. **D.** Advanced airways are indicated for patients who have lost the ability to protect their own airway. In seizure patients, intubation is usually delayed to allow the patient to pass naturally through the postictal period. To intubate this patient immediately following his seizure will cause potentially life-threatening complications if the patient wakes up. The patient described in Choice B coughs when suctioned, indicating that the patient's own airway reflexes are still intact and functioning. Choice C gives us the least information, but most patients with a GCS of 13 can easily manage their own airway. "Less than 8, intubate" is a common mantra for using a GCS score to aid in the decision of when to use an advanced airway. Therefore, Choice D is the best answer. *(Chapter XII)*

100. **A.** *MacIntosh* blades are curved to follow the natural curvature of the tongue and oropharynx. The tip is placed in the *vallecula* and elevated, causing the hyoepiglottic ligament to pull the epiglottis anteriorly and away from the axis of the trachea. Miller and Wisconsin blades are straight blades that are designed to directly manipulate the epiglottis. *(Chapter XII: Section A.1)*

II. Two-Month Cram Plan

	Airway and Breathing	Cardiology	Trauma
8 weeks before the test	**Study Time:** 2½ hours ❑ Take **Diagnostic Test** and review answer explanations. 　❑ Based on your errors on the **Diagnostic Test,** identify difficult topics and their corresponding chapters. These are your targeted chapters.		
7 weeks before the test	**Study Time:** 2 hours ❑ **Airway:** Chapter VI 　❑ Read sections A and B. 　❑ Do practice questions 1 and 2 in each section. 　❑ For targeted areas, do three questions in each section. ❑ **Advanced Airway:** Chapter XII 　❑ Read section A. 　❑ Do practice questions 1–5 in this section. 　❑ For targeted areas, do seven practice questions in this section.	**Study Time:** 1 hour ❑ **Medical Emergencies:** Chapter VIII 　❑ Read section C. 　❑ Do practice questions 1 and 2 in this section. 　❑ For targeted areas, do three questions in this section.	**Study Time:** 1 hour ❑ **Trauma:** Chapter IX 　❑ Read sections A and B. 　❑ Do practice questions 1 and 2 in each section. 　❑ For targeted areas, do three questions in each section.
6 weeks before the test	**Study Time:** 2 hours ❑ **Airway:** Chapter VI 　❑ Read section C. 　❑ Do practice questions 1 and 2 in this section. 　❑ For targeted areas, do all five practice questions in this section. ❑ **Advanced Airway:** Chapter XII 　❑ Read section B. 　❑ Do practice questions 1–5 in this section. 　❑ For targeted areas, do seven practice questions in this section.	**Study Time:** 1 hour ❑ **Medical Emergencies:** Chapter VIII ❑ Review section C. ❑ Do practice questions 3–5 in this section.	**Study Time:** 1 hour ❑ **Trauma:** Chapter IX 　❑ Read sections C and D. 　❑ Do practice questions 1 and 2 in each section. 　❑ For targeted areas, do three questions in each section.
5 weeks before the test	**Study Time:** 2 hours ❑ **Practical Skills:** Chapter XIII 　❑ Read section B. ❑ **Anatomy and Physiology:** Chapter XIV 　❑ Review relevant terms in section A. Highlight any difficult terms. ❑ **Medical Emergencies:** Chapter VIII 　❑ Read section B. 　❑ Do practice questions 1–5 in this section.	**Study Time:** 1 hour ❑ **Anatomy and Physiology:** Chapter XIV ❑ Read section C2. ❑ **Practical Skills:** Chapter XIII ❑ Read section C.	**Study Time:** 1 hour ❑ **Practical Skills:** Chapter XIII 　❑ Read sections D and E. ❑ **Anatomy and Physiology:** Chapter XIV 　❑ Review relevant terms in section A. Highlight any difficult terms. 　❑ Review the terms in section B. 　❑ Do practice questions 1, 3, and 4 in this section.

Medical Emergencies	Obstetrics and Pediatrics	Operations

Study Time: 2 hours
❏ **Medical Emergencies:** Chapter VIII
  ❏ Read sections A, D, and E.
  ❏ Do practice questions 1 and 2 in each section.
  ❏ For targeted areas, do three questions in each section.
❏ **Anatomy and Physiology:** Chapter XIV
  ❏ Read section A.
  ❏ Do practice questions 1–4.
	Study Time: 1 hour
	❏ **Infants and Children:** Chapter X
	  ❏ Read section A.
	  ❏ Do practice questions 1 and 2 in this section.
	  ❏ For targeted areas, do three questions in this section.
		Study Time: 2 hours
		❏ **Preparatory:** Chapter V
		  ❏ Read sections A and B.
		  ❏ Do practice questions 1 and 2 in each section.
		  ❏ For targeted areas, do three questions in each section.
		❏ **Patient Assessment:** Chapter VII
		  ❏ Read sections A–C.
		  ❏ Do practice questions 1 and 2 in each section.
		  ❏ For targeted areas, do all questions in these sections.

Study Time: 2 hours
❏ **Medical Emergencies:** Chapter VIII
  ❏ Read sections F–H.
  ❏ Do practice questions 1 and 2 in each section.
  ❏ For targeted areas, do three questions in each section.
❏ **Anatomy and Physiology:** Chapter XIV
  ❏ Read section A.
  ❏ Do practice questions 5–8.
	Study Time: 1 hour
	❏ **Infants and Children:** Chapter X
	  ❏ Read section B.
	  ❏ Do practice questions 1 and 2 in this section.
	  ❏ For targeted areas, do three questions in this section.
		Study Time: 2 hours
		❏ **Patient Assessment:** Chapter VII
		  ❏ Read sections A–C.
		  ❏ Do the remaining practice questions in each section.
		❏ **Operations:** Chapter XI
		  ❏ Read sections A and B.
		  ❏ Do practice questions 1 and 2 in each section.
		  ❏ For targeted areas, do three questions in these sections.

Study Time: 1 hour
❏ **Medical Emergencies:** Chapter VIII
  ❏ Read sections A, D, and E.
  ❏ Do practice questions 3–5 in each section.
	Study Time: 1 hour
	❏ **Medical Emergencies:** Chapter VIII
	  ❏ Read section I.
	  ❏ Do practice questions 1–5 in this section.
		Study Time: 2 hours
		❏ **Patient Assessment:** Chapter VII
		  ❏ Read sections D and E.
		  ❏ Do practice questions 1 and 2 in each section.
		  ❏ For targeted areas, do all questions in these sections.
		❏ **Operations:** Chapter XI
		  ❏ Read sections A and B.
		  ❏ Do practice questions 3–5 in each section.

continued

	Airway and Breathing	Cardiology	Trauma

4 weeks before the test	**Study Time:** 1 hour
	❏ **Anatomy and Physiology:** Chapter XIV
	  ❏ Read section C1.
	❏ **Airway:** Chapter VI
	  ❏ Read sections A and B.
	  ❏ Do practice questions 3–5 in this section.
		Study Time: 1 hour
		❏ **Anatomy and Physiology:** Chapter XIV
		  ❏ Review relevant terms in section A. Highlight any difficult terms.
			Study Time: 1 hour
			❏ **Trauma:** Chapter IX
			  ❏ Read sections A and B.
			  ❏ Do practice questions 3–5 in each section.

3 weeks before the test	**Study Time:** 1 hour
	❏ **Advanced Airway:** Chapter XII
	  ❏ Read sections A and B.
	  ❏ Do practice questions 6–10 in each section.
		Study Time: 1 hour
		❏ **Anatomy and Physiology:** Chapter XIV
		  ❏ Review highlighted terms in section A.
			Study Time: 1 hour
			❏ **Trauma:** Chapter IX
			  ❏ Read sections C and D.
			  ❏ Do practice questions 4 and 5 in each section.

2 weeks before the test	**Study Time:** 6 hours ❏ Take **Practice Test** and review answer explanations. ❏ Based on your errors on the **Practice Test,** identify difficult topics and their corresponding chapters. These chapters are your targeted areas.		
	Study Time: 1 hour ❏ Based on the Practice Test, review the chapters or sections for all targeted areas. ❏ Redo those questions that you answered incorrectly on the Practice Test.	**Study Time:** 1 hour ❏ Review the questions related to Cardiology that you missed on the Practice Test. ❏ Redo practice questions 1 and 2 in Chapter VIII, Medical Emergencies.	**Study Time:** 1 hour ❏ Review the questions related to Trauma that you missed on the Practice Test. ❏ **Anatomy and Physiology:** Chapter XIV ❏ Review highlighted terms.

7 days before the test	**Study Time:** 30 minutes
	❏ **Airway:** Chapter VI
	  ❏ Review sections A–C.
	  ❏ Do practice question 5 in each section.
		Study Time: 30 minutes
		❏ **Medical Emergencies:** Chapter VIII
		  ❏ Read section C.
			Study Time: 30 minutes
			❏ **Trauma:** Chapter IX
			  ❏ Review sections A and B.
			  ❏ Redo practice questions 1 and 2 in each section.

6 days before the test	**Study Time:** 30 minutes
	❏ **Advanced Airway:** Chapter XII
	  ❏ Read sections A and B.
	  ❏ Do practice question 6 in these sections.
		Study Time: 30 minutes
		❏ **Medical Emergencies:** Chapter VIII
		  ❏ Redo practice questions 3–5 in section C.
			Study Time: 30 minutes
			❏ **Trauma:** Chapter IX
			  ❏ Review sections C and D.
			  ❏ Redo practice questions 1 and 2 in each section.

Medical Emergencies	Obstetrics and Pediatrics	Operations

Study Time: 1 hour
❏ **Medical Emergencies:** Chapter VIII
   ❏ Read sections F–H.
   ❏ Do practice questions 3–5 in each section.
	Study Time: 1 hour
	❏ **Infants and Children:** Chapter X
	   ❏ Read section A.
	   ❏ Do practice questions 3–5 in this section.
		Study Time: 2 hours
		❏ **Preparatory:** Chapter V
		   ❏ Read sections A and B.
		   ❏ Do the remaining practice questions in each section.
		❏ **Operations:** Chapter XI
		   ❏ Read sections C and D.
		   ❏ Do three practice questions in each section.

Study Time: 1 hour
❏ **Anatomy and Physiology:** Chapter XIV
   ❏ Read section B.
   ❏ Do practice questions 2 and 5.
	Study Time: 1 hour
	❏ **Infants and Children:** Chapter X
	   ❏ Read section B.
	   ❏ Do practice questions 3–5 in this section.
		Study Time: 2 hours
		❏ **Patient Assessment:** Chapter VII
		   ❏ Read sections D and E.
		   ❏ Do the remaining practice questions in each section.
		❏ **Preparatory:** Chapter V
		   ❏ Read sections C and D.
		   ❏ Do practice questions 1 and 2 in each section.

Study Time: 1 hour ❏ Review the questions related to Medical Emergencies that you missed on the Practice Test.	**Study Time:** 1 hour ❏ Review the questions related to Infants and Children that you missed on the Practice Test.	**Study Time:** 1 hour ❏ Review the questions related to Operations that you missed on the Practice Test.

Study Time: 30 minutes
❏ **Anatomy and Physiology:** Chapter XIV
   ❏ Read sections C3–C9.
   ❏ Do practice questions 1–5.
	Study Time: 30 minutes
	❏ **Infants and Children:** Chapter X
	   ❏ Review section A.
		Study Time: 30 minutes
		❏ **Preparatory:** Chapter V
		   ❏ Do remaining practice questions in sections C and D.

Study Time: 30 minutes
❏ **Anatomy and Physiology:** Chapter XIV
   ❏ Read sections C3–C9.
   ❏ Do practice questions 1–5.
	Study Time: 30 minutes
	❏ **Infants and Children:** Chapter X
	   ❏ Review section B.
		Study Time: 30 minutes
		❏ **Preparatory:** Chapter V
		   ❏ Review chapter.

continued

	Airway and Breathing	Cardiology	Trauma
5 days before the test	**Study Time:** 30 minutes ❏ **Anatomy and Physiology:** Chapter XIV ❏ Read section C1. ❏ **Medical Emergencies:** Chapter VIII ❏ Read section B. ❏ Review practice questions 1–5 in this section.	**Study Time:** 30 minutes ❏ **Anatomy and Physiology:** Chapter XIV ❏ Review section C2 of this chapter. ❏ Do practice question 3.	**Study Time:** 30 minutes ❏ **Trauma:** Chapter IX ❏ Review sections A and B. ❏ Redo practice questions 3–5 in each section.
4 days before the test	**Study Time:** 30 minutes ❏ **Practical Skills:** Chapter XIII ❏ Read section B.	**Study Time:** 30 minutes ❏ **Practical Skills:** Chapter XIII ❏ Review section C.	**Study Time:** 30 minutes ❏ **Trauma:** Chapter IX ❏ Review sections C and D. ❏ Redo practice questions 3–5 in each section.
3 days before the test	**Study Time:** 30 minutes ❏ Review any questions concerning Airway and Breathing on the Diagnostic Test.	**Study Time:** 30 minutes ❏ Review any questions concerning Cardiology on the Diagnostic Test.	**Study Time:** 30 minutes ❏ Review any questions concerning Trauma on the Diagnostic Test.
2 days before the test	**Study Time:** 30 minutes ❏ Review any questions concerning Airway and Breathing on the Practice Test.	**Study Time:** 30 minutes ❏ Review any questions concerning Cardiology on the Practice Test.	**Study Time:** 30 minutes ❏ Review any questions concerning Trauma on the Practice Test.
1 day before the test	❏ Relax . . . .You're well prepared for the test. ❏ Have confidence in your ability to do well.		
Morning of the test	**Reminders:** ❏ Eat a healthy breakfast. ❏ Give yourself extra time to reach the testing facility. If you get there early, you'll have time to review some of your notes. ❏ Take your Authorization to Test letter with you to the exam along with your photo ID. ❏ Try to go outside for a few minutes and walk around before the test. ❏ Most important: Stay calm and confident during the test. Take deep, slow breaths if you feel at all nervous.		

Medical Emergencies	Obstetrics and Pediatrics	Operations
Study Time: 30 minutes ❑ **Medical Emergencies:** Chapter VIII 　❑ Review sections A, D, and E.	**Study Time:** 30 minutes ❑ **Medical Emergencies:** Chapter VIII 　❑ Review section I. 　❑ Redo practice questions 1–5.	**Study Time:** 30 minutes ❑ **Patient Assessment:** Chapter VII 　❑ Review chapter. 　❑ Redo practice questions 1 and 2 in section A.
Study Time: 30 minutes ❑ **Medical Emergencies:** Chapter VIII 　❑ Review sections F–H.	**Study Time:** 30 minutes ❑ **Infants and Children:** Chapter X 　❑ Review sections A and B. 　❑ Redo practice questions 3–5 in this section.	**Study Time:** 30 minutes ❑ **Operations:** Chapter XI 　❑ Review chapter. 　❑ Redo any questions that you originally got wrong in the section practices.
Study Time: 30 minutes ❑ Review any questions concerning Medical Emergencies on the Diagnostic Test.	**Study Time:** 30 minutes ❑ Review any questions concerning Infants and Children on the Diagnostic Test.	**Study Time:** 30 minutes ❑ Review any questions concerning Operations on the Diagnostic Test.
Study Time: 30 minutes ❑ Review any questions concerning Medical Emergencies on the Practice Test.	**Study Time:** 30 minutes ❑ Review any questions concerning Infants and Children on the Practice Test.	**Study Time:** 30 minutes ❑ Review any questions concerning Operations on the Practice Test.

III. One-Month Cram Plan

	Airway and Breathing	Cardiology	Trauma

4 weeks before the test	**Study Time:** 2½ hours
	❑ Take **Diagnostic Test** and review answer explanations.
	  ❑ Based on your errors on the **Diagnostic Test,** identify difficult topics and their corresponding chapters. These are your targeted chapters.
	  ❑ Read your target chapters first.
	  ❑ Focus on practice questions that are similar to the questions you answered incorrectly on the Diagnostic Test.		

3 weeks before the test	**Study Time:** 1 hour
	❑ **Airway:** Chapter VI
	  ❑ Read chapter.
	  ❑ Do practice questions 1–5 in each section.
		Study Time: 1 hour
		❑ **Medical Emergencies:** Chapter VIII
		  ❑ Read section C.
		  ❑ Do practice questions 1–5 in this section.
			Study Time: 1 hour
			❑ **Trauma:** Chapter IX
			  ❑ Read sections A and B.
			  ❑ Do the practice questions in each section.

2 weeks before the test	**Study Time:** 1 hour
	❑ **Advanced Airway:** Chapter XII
	  ❑ Read chapter.
	  ❑ Do practice questions 1–10 in each section.
		Study Time: 30 minutes
		❑ **Anatomy and Physiology:** Chapter XIV
		  ❑ Read section C2.
		  ❑ Answer practice questions 4 and 6 in this section.
			Study Time: 1 hour
			❑ **Trauma:** Chapter IX
			  ❑ Read sections C and D.
			  ❑ Do the practice questions in each section.

7 days before the test	**Study Time:** 30 minutes
	❑ **Practical Skills:** Chapter XIII
	  ❑ Read section B.
		Study Time: 30 minutes
		❑ **Practical Skills:** Chapter XIII
		  ❑ Read section C.
			Study Time: 30 minutes
			❑ **Practical Skills:** Chapter XIII
			  ❑ Read section D.

6 days before the test	**Study Time:** 30 minutes
	❑ **Anatomy and Physiology:** Chapter XIV
	  ❑ Read section C1.
		Study Time: 30 minutes
		❑ **Anatomy and Physiology:** Chapter XIV
		  ❑ Review relevant terms in section A. Highlight any difficult terms.
			Study Time: 30 minutes
			❑ **Practical Skills:** Chapter XIII
			  ❑ Read section E.

5 days before the test	**Study Time:** 30 minutes
	❑ **Practical Skills:** Chapter XIII
	  ❑ Read section E.
		Study Time: 30 minutes
		❑ **Anatomy and Physiology:** Chapter XIV
		  ❑ Review highlighted terms.
			Study Time: 30 minutes
			❑ **Anatomy and Physiology:** Chapter XIV
			  ❑ Read sections A and B. Highlight any difficult terms.
			  ❑ Review highlighted terms.

4 days before the test	**Study Time:** 30 minutes
	❑ **Airway:** Chapter VI
	  ❑ Review chapter.
	  ❑ Review practice questions 1–5 in each section.
		Study Time: 30 minutes
		❑ **Medical Emergencies:** Chapter VIII
		  ❑ Review section C.
			Study Time: 30 minutes
			❑ **Trauma:** Chapter IX
			  ❑ Review sections A and B.

Medical Emergencies	Obstetrics and Pediatrics	Operations
Study Time: 1 hour ❑ **Medical Emergencies:** Chapter VIII 　❑ Read sections A, D, and E. 　❑ Do the practice questions in each section.	**Study Time:** 30 minutes ❑ **Infants and Children:** Chapter X 　❑ Read section A. 　❑ Do the practice questions in this section.	**Study Time:** 2 hours ❑ **Preparatory:** Chapter V 　❑ Read chapter. 　❑ Do the practice questions in each section.
Study Time: 1 hour ❑ **Medical Emergencies:** Chapter VIII 　❑ Read sections F–H. 　❑ Do the practice questions in each section.	**Study Time:** 30 minutes ❑ **Infants and Children:** Chapter X 　❑ Read section B. 　❑ Do the practice questions in this section.	**Study Time:** 2 hours ❑ **Patient Assessment:** Chapter VII 　❑ Read chapter. 　❑ Do the practice questions in each section.
Study Time: 1 hour ❑ **Anatomy and Physiology:** Chapter XIV 　❑ Read sections A–C. 　❑ Do three practice questions in each section.	**Study Time:** 30 minutes ❑ **Medical Emergencies:** Chapter VIII 　❑ Read section I. 　❑ Do the practice questions in this section.	**Study Time:** 2 hours ❑ **Operations:** Chapter XI 　❑ Read chapter. 　❑ Do the practice questions in each section.
Study Time: 30 minutes ❑ **Medical Emergencies:** Chapter VIII 　❑ Review sections A and D.	**Study Time:** 30 minutes ❑ **Infants and Children:** Chapter X 　❑ Review section A.	**Study Time:** 30 minutes ❑ **Preparatory:** Chapter V 　❑ Review chapter.
Study Time: 30 minutes ❑ **Medical Emergencies:** Chapter VIII 　❑ Review sections E and F.	**Study Time:** 30 minutes ❑ **Infants and Children:** Chapter X 　❑ Review section B.	**Study Time:** 30 minutes ❑ **Patient Assessment:** Chapter VII 　❑ Review chapter.
Study Time: 30 minutes ❑ **Medical Emergencies:** Chapter VIII 　❑ Review sections G and H.	**Study Time:** 30 minutes ❑ **Medical Emergencies:** Chapter VIII 　❑ Review section I.	**Study Time:** 30 minutes ❑ **Operations:** Chapter XI 　❑ Review sections A–C.

continued

	Airway and Breathing	Cardiology	Trauma

3 days before the test	**Study Time:** 30 minutes
	❏ **Advanced Airway:** Chapter XII
	  ❏ Review chapter.
	  ❏ Review practice questions 1–10 in each section.
		Study Time: 30 minutes
		❏ **Anatomy and Physiology:** Chapter XIV
		  ❏ Review section C2.
			Study Time: 30 minutes
			❏ **Trauma:** Chapter IX
			  ❏ Review sections C and D.

2 days before the test	**Study Time:** 2½ hours ❏ Take **Practice Test** and review answer explanations. ❏ Make sure you understand your errors.		
1 day before the test	**Study Time:** 30 minutes ❏ Review your target chapters. ❏ Redo some of the questions concerning Airway and Breathing from the Practice Test.	**Study Time:** 30 minutes ❏ Review your target chapters. ❏ Redo the practice questions that focus on Cardiology in Chapter VIII, Medical Emergencies.	**Study Time:** 30 minutes ❏ Review your target chapters. ❏ Redo the some of the questions concerning Trauma from the Diagnostic Test.
Morning of the test	**Reminders:** ❏ Eat a healthy breakfast. ❏ Give yourself extra time to reach the testing facility. If you get there early, you'll have time to review some of your notes. ❏ Take your Authorization to Test letter with you to the exam along with your photo ID. ❏ Try to go outside for a few minutes and walk around before the test. ❏ Most important: Stay calm and confident during the test. Take deep, slow breaths if you feel at all nervous.		

Medical Emergencies	Obstetrics and Pediatrics	Operations

Study Time: 1 hour
❏ **Anatomy and Physiology:** Chapter XIV
   ❏ Review sections A–C.
	Study Time: 30 minutes
	❏ **Infants and Children:** Chapter X
	   ❏ Review any practice questions you answered incorrectly.
		Study Time: 30 minutes
		❏ **Operations:** Chapter XI
		   ❏ Review sections D and E.
		   ❏ Review any practice questions you answered incorrectly in these sections.

Study Time: 1 hour ❏ Review your target chapters. ❏ Redo the practice questions in Chapter VIII, Medical Emergencies.	**Study Time:** 30 minutes ❏ Review your target chapters. ❏ Redo some of the questions concerning Obstetrics and Pediatrics from the Practice Test.	**Study Time:** 1 hour ❏ Review your target chapters. ❏ Redo the practice questions in sections A and B of Chapter XI, Operations.

IV. One-Week Cram Plan

	Airway and Breathing	Cardiology	Trauma

7 days before the test	**Study Time:** 2½ hours
	❑ Take **Diagnostic Test** and review answer explanations.
	    ❑ Based on your errors on the **Diagnostic Test,** identify difficult topics and their corresponding chapters. These are your targeted chapters.
	    ❑ Read your target chapters first.		

6 days before the test	**Study Time:** 2 hours
	❑ **Airway:** Chapter VI
	    ❑ Read chapter.
	    ❑ Do practice question 1 in each section.
	    ❑ For targeted areas, do practice questions 1 and 2.
	❑ **Advanced Airway:** Chapter XII
	    ❑ Read chapter.
	    ❑ Do practice question 1 in each section.
	    ❑ For targeted areas, do practice questions 1 and 2.
		Study Time: 1 hour
		❑ **Medical Emergencies:** Chapter VIII
		    ❑ Read section C.
		    ❑ Do practice questions 1–5 in this section.
		❑ **Anatomy and Physiology:** Chapter XIV
		    ❑ Read section C2.
		    ❑ Answer practice questions 4 and 6 in this section.
			Study Time: 1 hour
			❑ **Trauma:** Chapter IX
			    ❑ Read sections A and B.
			    ❑ Do the practice questions 1 and 2 in each section.
			    ❑ For targeted areas, do practice questions 1–3.
			❑ **Practical Skills:** Chapter XIII
			    ❑ Read section D.

5 days before the test	**Study Time:** 2 hours
	❑ **Practical Skills:** Chapter XIII
	    ❑ Read section B.
	    ❑ **Anatomy and Physiology:** Chapter XIV
	    ❑ Read section C1.
	❑ **Medical Emergencies:** Chapter VIII
	    ❑ Read section C.
	    ❑ Do practice questions 1–5.
		Study Time: 1 hour
		❑ **Practical Skills:** Chapter XIII
		    ❑ Read section C.
		❑ **Anatomy and Physiology:** Chapter XIV
		    ❑ Review relevant terms in section A. Highlight any difficult terms.
		    ❑ Create flashcards to review difficult terms.
			Study Time: 1 hour
			❑ **Trauma:** Chapter IX
			    ❑ Read sections C and D.
			    ❑ Do the practice questions 1 and 2 in each section.
			    ❑ For targeted areas, do practice questions 1–3.
			❑ **Practical Skills:** Chapter XIII
			    ❑ Read section E.

4 days before the test	**Study Time:** 2 hours
	❑ **Airway:** Chapter VI
	    ❑ Read chapter.
	    ❑ Do remaining practice questions in each section.
	❑ **Advanced Airway:** Chapter XII
	    ❑ Read chapter.
	    ❑ Do remaining practice questions in each section.
		Study Time: 1 hour
		❑ **Practical Skills:** Chapter XIII
		    ❑ Review section C.
		❑ **Anatomy and Physiology:** Chapter XIV
		    ❑ Review the flashcards you created.
			Study Time: 1 hour
			❑ **Trauma:** Chapter IX
			    ❑ Review sections A–D.
			    ❑ Do the remaining practice questions in each section.

Medical Emergencies	Obstetrics and Pediatrics	Operations

Study Time: 1 hour
❏ **Medical Emergencies:**
Chapter VIII
  ❏ Read sections A, D, and E.
  ❏ Do practice questions 1 and 2 in each section.
  ❏ For targeted areas, do practice questions 1–3.
	Study Time: 1 hour
	❏ **Infants and Children:** Chapter X
	  ❏ Read section A.
	  ❏ Do practice questions 1 and 2 in this section.
	  ❏ For targeted areas, do practice questions 1–3.
		Study Time: 2 hours
		❏ **Preparatory:** Chapter V
		  ❏ Read chapter.
		  ❏ Do practice questions 1 and 2 in each section.
		  ❏ For targeted areas, do practice questions 1–3.

Study Time: 1 hour
❏ **Medical Emergencies:**
Chapter VIII
  ❏ Read sections F–H.
  ❏ Do practice questions 1 and 2 in each section.
  ❏ For targeted areas, do practice questions 1–3.
	Study Time: 1 hour
	❏ **Infants and Children:** Chapter X
	  ❏ Read section B.
	  ❏ Do practice questions 1 and 2 in this section.
	  ❏ For targeted areas, do practice questions 1–3.
		Study Time: 2 hours
		❏ **Patient Assessment:** Chapter VII
		  ❏ Read chapter.
		  ❏ Do practice questions 1 and 2 in each section.
		  ❏ For targeted areas, do practice questions 1–3.

Study Time: 1 hour
❏ **Anatomy and Physiology:**
Chapter XIV
  ❏ Read sections A–C.
  ❏ Do two practice questions in each section.
	Study Time: 1 hour
	❏ **Medical Emergencies:**
	Chapter VIII
	  ❏ Read section I.
	  ❏ Do the practice questions in this section.
		Study Time: 2 hours
		❏ **Operations:** Chapter XI
		  ❏ Read chapter.
		  ❏ Do practice questions 1 and 2 in each section.
		  ❏ For targeted areas, do practice questions 1–3.

continued

	Airway and Breathing	Cardiology	Trauma
3 days before the test	**Study Time:** 2½ hours ❏ Take **Practice Test** and review answer explanations. ❏ Based on your errors on the **Practice Test,** identify difficult topics and their corresponding chapters. These are your targeted areas.		
2 days before the test	**Study Time:** 2 hours ❏ Based on Practice Test, review sections that still need attention. ❏ **Airway:** Chapter VI ❏ Review sections A and B. ❏ Do practice question 5 in each section. ❏ **Advanced Airway:** Chapter XII ❏ Review section A. ❏ Do practice questions 1–10.	**Study Time:** 1 hour ❏ Based on Practice Test, review any topics that still require your attention. ❏ **Medical Emergencies:** Chapter VIII ❏ Review section C. ❏ Do practice question 3 in this section. ❏ **Anatomy and Physiology:** Chapter XIV ❏ Review section C2.	**Study Time:** 1 hour ❏ Based on Practice Test, review sections that still present difficulties. ❏ **Anatomy and Physiology:** Chapter XIV ❏ Read sections A and B. Highlight any difficult terms. ❏ Review highlighted terms.
1 day before the test	**Study Time:** 2 hours ❏ **Airway:** Chapter VI ❏ Review section C. ❏ Do practice questions 1–3. ❏ **Advanced Airway:** Chapter XII ❏ Read section B. ❏ Do practice questions 1–10.	**Study Time:** 1 hour ❏ **Medical Emergencies:** Chapter VIII ❏ Review section C. ❏ Do practice questions 4 and 5 in this section. ❏ **Anatomy and Physiology:** Chapter XIV ❏ Review section C2. ❏ Answer practice question 4 in this section.	**Study Time:** 1 hour ❏ **Practical Skills:** Chapter XIII ❏ Read sections D and E. ❏ **Anatomy and Physiology:** Chapter XIV ❏ Review highlighted terms in sections A and B.
Morning of the test	**Reminders:** ❏ Eat a healthy breakfast. ❏ Give yourself extra time to reach the testing facility. If you get there early, you'll have time to review some of your notes. ❏ Bring your Authorization to Test letter and your photo ID with you to the test facility. ❏ Try to go outside for a few minutes and walk around before the test. ❏ Most important: Stay calm and confident during the test. Take deep, slow breaths if you feel at all nervous.		

Medical Emergencies	Obstetrics and Pediatrics	Operations

Study Time: 1 hour
❑ Based on Practice Test, review any sections that you still have trouble with.
❑ **Medical Emergencies:** Chapter VIII
    ❑ Review sections A, D, and E.
    ❑ Do practice questions 3–5 in each section.
	Study Time: 2 hours
	❑ Review the questions concerning Infants and Children that you answered incorrectly on the Practice Test.
	❑ **Infants and Children:** Chapter X
	    ❑ Review sections A and B.
	    ❑ Do practice question 4 in each section.
		Study Time: 2 hours
		❑ Based on Practice Test, review any sections that you still have trouble with.
		❑ **Preparatory:** Chapter V
		    ❑ Review chapter.
		    ❑ Do practice question 3 in each section.

Study Time: 1 hour
❑ **Medical Emergencies:** Chapter VIII
    ❑ Review sections F–H.
    ❑ Do practice questions 3–5 in each section.
	Study Time: 1 hour
	❑ **Medical Emergencies:** Chapter VIII
	    ❑ Review section I.
	    ❑ Do two practice questions in this section.
		Study Time: 2 hours
		❑ **Patient Assessment:** Chapter VII
		    ❑ Read chapter.
		    ❑ Do practice question 4 in each section.
		❑ **Operations:** Chapter XI
		    ❑ Read chapter.
		    ❑ Do three practice questions in each section.

V. Preparatory

Some questions on the EMT-Basic exam assess your knowledge of what do to *before* you administer patient care. These questions are called *preparatory questions*, and they assess your knowledge of what to do when you arrive at a scene. They also assess your knowledge of legal and ethical issues as well as your understanding of the different stress-management techniques EMT-Basics employ to stay healthy.

Remember, the test you take may differ from the NREMT exam. This means that you may see questions on state or municipal EMT-Basic exams that include additional questions regarding preparatory topics and other subjects not covered on the NREMT exam. This is why it is important to examine the "Additional Topics to Review" sections in this chapter and go over your notes from class in addition to reading this chapter.

A. Basics of Emergency Care

Suppose you respond to the scene of an automobile crash. The two cars involved in the crash appear to have crashed head-on. Several bystanders are on the scene, and shattered glass is on the road. A passenger in one of the vehicles has crawled out of the car and appears to be fine. She tells you that she believes the driver of the car, who is still inside the car, is seriously injured and needs immediate attention. You notice smoke coming from under the hood of the car.

As an EMT, you have many responsibilities—you need to assess the driver of the car as well as others in the vehicles who may be injured. You need to keep the bystanders safe and away from the glass and call for assistance. What do you do first?

As an EMT, your primary responsibility in an emergency is to protect yourself. This is especially difficult to do when others need your help. However, if you don't take the necessary precautions, you may become injured and unable to help those in need. What should you do *first* in the scenario above? Call the fire department for assistance. The car with smoke coming from under its hood may be on fire. Next, you should try to move any bystanders away from the scene of the accident. In some cases, EMT-Basics must have special training to extricate, or remove, a patient who is trapped in a motor vehicle or other dangerous situation. This process is further discussed in Chapter XI, "Operations." If you do not have the proper training to extricate the patient from the vehicle, it is important for you to wait for the fire department to arrive and secure the scene before you attempt to assess the trapped patient. Questions about the EMT-Basic's primary responsibilities will be part of the EMT-Basic exam.

1. Personal Protection

EMT-Basics can protect themselves in several ways. One way is to avoid coming into contact with hazardous materials. Hazardous materials, such as high levels of carbon monoxide, should be dealt with by a hazmat team. You may remember from your training that a *hot zone* is an area containing hazardous materials. EMT-Basics should never go into a hot zone even if a patient has been decontaminated.

EMT-Basics should also be on the lookout for other life-threatening situations such as fires, potential explosions, and electricity, such as from downed power lines. They should not enter areas when such dangers are present. EMT-Basics should also be on the lookout for people who are upset or angry. EMT-Basics should not intervene in violent situations. Domestic disturbances are particularly dangerous and often escalate into violence. Police presence is necessary before treating patients in these situations. Some questions on the EMT-Basic exam may ask what an EMT-Basic should do to stay safe in a dangerous situation.

2. Body Substance Isolation (BSI)

Body substance isolation (BSI) precautions are designed to keep you from coming into contact with blood and bodily fluids. Because you can't always tell if a patient is ill or has a contagious disease, it's important for EMT-Basics to follow BSI precautions. Because this is so important, expect to answer test questions about BSI.

BSI precautions include washing hands, wearing gloves, and wearing eye protection, masks, and gowns, when appropriate. BSI precautions should be followed whenever an EMT-Basic responds to an incident and before coming into contact with a patient.

Hand washing is important in preventing the spread of infection and disease. Before you treat a patient and whenever you change your gloves, use a liquid disinfecting agent that doesn't require water. After transporting a patient to a hospital, remove your gloves and wash your hands thoroughly. Also wash your wrists and forearms. Wash your hands for at least 10–15 seconds and then dry them with a disposable towel.

EMT-Basics should make a habit of wearing gloves at all times in the field to protect themselves from blood or bodily fluids. Most gloves are either vinyl or nitrile. EMTs today rarely wear latex gloves. Always remember to change your gloves when moving from one patient to another to prevent cross-contamination.

EMT-Basics should wear eye protection, masks, and gowns whenever there is a possibility that they'll be splashed with blood or bodily fluids. This includes treating patients who are spurting blood or giving birth. EMT-Basics should also wear a mask when performing endotracheal intubation and when their patient may have an airborne infectious disease, such as tuberculosis.

3. Lifting and Carrying Patients

The job of an EMT-Basic is physically demanding. EMT-Basics routinely transport patients, which requires lifting and carrying them. Some test questions ask how you should move a patient without becoming injured. To avoid a lower-back injury, follow these guidelines when lifting a patient:

- Assess a patient's weight before lifting and note whether you need assistance.
- Keep your back straight and use your legs and not your back. Don't twist your torso. Bend slightly at the knees.
- Keep your feet shoulder-length apart and make sure you have traction under your feet. Keep your feet flat on the ground. Straddle the patient and distribute the weight to the balls of your feet.
- Use the power lift (squat lift) when lifting from the ground.
- Use the power grip. With this grip, your palm and fingers are in contact with the person or object being lifted, and your fingers are bent at the same angle.

EMT-Basics frequently carry patients from the scene to an ambulance. Follow these guidelines when carrying a patient:

- Use a wheeled stretcher whenever possible.
- When a patient must be carried on a stretcher or backboard, use as many emergency personnel as possible. A one-handed carry using more than two persons is safer than two EMT-Basics using a two-handed carry.
- Use a stair chair to carry a patient down stairs.

Tip: Before you take the EMT-Basic exam, carefully review these techniques: rapid extrication of a patient from a vehicle, direct ground lift, direct carry method, and the draw sheet method. Be sure to know which technique should be used with which type of injury. For example, the direct ground lift should only be used when a spinal injury is not suspected.

The following equipment is used to lift and transport patients:

- *Wheeled stretcher*—Used to transport patients from the scene to an ambulance.
- *Portable stretcher*—Used in places that are too small for a wheeled stretcher.
- *Scoop stretcher*—Used to lift a patient into a supine position onto a wheeled stretcher.
- *Backboard*—Used to immobilize a patient; long backboards immobilize the entire patient while short backboards are used to immobilize the patient's spine as the patient is being extricated.
- *Stair chair*—Used to transport a patient down stairs; most have wheels used to roll the patient onto a stretcher once the patient is safely down the stairs.
- *Basket stretcher*—Used in rescues; ropes and lifting devices are easily attached.
- *Flexible stretcher*—Used to carry a patient from an upper floor from to a ground floor; should only be used when there is no suspected spinal injury.

4. Patient Positioning

The EMT-Basic exam often includes questions about patient positioning. The way in which a patient is positioned depends on his or her condition:

- Unresponsive patients are usually placed in the recovery position (on left side, left arm under head, bent left knee).
- Pediatric patients may be placed in a safety seat designed for an ambulance.
- Patients with a spinal injury must be immobilized.
- Patients in shock should be placed in Trendelenburg position (supine, legs bent at hip, with feet lifted 8–12 inches).
- Patients with chest pain are usually more comfortable sitting than lying down.

5. Medical Direction Physician

On the EMT-Basic exam and in this book, you'll see references to *medical direction*, or medical control. This is a process by which physicians monitor and assist EMT-Basics in the field. There are two types of medical direction.

On-line medical direction involves direct communication between the EMT-Basic and the physician. Medical direction can offer advice about specific treatments. In some cases, EMT-Basics must receive authorization from medical direction before performing certain interventions. EMT-Basics will often contact medical direction via cellular phone or radio.

Physicians also assist EMT-Basics through *indirect medical direction*, or off-line medical control. This involves the ways in which physicians develop protocols for EMS systems and influence the education of EMT-Basics.

As an EMT-Basic, it's important that you cultivate a good working relationship with medical direction. Medical direction is a valuable resource for EMT-Basics, so it's important for you to treat the physician on call with respect and to always abide by his or her instructions.

Additional Topics to Review

- Reaching, pushing, and pulling
- Emergency moves

Practice

Directions (1–5): Select the best answer for each question or incomplete statement.

1. You respond to a call to assist a patient who has gone into labor. To follow body substance isolation (BSI) precautions, you should put on

   A. a mask.
   B. gloves.
   C. eye protection.
   D. all of the above

2. When lifting a patient on a stretcher, you should

   A. bend slightly at the knees.
   B. twist your torso slightly.
   C. distribute the weight in your fingers.
   D. keep your feet together.

3. The preferred device to transport a patient with a suspected spinal injury is a

   A. wheeled stretcher.
   B. flexible stretcher.
   C. long backboard.
   D. basket stretcher.

4. You arrive on the scene to find a tractor-trailer on its side. Gasoline is leaking onto the roadway. The driver is still inside the vehicle and appears to be unconscious. A passenger is out of the tractor-trailer and lying on the ground. You should first

    A. treat the passenger.

    B. remove the driver from the vehicle.

    C. call for assistance.

    D. remove the gasoline from the road.

5. You arrive on the scene to find a patient experiencing an attack of angina. The patient has a prescription for nitroglycerin. You call medical direction for assistance. The medical direction physician advises you to assist the patient in taking the nitroglycerin. This is an example of

    A. on-line medical direction.

    B. indirect medical direction.

    C. quality improvement.

    D. quality care.

Answers

1. **D.** When assisting a woman in childbirth, an EMT-Basic is at risk of being splashed with blood or bodily fluids. EMT-Basics in this situation should wear *a mask*, *gloves*, *eye protection*, and a gown.

2. **A.** When lifting a patient on a stretcher, an EMT-Basic should keep his or her back straight and *bend slightly at the knees*. Feet should be shoulder-length apart and weight should be distributed on the balls of the feet.

3. **C.** A patient with a suspected spinal injury should be immobilized. Therefore, he or she should be transported on a *long backboard.*

4. **C.** The gasoline leaking from the tractor-trailer is a serious hazard. EMT-Basics should *call for assistance* and never go into a hot zone.

5. **A.** Because the EMT-Basic had direct contact with the medical direction physician, this is a case of *on-line medical direction.*

B. Dealing with Stress

You already know that an EMT's job can be extremely stressful. EMT-Basics deal with dangerous and mentally draining situations every day. They must not only treat injuries and illnesses, but also help patients who are extremely emotional.

Although EMT-Basics learn how to compartmentalize their emotions on the job, there is no way to avoid stress altogether. In this section, you'll review the ways in which EMT-Basics learn how to cope with the stress they encounter on the job.

1. Managing Stress

Stress is any factor that results in physical or mental tension. Many people think of stress as something negative, but stress can also be positive. Without stress, there would be little motivation to complete our daily tasks. Stress becomes negative when it starts to consume your life, preventing you from functioning in a normal manner. People experience stress in different ways. Symptoms of stress can be physical, emotional, and mental. This is why it's important for you to understand how you can manage stress and prevent it from becoming a serious issue.

There are many situations that cause EMT-Basics to feel stress. Cases involving mass casualties, trauma or abuse of children, or grotesque injuries can have a serious effect on EMS workers. The stress caused by these incidents doesn't always manifest right away. Particularly traumatic cases can continue to affect EMT-Basics for weeks or even months after the initial incident.

While it's impossible to avoid stress altogether, there are simple steps you can take to deal with stress in an effective manner, as summarized in the following figure.

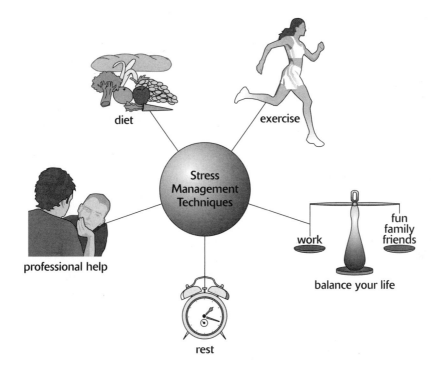

EMT-Basics need to maintain a balanced lifestyle to deal with the stress they encounter on the job.

a. Diet

One of the most important things you can do to manage stress is to eat a well-balanced diet. Eating balanced meals will provide you with the vitamins and nutrients you need to stay healthy. Incorporate fruits, vegetables, and whole grains into your diet. Avoid fatty foods and excessive sugar and salt. These foods can increase your blood pressure, which can contribute to stress.

EMT-Basics are extremely busy, so eating regular meals can be challenging. Skipping meals can cause your blood sugar to drop, making you feel tired and irritable. This is why it's important to eat healthy meals regularly. If you can't find time to eat an entire meal, grab a healthy snack. A banana or a cup of yogurt can help regulate your blood sugar levels until you find the time to eat.

b. Exercise

Getting regular exercise isn't just about staying in shape—it's also an important factor in managing stress. Studies show that regular exercise reduces the risk of a number of serious diseases and greatly contributes to emotional well-being. You don't need to spend hours in the gym to get a good workout. Take your dog for a walk or go for a hike in a nearby park. Any activity that elevates your heart rate will contribute to your overall health.

c. Balance Your Life

EMT-Basics are extremely dedicated to their jobs. However, EMT-Basics need to maintain a balance between their professional and personal lives. It's important for EMT-Basics to involve themselves in activities outside of EMS. Spending time with family and friends and engaging in entertaining activities will help relieve stress and provide the EMT-Basic with an emotional and mental break from job-related stressors.

d. Rest

Getting enough sleep is one of the most important things that an EMT-Basic can do to relieve stress. A lack of sleep adds to stress and could affect your performance on the job. Doctors recommend getting at least eight hours of sleep every night to maintain a healthy lifestyle. Keep yourself on a regular sleep schedule. If you can, try to go to sleep and wake up at the same time every day. This will help your body maintain a normal sleeping pattern and can help prevent insomnia.

e. Professional Help

You may find that you can't deal with symptoms of stress on your own. If this happens, it's important for you to seek professional help. There's no shame in speaking with a counselor, physiologist, or other mental health professional about how you're feeling. Often, these professionals can provide you with the tools you need to better manage the stressors you encounter on the job and in your personal life.

Don't wait until the stress becomes too much to handle. If you suspect that something isn't right, contact your doctor for a referral to a mental health professional. You can also ask for referrals from coworkers or friends who have dealt with these issues in the past.

2. Critical Incident Stress Debriefing

Certain situations can cause great stress for EMS workers. A *critical incident* is a situation that causes EMS workers to experience serious emotional reactions and may inhibit their ability to perform their duties. These incidents may include situations involving the death or injury of a coworker or loved one. Critical incidents may also include mass-casualty emergencies and situations in which the patient dies after a long rescue attempt.

To help EMS workers deal with these situations, many systems have implemented a process called *critical incident stress debriefing* (CISD). CISDs are initiated within 24 to 72 hours after the initial incident. The debriefing, which is conducted by peer counselors and mental health professionals, allows EMS workers to discuss their feelings about the incident. These debriefings don't involve any discussion about the technical aspects of a case. Rather, it is a confidential discussion about how the incident has affected the emotional and mental well-being of the EMT-Basics. Everyone who was involved in the incident is invited to participate in the CISD.

CISDs can also involve discussion of general job-related stresses that most EMS workers experience. The important thing to remember is that the CISD is designed to be a safe environment for EMS workers to discuss their feelings. The main goal of the CISD is to expedite the recovery process after a critical incident. The debriefing process can help individuals process their emotions more quickly than they would be able to on their own. The professionals involved in CISD can also recommend further treatment for EMS workers who are particularly affected by certain cases.

3. Cases Involving Death and Dying

Some of the most difficult cases that EMT-Basics deal with involve patients who are dying. It's important to remember that people deal with death in different ways. You should always treat patients and family members who are dealing with this situation with the utmost respect and compassion.

While you should never offer false hope in a serious situation, you can show your support through simple gestures. Holding a patient's hand or simply listening to the patient's concerns can mean a lot. Always do your best to help friends and family members through this difficult time. Allow them to express their feelings through whatever means necessary. Some people may cry, scream, or show very little reaction to the news of a loved one's death. Do what you can to comfort them.

Remember, these cases can also have a serious effect on you and your coworkers. Don't ignore feelings of grief or sadness. Discuss your emotions with your coworkers. If you are particularly affected by a case, ask your supervisor for a CISD or seek professional help.

Additional Topics to Review

- Elisabeth Kübler-Ross's five stages of grief
- Comprehensive critical incident stress management

Practice

Directions (1–4): Select the best answer for each question or incomplete statement.

1. You are called to the home of an elderly woman with terminal cancer. Her daughter says that the woman has been silent and sometimes doesn't acknowledge her presence. This woman is likely exhibiting

    A. acceptance.
    B. denial.
    C. depression.
    D. bargaining.

2. EMS workers who cannot deal with stress on their own should

    A.   get more sleep.
    B.   eat healthy foods.
    C.   spend time with their friends.
    D.   seek professional help.

3. EMS workers can maintain their blood sugar levels by

    A.   eating regular meals.
    B.   taking long walks.
    C.   taking a vacation.
    D.   discussing their feelings.

4. What is the main goal of the CISD?

    A.   to place blame on coworkers
    B.   to expedite the recovery process
    C.   to discuss job-related stressors
    D.   to identify EMT-Basics who need professional help

Answers

1. **C.** According to Elisabeth Kübler-Ross's five stages of grief, silence can be a sign of *depression* in patients who are dealing with terminal illnesses.

2. **D.** EMS workers who cannot deal with stress on their own should *seek professional help*.

3. **A.** *Eating regular meals* can help EMS workers maintain their blood sugar levels.

4. **B.** The main goal of the CISD is *to expedite the recovery process*, although job-related stressors may also be discussed during these meetings.

C. Legal and Ethical Issues

EMT-Basics must obey laws pertaining to patient care and behave in an ethical manner. When EMT-Basics demonstrate ethics, they treat their patients with respect and offer them the best possible care. Suppose an EMT-Basic responds to a call to help an elderly man who may be suffering a heart attack. He assesses the patient and helps him take his nitroglycerine. When the EMT's cell phone rings, he steps away from the patient to speak to a friend. Is this EMT's behavior legal? Is it ethical? No! The EMT-Basic could be charged with abandonment, and his behavior is definitely not ethical. Some questions on the EMT-Basic exam will assess your knowledge of legal and ethical issues.

1. Consent

As you may recall from your training, patients have the right to consent to or refuse medical treatment. An adult who is mentally competent and of legal age must give *expressed consent* before receiving treatment. A patient may give expressed consent verbally or may simply nod his or her head. In some situations, expressed consent involves a written document that is signed by the patient. Prior to receiving the treatment, the patient should obtain details about the procedure and the risks involved. Once the patient has all the necessary information, he or she can give the EMT-Basic *informed consent*. If a patient is unconscious and no family members are available to consult, the EMT-Basic may initiate medical treatment if it's in the patient's best interest. This is called *implied consent*.

A parent or guardian must give consent for a child or a mentally incompetent adult to receive treatment. However, if a life-threatening situation exists and the parent or guardian isn't available, you may assume implied consent. You don't need to consult a parent or guardian for a child who is *emancipated*. An emancipated child may not be of legal age, but may be pregnant, a parent, or married. An emancipated child may also be a member of the armed services, or he or she may be a financially independent individual who no longer lives with his or her parents.

Tip: Patients under the influence of drugs or alcohol can't give expressed consent because they are unable to make rational decisions. If a scenario is given on the EMT-Basic exam in which the patient is intoxicated and the question asks what type of consent you need to administer medical treatment, don't choose expressed consent. Implied consent is a better choice.

2. Confidentiality

The Health Insurance Portability and Accountability Act, or HIPAA, has made rules regarding patient confidentiality more strict. While laws regarding patient confidentiality vary from state to state, most states consider the following information confidential:

- Patient interviews
- Patient assessments
- Treatments that a patient has undergone

You can't release this information to a patient's friends or family without the patient's permission. In most states, you may release patient information to other health care professionals and insurance companies. When a crime is involved, such as a rape or a shooting, you must report it to legal authorities. You can also be subpoenaed for information. If this is the case, you're legally bound to release the information.

3. Refusal of Care

Suppose you're administering care to an unconscious patient who awakens and refuses to let you continue the medical treatment. What should you do? You must respect the patient's wishes and stop treatment. You should also have the patient sign a "release from liability" form, which states that the patient has been advised to undergo medical treatment but has refused to do so. This form protects EMT-Basics and other health care professionals from being sued if the patient suffers additional illness or injury resulting from the refusal of care. If the patient refuses to sign the form, have a family member or a police officer sign the form and indicate that they have witnessed the patient refusing treatment. If you continue to treat a patient who has refused care, you may be charged with assault and battery. If you *assault* a patient, you threaten him or her or try to touch the patient in an offensive way. If you do touch the patient in an offensive way, you're guilty of battery. The EMT-Basic exam often includes questions about what an EMT-Basic should do when a patient refuses care.

Patients may only refuse care if they're mentally competent and of legal age. If a patient is intoxicated or in shock, the patient's judgment may be impaired. When this is the case, ask a family member to allow you to continue treatment.

The following might help you convince a patient to undergo treatment if the patient refuses to do so:

- Inform the patient of the potential consequences of refusing medical treatment.
- Ask the patient's family or friends to help you convince the patient of the benefits of treatment. However, be careful not to betray the patient's confidentiality.
- Ask the patient to go to the hospital to receive further care.
- Consult with your medical direction physician and have him or her speak to the patient.
- Remain on the scene in case the patient changes his or her mind.

4. Advanced Directives

Because EMT-Basics treat patients who may be in life-threatening situations, they should be familiar with advanced directives. You may be asked questions about these directives on the EMT-Basic exam. *Advanced directives* are documents patients use to convey their wishes when they are unable to do so.

a. Do Not Resuscitate (DNR) Orders

A physician usually writes *Do Not Resuscitate (DNR) orders* at the patient's request. These orders state that few, if any, measures should be taken if the patient suffers cardiac arrest. Terminally ill patients often have DNR orders. When examining a DNR order, check to ensure that it has been signed by a physician and that it's in effect and not past an expiration date. You must see the order—it's not enough for the patient or a family member to tell you that one exists. Whenever you're in doubt, begin resuscitating the patient and consult your medical direction physician.

b. Living Wills

A *living will* states what medical treatments a patient wants, or doesn't want, if he or she becomes incapacitated. A living will might state that a patient wants only basic life support or it may state that the patient wants all efforts to be made to save his or her life. Living wills only apply in the administration of life-sustaining treatment, meaning situations of life or death. If a patient suffers a moderate or severe injury that is not life-threatening, always administer treatment.

5. Organ Donation

EMT-Basics must be familiar with laws regarding organ donation. Patients who are organ donors must have a legal, signed document stating this. This document may be a sticker on the patient's driver's license or an organ donor card. Be aware that saving a patient's life must always be your first priority regardless of whether the patient wishes to donate his or her organs.

6. Negligence

EMT-Basics have a *duty to act*. This means that they are legally bound to provide emergency medical care when the need arises. If an EMT-Basic does not do this, he or she may be charged with *negligence*. The following must be proven before an EMT-Basic is considered negligent:

1. The EMT-Basic had a duty to act. This means it was the EMT-Basic's responsibility to provide a patient with medical treatment. (Whether an EMT-Basic has a duty to act when off duty depends on the laws in his or her state.)
2. The EMT-Basic failed to act. This might also mean that the EMT-Basic failed to provide satisfactory medical treatment.
3. Damage occurred because the EMT-Basic did not act. This means that the patient suffered physical or emotional injury because the EMT-Basic didn't act.
4. The injury the patient suffered was caused by the EMT-Basic's inaction. This is called *proximate cause*.

7. Abandonment

If an EMT-Basic starts to provide patient care but then stops without the patient's consent, the EMT-Basic may be guilty of *abandonment*. The only time EMT-Basics are allowed to stop giving a patient care is if another EMT-Basic or a person with equal or higher medical training takes over the patient's care. EMT-Basics may stop patient care once a patient arrives at a hospital, if the patient no longer needs or wants treatment, or if the EMT-Basic's safety is threatened.

Additional Topics to Review

- Crime scenes
- Identification insignia (a bracelet, necklace, or card indicating that a person has a pre-existing condition)

Practice

Directions (1–5): Select the best answer for each question or incomplete statement.

1. If a patient tells you that it's okay to perform a medical procedure, this patient has given you

   A. implied consent.
   B. an advanced directive.
   C. expressed consent.
   D. a release from liability.

2. Which patient is most capable of refusing treatment?

   A. a semiconscious woman with a head injury
   B. a middle-aged man who is drunk
   C. a teenage girl under the influence of drugs
   D. a man in his 20s with a cut on his arm

3. An EMT-Basic refuses to treat a patient. The EMT-Basic may be guilty of

    A. abandonment.
    B. assault.
    C. negligence.
    D. battery.

4. A woman you're treating demands that you stop treatment and refuses to sign a release from liability form. She does not appear to be under the influence of drugs or alcohol and seems mentally stable. You should

    A. continue to treat her anyway.
    B. try to convince her to let you or someone else treat her.
    C. leave the scene and tell your supervisor.
    D. tell her she is legally obligated to sign the form.

5. In most states, you can release a patient's information to a patient's

    A. doctor.
    B. insurance company.
    C. both A and B.
    D. neither A nor B

Answers

1. **C.** Verbal consent is *expressed consent*. If a patient is unable to give verbal consent, in most cases, you may assume implied consent.

2. **D.** Patients must not have impaired judgment when refusing treatment. Only the *man in his 20s with a cut on his arm* is of sound mind.

3. **C.** An EMT-Basic who refuses to treat a patient may be guilty of *negligence*. If the EMT-Basic starts treating a patient and then stops, the EMT-Basic may be guilty of abandonment.

4. **B.** EMT-Basics can't treat patients who refuse treatment and do not appear to be impaired. The best option here is *try to convince the woman to undergo the treatment*.

5. **C.** In most states, EMT-Basics may release confidential patient information to *other health care professionals and to insurance companies*.

D. Baseline Vital Signs and SAMPLE History

Preparatory questions also assess your knowledge of taking baseline vital signs and completing a SAMPLE history. Remember that baseline vital signs are those you take when you first come into contact with a patient. You later use these signs when you reassess the patient. Changes in vital signs indicate changes in the patient's condition. The SAMPLE history is information you gather about a patient and his or her medical condition.

1. Baseline Vital Signs

Note the following when you are assessing baseline vital signs:

Breathing: Watch the patient breathe. During one complete breath, the patient's chest will rise and then fall. Count the number of breaths the patient takes in 30 seconds, and then multiply this number by 2 to determine the number of breaths per minute. Note that breathing is also referred to as *respiration.* The following are normal respiration rates:

- Adults: 12–20 respirations per minute
- Small children: 20–30 respirations per minute
- Infants: greater than 30 respirations per minute

Also note the quality of a patient's respirations. The patient's chest should expand. Breathing should sound clear and not noisy.

Pulse: When you take a patient's pulse, note that a rate of 60–100 is normal for adults. The pulse of children and elderly patients may be faster. A patient's pulse should be strong and regular. A weak pulse is a sign of shock.

Skin: EMT-Basics note the patient's skin color when assessing baseline vital signs. Skin color is assessed in the nail beds, inside the mouth (*oral mucosa*), and inside the lower eyelid (*conjunctiva*). The normal color of skin in these areas is pink, regardless of whether the patient has light or dark skin. Assess the soles of the feet or the palms in children and infants for capillary refill time. Pale skin color indicates a lack of blood flow. A patient with flushed skin may have been exposed to heat or carbon monoxide.

Pupils: A patient's pupils should be normal and equal in size. The pupils should constrict when you shine a penlight in the eyes and then dilate when the light is removed. A patient whose pupils don't react to light may have a head injury or may have ingested medications that affect pupil dilation.

Blood pressure: As you may remember, *systolic blood pressure* is a measurement of the pressure against the walls of the arteries as the heart contracts. *Diastolic blood pressure* is a measurement of the pressure against the walls of the blood vessels as the heart relaxes. In adults, normal blood pressure is 120/80 (systolic/diastolic). Blood pressure is lower in children but increases as they grow older. In a 5-year-old child, normal blood pressure is 90/52, and in a 10-year-old child, normal blood pressure is 100/60.

2. SAMPLE History

A SAMPLE history is a medical history, which EMT-Basics obtain from the patient, his or her family, and bystanders. The information you obtain during a SAMPLE history should be documented accurately, clearly, and concisely. SAMPLE is an acronym to help you remember the six elements of this history:

Signs and symptoms: A *sign* is a medical condition you can observe in a patient, such as skin color. A *symptom* is a condition that the patient describes, such as nausea, that you can't see.

Allergies: Always ask patients if they are allergic to medications, foods, or anything in the environment. Some people are allergic to penicillin or sulfa drugs. Others are allergic to milk or shellfish. Common allergens in the environment include grass and other plants. Check for medical alert tags. Determining a patient's allergies can help you determine if the patient has had an allergic reaction.

Medications: Ask a patient what medications he or she is taking. Inquire as to both prescribed and over-the-counter medications. If medication is prescribed, ask if it is being taken as directed.

Pertinent past medical history: Ask the patient about past medical problems, surgeries, and injuries.

Last oral intake (solid or liquid): Ask the patient to indicate the time and amount of food and liquid he or she last consumed.

Events leading to the injury or illness: Have the patient identify the events leading to the injury or illness. If the patient has chest pain, note whether the patient was active or resting when the pain first occurred. Use the acronym OPQRST to help you question the patient:

- **O—onset** (when the problem first occurred)
- **P—provocation** (what makes it better or worse)
- **Q—quality** (the patient's description of signs or symptoms)
- **R—radiation** (whether the pain moves to another location)
- **S—severity** (on a scale from 0 to 10, with 0 meaning no symptoms)
- **T—time** (the length of time the condition has been present)

Additional Topic to Review

- Vital sign reassessment

Practice

Directions (1–5): Select the best answer for each question or incomplete statement.

1. You and your partner assess a 40-year-old woman's breathing while assessing her baseline vital signs. A normal number of respirations per minute for this woman is

   A. 11.
   B. 15.
   C. 25.
   D. 40.

2. A patient tells you that he has pain in his right leg. This pain is a

   A. symptom.
   B. past medical history.
   C. sign.
   D. reaction.

3. The M in SAMPLE stands for

    A. medical.
    B. muscles.
    C. maintenance.
    D. medications.

4. While assessing a teenage boy's baseline vital signs, you suspect he has suffered a head injury because his

    A. skin is flushed.
    B. pupils don't react to light.
    C. pulse is irregular.
    D. blood pressure is high.

5. A normal pulse rate for an average adult would be

    A. 45.
    B. 50.
    C. 70.
    D. 110.

Answers

1. **B.** A normal adult should have *12–20 respirations per minute*.

2. **A.** A *symptom* is a description from the patient that can't be seen by the EMT-Basic, such as pain. A sign is a medical condition that can be observed in a patient, such as a bruise.

3. **D.** The M in SAMPLE stands for *medications*.

4. **B.** If a patient's *pupils don't react to light*, the patient may have a head injury.

5. **C.** The normal pulse rate for an average adult would be *60–100*.

VI. Airway

The airway section of the EMT-Basic exam tests your knowledge of the different parts and functions of the respiratory system. You'll also be tested on what to do when the airway is obstructed (blocked) and on your knowledge of different artificial ventilation techniques.

About 18 percent of the NREMT cognitive exam tests your knowledge of the respiratory system using fact-based and scenario-based questions. The fact-based questions are designed to test your comprehension skills, while the scenario-based questions present a situation and ask you what needs to be done next. These types of questions assess your ability to apply what you've learned to real-life situations.

The information and practice questions in this section should be used to review what you've already learned about the respiratory system. This section does not cover everything that you will see on the exam, so remember to read the "Additional Topics to Review" sections in this chapter for more information.

A. The Respiratory System

The respiratory system is made up of the parts of the body in which air passes through, including the mouth, nose, lungs, pharynx, trachea, and bronchi. Collectively, these passageways are known as the airway. The main function of the respiratory system is to take oxygen into the lungs by way of either the nose or the mouth and then release carbon dioxide back out through the nose or the mouth. An obstructed (blocked) airway is an extremely dangerous situation that can result in death if left untreated. As an EMT-Basic, one of your most important jobs is to ensure that the patient's airway remains open and clear at all times.

1. Parts of the Respiratory System

You are probably already familiar with the different parts of the respiratory system. In this section, you'll find an overview of the function of the organs in the respiratory system.

When you breathe in air through your *mouth* or *nose*, air travels to the *pharynx* (throat), which is located directly behind your mouth and nasal cavity. The pharynx connects the nasal and oral cavities to the *larynx*, or voice box. The pharynx is divided into two parts: the *nasopharynx*, which is located behind the nasal cavity, and the *oropharynx* (back of the throat), which is located below the nasopharynx.

Air flows from the pharynx to the *trachea*, or windpipe, through the *glottis*, the middle of the larynx that houses the vocal cords. A flaplike structure above the glottis called the *epiglottis* prevents food or liquid from entering the trachea. The air continues through the trachea and passes the *cricoid ring*, which is the first tracheal ring. EMT-Basics should be familiar with the location of the cricoid ring because it is the only complete ring of cartilage in the trachea.

After that, air continues to flow into the right and left *bronchi*, the large tubes that connect the trachea to the lungs. The air passes through the bronchi and eventually reaches the *alveoli*, which are tiny air sacs where oxygen and carbon dioxide are exchanged.

Two muscle groups aid in respiration: the diaphragm and the intercostal muscles. The *diaphragm* is a large muscle that extends across the bottom of the rib cage. The *intercostal muscles* are located between the ribs and help move the chest cavity outward during inhalation and inward during exhalation. During inhalation, the diaphragm and the intercostal muscles contract to increase the size of the chest cavity. The diaphragm moves downward as the ribs move outward to allow air to flow into the lungs. During exhalation, the diaphragm and the intercostal muscles relax to decrease the size of the chest cavity. The diaphragm moves upward and the ribs move inward to push air out of the lungs.

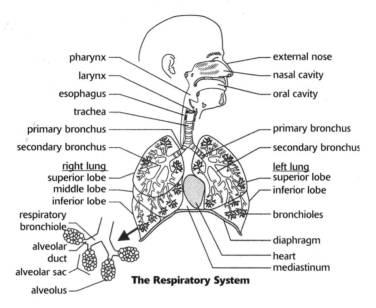

A view of the respiratory system.

2. Adequate Breathing

Two types of breathing rhythms exist: adequate and inadequate. *Adequate*, or normal, breathing occurs when a person breathes at an adequate, or normal, depth and rate to meet the oxygen demands of the body. The number of breaths a person takes per minute is called the *respiratory rate*. The following are normal respiratory rates:

- Adults: 12–20 breaths per minute
- Children: 15–30 breaths per minute
- Infants: 25–50 breaths per minute

The amount of air a person inhales and exhales in a single breath varies. The air breathed in and out is called the *tidal volume*. The normal tidal volume for an average adult is 500 ml.

Adequate breathing is relaxed and quiet. A person who exhibits an adequate breathing rhythm produces equal breath sounds, exerts minimal effort when breathing, and expands the chest equally.

3. Inadequate Breathing

Inadequate, or irregular, breathing is defined as stressed or labored. A person who exhibits an inadequate breathing rhythm produces no breath sounds, exerts effort when breathing, and may expand the chest unequally.

Tip: All inadequate breathing cases are emergency situations.

As an EMT-Basic, one of the most important skills you'll learn is to recognize the signs of inadequate breathing patterns. A person who is having difficulty breathing may exhibit one or more of the following signs:

- Shortness of breath
- Too fast or too slow respiratory rates
- Irregular rhythm
- Nonexistent breath sounds
- Shallow, unequal chest expansion
- Pale, cyanotic (blue), or clammy skin
- Retractions above clavicles or between ribs
- Nasal flaring or seesaw breathing in children or infants
- Gasping breaths
- Changes in consciousness

Additional Topics to Review

- Respiratory anatomy: location of the different parts of the respiratory system
- Respiratory physiology: the process of exchanging oxygen and carbon dioxide
- Functions of the alveolar sac and capillaries during gas exchange
- Differences in airway structure for adults, children, and infants, such as tongue, trachea, and chest wall size, and cricoids ring development
- Hypoxia: condition in which the body's tissues and cells don't get adequate oxygen

Practice

Directions (1–5): Select the best answer for each question or incomplete statement.

1. A sign of inadequate breathing in a 50-year-old male is

   A. a seesaw breathing motion.
   B. flared nostrils.
   C. a respiratory rate of 12–20 breaths per minute.
   D. cyanotic skin.

2. The normal tidal volume for an average adult is

   A. 500 ml.
   B. 400 ml.
   C. 250 ml.
   D. 200 ml.

3. Which of the following takes place during exhalation?

   A. Oxygen is pushed out of the lungs.
   B. The size of the chest increases.
   C. The diaphragm moves upward.
   D. The intercostal muscles moves outward.

4. The trachea is commonly referred to as the

   A. voice box.
   B. windpipe.
   C. throat.
   D. vocal cords.

5. You arrive on the scene to find a 3-year-old child lying flat on the ground. You know that her breathing is inadequate because

   A. her chest is not rising and falling.
   B. you can hear her breath sounds.
   C. she does not exhibit cyanotic skin.
   D. her respiratory rate is 15–30 breaths per minute.

Answers

1. **D.** *Cyanotic* or blue skin is a sign of inadequate breathing in a 50-year-old male.

2. **A.** The normal tidal volume for an average adult is *500 ml*.

3. **C.** During exhalation, *the diaphragm moves upward* and the intercostal muscles relax.

4. **B.** The *windpipe* is another name for the trachea.

5. **A.** You can tell that the child's breathing is inadequate because *her chest is not rising and falling*. If she was breathing normally, you'd be able to hear breath sounds and her respiratory rate would be 15–30 breaths per minute.

B. Opening the Airway

Once you've established that the patient is suffering from inadequate breathing, you should ensure that the patient's airway remains open. A blocked or closed airway can lead to death. In the following section, you'll review the different ways to open the airway in an emergency situation.

1. Manual Positioning

Whether a patient is conscious or unconscious, the first thing you should do is get him or her into the *supine* position (lying on his or her back and facing up). Unconscious patients sometimes lose control of their jaw, which may cause the tongue to fall to the back of their throat. This can cause the epiglottis to block the glottic opening and close the airway. In situations where there is no suspected trauma, use the *head-tilt chin-lift* technique to open the airway. This technique helps pull the tongue out of the oropharynx and moves the epiglottis away from the glottis. Remember, you should use two fingers to slowly tilt the head back and lift the chin when performing the head-tilt chin-lift technique.

If you suspect the patient has suffered trauma, you should avoid moving the neck, which could damage the spinal cord. Instead, perform the *jaw thrust* maneuver. This technique is used to move the jaw forward, which opens the airway. To perform this technique, carefully push the jaw forward using your thumbs, keeping your index fingers near the mouth opening.

After the airway is opened, check the patient for signs of breathing by listening for breath sounds and feeling the patient's chest for movement. If the patient is unable to maintain regular breathing, you should use an airway adjunct to keep the airway open.

2. Airway Adjuncts

An airway adjunct is a device that helps keep the airway open. There are two types of airway adjuncts: oropharyngeal airways and nasopharyngeal airways. The *oropharyngeal airway* is inserted into the mouth, while the *nasopharyngeal airway* is inserted into the nose.

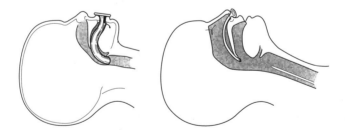

The oropharyngeal (left) and nasopharyngeal (right) airways.

a. Oropharyngeal Airway

The oropharyngeal airway is a curved piece of plastic that is inserted into the patient's mouth. This device lifts the tongue out of the oropharynx. Also called the oral airway or OP airway, the oropharyngeal airway comes in a range of sizes. The oropharyngeal airway is usually used on unresponsive patients who have no gag reflex. The *gag reflex* causes a person to gag when something stimulates the back of the throat, preventing foreign materials from getting caught in the airway. You should not use this type of airway adjunct on a patient who has a gag reflex because the position of the device could cause the patient to vomit or gag. Remember to review the different ways to insert an oropharyngeal airway on adults, children, and infants.

b. Nasopharyngeal Airway

The nasopharyngeal airway, also called the nasal airway or NP airway, is made of flexible rubber or plastic that is inserted into the patient's nostril to provide an airway. Like the oropharyngeal airway, the nasopharyngeal airway comes in a range of sizes. This device is usually used on responsive patients who need help maintaining a clear airway. This airway is a good choice for responsive patients who need assistance breathing because it doesn't stimulate the gag reflex. You can use the same technique to insert the nasopharyngeal airway on adults, children, or infants. Remember to choose the correct size and use lubrication because insertion of the nasopharyngeal airway can be painful to a responsive patient.

3. Suctioning Techniques

After an airway is established, it can sometimes become blocked by liquids such as blood, mucus, or saliva; small particles of vomit; broken teeth; or food. If this happens, you must clear the airway. Any material inhaled into the lungs can cause damage to lung tissue, so it's important to monitor the patient carefully to avoid this.

Tip: If you hear a gurgling sound coming from the patient, this could be a sign that the airway is blocked.

You can clear the airway by rolling the patient onto his or her side and allowing fluids to drain from the mouth. Sometimes you may need to use suction to remove fluids and small particles from the airway.

a. Suction Units

Suction units are important when treating patients with obstructed airways. EMT-Basics should be familiar with three types of suction units: mounted, portable, and hand-operated devices. Most ambulances have mounted, or built-in, suction units powered by the vehicle's battery, portable suction units powered by batteries, and hand-operated suction units. These different suction units can either be used on scene or while transporting patients.

Suction units work by using a vacuum pump to suction, or suck, materials out of the patient's airway and into a canister. They are used in conjunction with a *suction catheter*, which is attached to the end of the tubing before it's placed into the patient's mouth.

The suction catheters used by EMT-Basics are either rigid or soft. Rigid catheters (also called *hard, tonsil tip, tonsil sucker,* or *Yankauer* catheters) are made of hard plastic and are easy to control. They're usually used on unresponsive patients. Rigid catheters can be used on patients of any age. With children and infants, however, it is important to avoid hitting the back of the throat because stimulation of this area can decrease the heart rate.

Soft catheters, also called *French* catheters, are made of long, flexible plastic and used to suction nasal passages. They are often used in situations where rigid catheters cannot be used, such as when the patient is responsive. A bulb syringe may be used in conjunction with a soft catheter for infants and children under 6 months of age. It's important to remember that you should never insert any catheter farther than the base of the tongue.

Before taking the EMT-Basic exam, be sure to review the proper techniques for using different types of suction units and catheters.

Tip: Oxygen is removed during suctioning, so you must limit suctioning to 10–15 seconds and administer oxygen before and after suctioning.

Additional Topics to Review

- Insertion of an oropharyngeal airway; noting the differences between adults, children, and infants
- Insertion of a nasopharyngeal airway
- Using suctioning units
- Proper suctioning techniques
- Using a soft catheter and bulb syringe to suction an infant's airway

Practice

Directions (1–5): Select the best answer for each question or incomplete statement.

1. Which device should be used to suction blood from the mouth of an unresponsive 4-month-old?
   - A. oropharyngeal airway
   - B. nasopharyngeal airway
   - C. tonsil tip
   - D. bulb syringe or soft catheter

2. When performing the jaw thrust maneuver, the EMT-Basic should ensure that the patient is in the
   - A. tripod position.
   - B. supine position.
   - C. prone position.
   - D. Fowler's position.

3. You arrive on the scene and find a 40-year-old woman who passed out and hit her head. She is lying on the kitchen floor and is unresponsive with no gag reflex. She has a pulse. You should use an oropharyngeal airway, which
   - A. provides an airway when inserted into the nose.
   - B. thrusts the jaw forward to open the airway.
   - C. suctions fluids and material from the airway.
   - D. lifts the tongue out of the oropharynx.

4. When opening the airway, the jaw thrust maneuver should be applied to

    A. patients who may have suffered trauma.
    B. all patients regardless of trauma.
    C. only infants and children.
    D. only patients who are conscious.

5. What should the EMT-Basic do immediately before and after suctioning an unresponsive patient?

    A. Clean the suction catheter.
    B. Recharge the suction unit.
    C. Administer oxygen.
    D. Attach a bulb syringe.

Answers

1. **D.** A *bulb syringe or soft catheter* should be used when suctioning fluids from the mouths of infants.

2. **B.** When performing the jaw thrust maneuver, an EMT-Basic should ensure the patient is in the *supine* position, which is lying on his or her back and facing up.

3. **D.** The oropharyngeal airway, which is inserted into the mouth, is used to *lift the tongue out of the oropharynx* to create an airway.

4. **A.** The jaw thrust maneuver should be applied to *patients who may have suffered trauma* because it carefully moves the jaw forward without moving the neck.

5. **C.** Because oxygen is removed during suctioning, the EMT-Basic should *administer oxygen* immediately before and after suctioning an unresponsive patient.

C. Artificial Ventilation

You've already learned about the different techniques that maintain and clear the airway. However, sometimes patients with cleared airways still have trouble breathing on their own and must be artificially ventilated. In this section, you'll review the different techniques of artificial ventilation, which include the following:

- Mouth-to-mouth
- Mouth-to-mask
- Bag-valve mask (BVM)
- Flow-restricted, oxygen-powered ventilation

You'll also learn about the different ways to administer oxygen to patients who have difficulty breathing on their own.

1. Mouth-to-Mouth

Although you probably learned about mouth-to-mouth, or rescue breathing, ventilation as part of your CPR training, take a few moments to review the basics. This technique is performed by placing your mouth over the patient's mouth to deliver oxygen to the patient. After you've ensured that the patient's airway is open, take a deep breath and pinch the patient's nose shut. Place your mouth over the patient's mouth, ensuring you have an airtight seal. Exhale just enough to make the patient's chest rise. Continue mouth-to-mouth ventilation at a rate of 1 breath every 5 seconds for an adult and 1 breath every 3–5 seconds for a child. For infants, place your mouth over the infant's nose *and* mouth, delivering 1 breath every 3 seconds.

Because of the direct physical contact that mouth-to-mouth ventilation requires, this technique is no longer one of the preferred artificial-ventilation methods used by EMT-Basics. However, all trainees are required to learn this method.

2. Mouth-to-Mask

Mouth-to-mask ventilation uses the same principle as mouth-to-mouth ventilation to deliver oxygen to a patient, but requires the use of a mask, such as a portable *pocket mask*. This mask can be used with or without supplemental oxygen. Pocket masks can be used on adults, children, and infants. They come in a variety of sizes, so it is important to choose the appropriate size for your patient. After clearing the airway and inserting either an oropharyngeal or a nasopharyngeal airway adjunct, place a mask over the patient's nose and mouth. (Oxygen could be connected to the mask at this point.) Seal the mask over the patient's face and place your mouth on the mask's valve. Exhale into the valve just enough to make the patient's chest rise. Continue at the same rate used for mouth-to-mouth ventilation.

3. Bag-Valve Mask (BVM)

The *bag-valve mask (BVM)* is a ventilation device that consists of a self-inflating bag, a one-way valve, a mask, and an oxygen reservoir. After clearing the airway and inserting either an oropharyngeal or a nasopharyngeal airway adjunct, connect the oxygen to the mask and place it over the patient's nose and mouth. Next, squeeze the bag to ventilate the patient. The one-way valve prevents the patient from rebreathing exhaled air. A BVM comes in different sizes and can be used on adults, children, and infants. Although it's possible for one EMT-Basic to provide adequate ventilation using a BVM, the technique is more effective when two EMT-Basics are present.

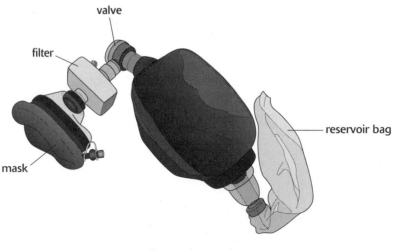

valve

filter

reservoir bag

mask

Bag-valve mask.

a. One-Person Bag-Valve Mask (BVM) Technique

Using a bag-valve mask (BVM) to ventilate a patient is no easy task. It's difficult for one person to keep the patient's airway open while also maintaining a proper seal and squeezing the bag. After clearing the airway and inserting either an oral or a nasal airway adjunct, attach the oxygen to the BVM, and then seal the mask over the patient's nose and mouth using your thumb and index finger. Maintain the patient's airway by keeping your middle, ring, and little fingers of the same hand under the jaw to gently lift the patient's chin. Squeeze the bag with your other hand to ventilate the patient. Adults should be ventilated once every 5 seconds and children and infants once every 3–5 seconds. Because this ventilation technique is difficult for one person to perform, it should only be used as a last resort if only one EMT-Basic is present.

b. Two-Person Bag-Valve Mask (BVM) Technique

Using the two-person bag-valve mask (BVM) technique to ventilate a patient is more effective than using the one-person BVM technique. After one EMT-Basic clears the airway and inserts either an oral or a nasal airway adjunct, the second EMT-Basic attaches the oxygen to the BVM and seals the mask over the patient's nose and mouth. The first EMT-Basic uses two hands to squeeze the bag to ventilate the patient, while the second EMT-Basic ensures that the patient's airway is maintained. Adults should be ventilated once every 5 seconds and children and infants once every 3–5 seconds.

c. Bag-Valve Mask-to-Stoma

Sometimes you'll be required to ventilate patients who have had a laryngectomy, the surgical removal of the larynx or voice box. When the larynx is removed, there is no longer a connection between the mouth and trachea. A new opening is made in the front of the neck called a *tracheal stoma*. The patient breathes through this new opening. To ventilate a patient with a tracheal stoma, attach the BVM directly to the stoma or place a small mask over the stoma. In some cases, you will need to cover the patient's mouth and pinch the patient's nose shut to properly ventilate the patient. You don't need to maintain the patient's airway in this situation. If this doesn't work, cover the tracheal stoma, maintain the patient's airway, and ventilate through the mouth.

4. Flow-Restricted, Oxygen-Powered Ventilation Device

The flow-restricted, oxygen-powered ventilation device is similar to the bag-valve mask. It operates on the same basic principle, except there is no bag. After clearing the airway and inserting either an oral or a nasal airway adjunct, attach the flow-restricted, oxygen-powered ventilation device to the mask, and then seal it over the patient's nose and mouth. Maintain the patient's airway by keeping your fourth and fifth digits (ring and little fingers) of the same hand under the jaw to gently lift the patient's chin. Depress the button to trigger the device and it will automatically administer oxygen. When you see the patient's chest rise, stop the device to allow for exhalation. Repeat once every 5 seconds. This device should never be used to ventilate children or infants because it could cause lung or tissue damage.

5. Oxygen

Patients may require oxygen in times of stress. As an EMT-Basic, you should immediately provide oxygen to any patient with inadequate breathing. Oxygen is stored in high-pressure tanks that contain gauges.

A full oxygen tank contains approximately 2,000 pounds of pressure per square inch. These tanks could explode if not handled properly.

> **Tip: Any patient who has difficulty breathing should be administered oxygen.**

a. Oxygen Delivery Devices

Oxygen is released from the tanks by a valve. A regulator is attached to the valve to control the flow of oxygen from the tank to the patient. Oxygen is delivered to patients through devices such as nonrebreather masks or nasal cannulas.

A *nonrebreather mask* delivers a high concentration of oxygen to a patient. The mask comes in different sizes and is attached to a bag that stores oxygen. The mask is placed over the patient's mouth and nose and the patient breathes in the oxygen from the bag. The bag must be full before the mask is placed on a patient. A nonrebreather mask is the preferred method of administering oxygen.

A *nasal cannula* delivers a lower concentration of oxygen to a patient. This small piece of tubing attaches to the patient's nose, administering oxygen directly into the nostrils. A nasal cannula is usually used on patients who require long-term oxygen use or for those who don't tolerate the nonrebreather mask.

Additional Topics to Review

- Ventilating children and infants
- Ventilating patients with facial injuries
- Ventilating patients with dental appliances
- Different sizes of oxygen cylinders
- Operating an oxygen tank

Practice

Directions (1–5): Select the best answer for each question or incomplete statement.

1. A portable mask that is used during mouth-to-mask ventilation is called a

   A. pocket mask.
   B. bag-valve mask.
   C. nasal cannula.
   D. one-way valve.

2. You arrive on scene and find an unconscious 9-month-old female with clammy skin. Which of the following ventilation techniques should NOT be used?

   A. mouth-to-mouth
   B. mouth-to-mask
   C. two-person bag-valve mask
   D. flow-restricted, oxygen-powered ventilation device

3. You're ventilating a 70-year-old man who has had a laryngectomy. You've attached the bag-valve mask directly to the stoma, but he's still not getting adequate oxygen. You should

   A. stop ventilation until you reach the hospital.
   B. cover the patient's mouth and nose before continuing ventilation.
   C. perform mouth-to-mouth ventilation.
   D. increase the amount of oxygen you are administering to him.

4. Which oxygen delivery device would be best to use on a patient who cannot tolerate the nonrebreather mask?

   A. an oropharyngeal airway
   B. a pocket mask
   C. a nasal cannula
   D. a tracheal stoma

5. When administering the two-person bag-valve mask ventilation technique, after the first EMT-Basic clears the patient's airway, the second EMT-Basic should

   A. insert the oropharyngeal airway or the nasopharyngeal airway.
   B. seal the mask over the patient's nose and mouth.
   C. start administering oxygen through a nonrebreather mask.
   D. squeeze the bag to ventilate the patient.

Answers

1. **A.** A portable mask that is used during mouth-to-mask ventilation is called a *pocket mask.*

2. **D.** The *flow-restricted, oxygen-powered ventilation device* should never be used to ventilate children or infants because it could cause lung or tissue damage.

3. **B.** When you're ventilating a patient with a laryngectomy, you may need to *cover the patient's mouth and nose before continuing ventilation* to prevent air from escaping.

4. **C.** Patients who don't tolerate oxygen through a nonrebreather mask should be given oxygen through *a nasal cannula.*

5. **A.** After the first EMT-Basic clears the patient's airway during the two-person bag-valve mask ventilation technique, the second EMT-Basic should *insert the oropharyngeal airway or the nasopharyngeal airway.*

VII. Patient Assessment

One of the most challenging parts of assessing and managing patients at the scene of an emergency is remembering to verbalize your actions, thoughts, and needs. This will help your fellow EMT-Basics understand what you need. Verbalizing the steps you are taking can also help to reassure scared or anxious patients. Communication is vital to an EMT-Basic's success in the field. Questions on the EMT-Basic exam will test your knowledge of sizing up the scene, assessing the patient, physically examining the patient, documenting your work, and communicating with the appropriate personnel.

Remember, state EMT-Basic exams may differ from the NREMT cognitive exam. While the NREMT exam does not list a percentage of questions that cover patient assessment, you may see a number of questions on this topic on state or municipal EMT-Basic exams. This is why it's important to review this chapter carefully. You'll also want to remember to read the "Additional Topics to Review" sections in this chapter and examine your notes from class for more information on patient assessment.

A. Assessing the Scene

Although caring for the patient is a high priority, you already know that the first thing an EMT-Basic must do is survey the scene of an emergency. This process is called *scene size-up*. The safety of the scene is important to the well-being of the victims, bystanders, witnesses, and emergency responders. The status of the scene will affect the way you respond to and care for the victims, possibly complicating or easing the process. EMT-Basics must observe the entire scene—every sight, sound, or smell could affect the safety of everyone at the scene. When on the scene, you will have to perform many duties quickly to ensure everyone's safety before assessing the patient.

1. Body Substance Isolation (BSI)

Before approaching a patient, you should take all necessary body substance isolation (BSI) precautions. As you may recall from Chapter V, "Preparatory," this includes wearing the appropriate gear to protect you from contagious diseases. This gear includes gloves, masks, gowns, and goggles. You may choose not to wear a gown because your uniform will protect most of your body, but you should always keep a spare gown or uniform nearby in case contamination occurs. Taking BSI precautions will not only protect you and your fellow emergency responders, but also your patients. Always remember to change your gloves when moving from one patient to the next to prevent cross-contamination.

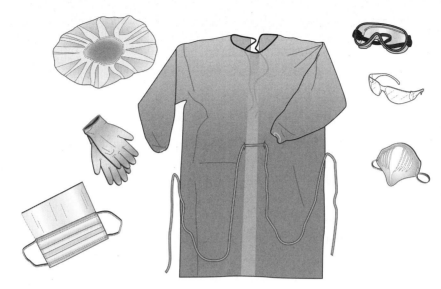

Body substance isolation (BSI) gear.

2. Scene Safety

As previously mentioned, safety at the scene is vital for the well-being of everyone present, including you. To ensure your safety, you should survey the entire environment before assessing the patient. Communication is another important component of safety on the scene. Talk yourself and your partner through the actions you're performing. This will ensure that your partner is up to date on the tasks you have completed and what you've found. Your partner will also be on the lookout for anything you may have overlooked.

Your personal roles and responsibilities will vary in different situations, but your personal safety should always be a top priority, especially in unusual emergencies. Wear *personal protective equipment* (PPE) that is appropriate for potentially dangerous situations, such as hazardous materials emergencies, rescue missions, and violent situations. This specialized equipment may include hazardous materials suits, puncture-proof gloves or pants, and helmets with ear protection. EMT-Basics are needed for a variety of emergencies, from car accidents to crime scenes. Although you will receive extensive training, there is no way to prepare for every possible emergency. This is why it is always important to assess the situation before attending to the patient.

As soon you determine that the scene is safe, you are responsible for the safety of the patient. This does not necessarily mean you should assess or treat patients at this time, but you must protect them from further injury. At a car accident, this might mean keeping them safe from glass or metal fragments, flames, or sparks. In the outdoors, you may need to protect the patient from snow, sleet, rain, extreme winds, heat, or cold.

Typically, police on the scene are responsible for bystander safety, but if EMT-Basics are first to arrive, you may need to ask the bystanders to move out of harm's way. Often, EMT-Basics will ask bystanders to assist them in basic tasks, such as moving patients from the ground onto stretchers. If you ask bystanders for help, provide detailed instructions on what needs to be done. If they are not fit to help, ask them to step away from the scene.

> Tip: Always be aware of your environment, especially the area that surrounds your patient.

3. Mechanism of Injury (MOI)

EMT-Basics typically note *mechanisms of injury* (MOIs) when working with unresponsive trauma patients. An MOI is the incident that led to the patient's injury. Sometimes the MOI is determined before EMT-Basics arrive on the scene, but most of the time the EMT-Basics must discover what caused the injury. Although some cases exist where an MOI is uncertain, you should always attempt to determine the MOI before leaving the scene.

Many times, a quick look at your surroundings will lead you to an MOI. A steep set of stairs may cause a fall, or ice on the road may lead to a car crash. The best way to figure out what happened is to question the patient. If the patient is unconscious or unresponsive, you should talk to friends, family members, or bystanders who witnessed the event.

Don't immediately trust the first MOI that comes to mind. Try to avoid making assumptions without proof. For example, even though the road was icy, a car accident could be the result of the driver suffering a seizure. A near-fatal fall down a flight of stairs could have been an accident, or it may have been attempted murder. Determining the right answer isn't always easy, so be sure to ask the witnesses and the police direct questions about the incident.

4. Number of Patients and the Need for Additional Help

As you survey the scene, count the number of patients you'll have to assess and treat. Medical calls often involve one patient, but trauma calls may include multiple patients with various injuries. Sometimes, it is difficult to locate a patient when you arrive on the scene. If you're called to a car accident, for example, the patient may have fled the scene for fear of getting in trouble, or the patient may have been thrown from the car. Look for possessions such as purses, wallets, or toys that may indicate the presence of other patients. If there are too many patients for your unit to handle responsibly, call for help. If you manage to gain control of the situation before help arrives, that's okay—it's better to have more people than not enough.

Additional Topics to Review

- How to use BSI precautions
- Types of PPE for every situation
- Nature of illnesses and chief complaints
- Labeling a patient as unresponsive
- Asking questions to determine MOI
- Working with other agencies and units

Practice

Directions (1–4): Select the best answer for each question or incomplete statement.

1. While on the scene of a single-car crash, the police tell you that the vehicle hydroplaned and hit a guard-rail. The driver is unresponsive and her head is bleeding. While searching the car, you find a prescription bottle in her purse. Based on this information, you should consider that the MOI may be the result of

   A. a malfunctioning car part.
   B. a reaction to the medication.
   C. a lapse in judgment by the driver.
   D. the fault of another driver.

2. Your first priority when you arrive on scene is to

   A. protect bystanders.
   B. determine the MOI.
   C. size up the scene.
   D. locate all patients.

3. You respond to a medical emergency in which the patient tells you that he thinks he is having a heart attack. After learning some distressing news, he started complaining of soreness in his arms and chest, shortness of breath, and excessive sweating. Which of the following is the patient's chief complaint?

   A. He has learned some distressing news.
   B. His arms and chest are sore.
   C. He's short of breath and sweating.
   D. He thinks he is having a heart attack.

4. A patient was thrown off his motorcycle during an accident involving multiple vehicles. It is raining and the patient is lying on the shoulder of the road. The road has been blocked off from traffic and the patient is conscious. What should you do first?

   A. Ask the patient how he was thrown from his motorcycle.
   B. Begin assessing the patient for life-threatening injuries.
   C. Cover the patient with a blanket or tarp to protect him from the rain.
   D. Place the patient on a gurney and move him to an ambulance.

Answers

1. **B.** The discovery of a prescription bottle in the patient's purse points to the possibility that the MOI may be the result of *a reaction to the medication*. If the patient took the pills and experienced side effects, the MOI would be medical, resulting in possible internal injuries. The question offers no proof that the car was malfunctioning or that another vehicle was involved.

2. **C.** Your first priority when you arrive is to *size up the scene*. This means that you should survey the environment, looking for anything that may make the scene unsafe for emergency personnel, patients, or bystanders.

3. **D.** The patient's chief complaint, or the reason he called EMS, is that *he thinks he is having a heart attack*. That patient's description of his of the chief complaint—his sore arms and chest and his difficulty breathing—is the nature of his illness.

4. **C.** Before you assess or treat the patient, you must first ensure his safety from the elements. *Cover the patient with a blanket or tarp to protect him from the rain* before proceeding. Although Choice D may seem correct, it is unwise to move the patient without first assessing his injuries.

B. Initial Assessment

Once the scene is declared safe and the patient is protected, you can perform your initial assessment. You should complete this process within a few minutes. The initial assessment includes forming a general impression; assessing mental status, airway, breathing, and circulation; and identifying priority patients. You will undoubtedly encounter questions about this process on the EMT-Basic exam because the initial assessment is an important part of every call.

1. General Impression of Patient

Your *general impression* is the way you interpret the safety of your surroundings and the patient's problem. General impressions form within seconds of approaching the patient. By observing the patient's body position, appearance, and attitude, you can usually determine whether the patient is suffering from a medical condition or an injury. You should also take the patient's gender, race, and age into consideration when forming your impression as certain conditions may be related to those factors. If the patient has a medical illness, you need to determine the *nature of illness* (NOI). The NOI is the way in which the patient describes his or her chief complaint, which is the reason why EMS was called. If the patient is injured, you need to determine the MOI. Finally, determine whether the patient's status is life threatening. If so, address the threat accordingly.

> **Tip:** If a patient's MOI suggests an injury to the spine, don't allow the patient to move before stabilizing the spine.

2. Assessing the Patient's Mental Status

To begin assessing a patient's mental status, try to start a conversation with the patient. Introduce yourself as an EMT-Basics and verbally walk the patient through the process as you go. The following are four categories of mental statuses. Many EMT-Basics remember these categories using the acronym *AVPU,* which stands for alert, verbal, painful, and unresponsive.

- *Alert*—These patients respond to the EMT-Basic's presence and answer questions with little difficulty. They may or may not be disoriented, however.

- *Verbal*—These patients respond to the EMT-Basic's voice, but may not be aware of the EMT-Basic's presence. Often, you must raise your voice or change your tone to invoke a response from this type of patient.

- *Painful*—These patients respond to painful stimuli, such as an appropriate stimulus performed by the EMT-Basic to elicit a response. EMT-Basics don't want to cause the patient pain; they only wish to see a response.

- *Unresponsive*—These patients do not respond to verbal or painful stimuli. Completely unresponsive patients are rare and always an indication for a priority transport, but EMT-Basics should always be prepared to assess them.

Tip: A patient's mental status may deteriorate over time, so you need to pay careful attention to the level of responsiveness as you assess the patient for injuries.

3. Assessing the Patient's Airway Status

The most important part of assessing the patient's airway status is determining whether the airway is blocked and, if so, clearing the airway to restore the flow of oxygen to the brain. Signs that a patient's airway may be blocked include coughing, gagging, wheezing, an inability to speak, clutching of the throat, and *cyanosis*, a condition in which the skin turns blue.

If the patient is alert and isn't experiencing these symptoms while you form your initial assessment, the airway is open and you can move on to assess the patient's breathing. If your patient is only responding to verbal or painful stimuli, or he or she is unresponsive, you need to open and assess the airway manually.

When treating a medical condition, perform a head-tilt chin-lift and check the airway. If it is blocked, clear it immediately. If the patient is injured and the MOI is unknown, stabilize the spine and complete a modified jaw thrust. Again, clear the airway and then assess the patient's breathing.

4. Assessing the Patient's Breathing

A healthy adult takes 12 to 20 breaths per minute. While performing your initial assessment, evaluate your patient's breathing rate and monitor breath sounds. If your patient is taking fewer than 12 breaths per minute or more than 20 breaths per minute, ask another crew member to place the patient on high-flow oxygen using a nonrebreather mask.

If the patient's responsiveness decreases during your evaluation, instruct a crew member to open the patient's airway and use a nonrebreather mask. If this doesn't help the patient's breathing, try using pocket masks, bag-valve masks, and flow-restricted, oxygen-powered ventilation devices. See Chapter VI, "Airway," for more information.

5. Assessing the Patient's Circulation

After assessing the patient's mental status, airway, and breathing, you have to check the patient's pulse. The pulse is a representation of the patient's heartbeat and is measured by pressing an artery against bone. The pulse is a strong indicator of a patient's overall health.

You must first check the patient's radial pulse, located at the wrist. If you discover a radial pulse, compare its rate to the pulse of the carotid artery, located in the patient's neck. If the radial pulse is weaker than the carotid pulse, the patient may be in shock.

Tip: You can feel the pulse in many areas of the body, including the neck (carotid artery), the wrist (radial artery), the inside of the elbow (brachial artery), behind the knee (popliteal artery), and at the ankle joint (posterior tibial artery).

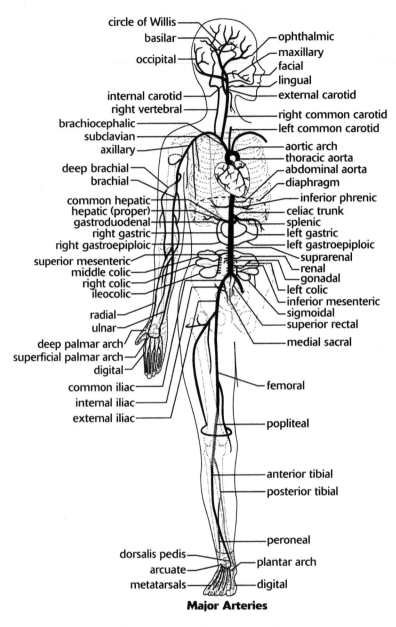

Major Arteries

The major arteries in the body.

6. Identifying Priority Patients

Your initial assessment should allow you to determine if your patient needs to be transported to a medical facility immediately. The following are common characteristics of priority patients:

- Difficulty breathing
- Severe pain

- Poor general impression
- Chest pain
- Uncontrolled bleeding
- Complicated childbirth
- Exhibiting signs of shock
- Responsive, but cannot follow instructions
- Unresponsive with no cough or gag reflex

The majority of trauma patients are priority patients. Your assessment of the scene and the patient's MOI will determine whether a patient is listed as trauma or medical. A trauma patient is someone who has suffered a serious or life-threatening injury and who may be at risk of shock, respiratory failure, or death. All unresponsive patients with unknown MOI should be assessed for potentially having both trauma and medical issues.

Additional Topics to Review

- Types of life-threatening injuries
- Determining mental status in children
- Further distinctions between mental statuses
- Performing the head-tilt chin-lift and modified jaw thrust
- Clearing an obstructed airway
- Oxygen administration techniques
- Assessing perfusion

Practice

Directions (1–4): Select the best answer for each question or incomplete statement.

1. At the scene of a motor vehicle accident, you discover a patient who was ejected from his car. He is off the road and not in danger from passing traffic. What should you do first?

   A.   Assess the patient's breathing rate.
   B.   Determine the patient's mental status.
   C.   Check his radial pulse.
   D.   Determine the MOI.

2. You have responded to a call for a house fire. At the scene, you find three victims seated on the curb across the street from their burning home. Two of the patients appear to be alert and answer your questions, but the third patient doesn't respond to your presence until you reach out and pinch his neck. What is this patient's mental status?

   A.   alert
   B.   verbal
   C.   painful
   D.   unresponsive

3. Which of the following does NOT affect your general impression of the patient?

    A. the patient's NOI

    B. the patient's attitude

    C. the patient's height

    D. the patient's age

4. Which of the following steps should you perform first when the MOI is unknown and you are assessing an unresponsive patient's airway?

    A. Ask witnesses what happened.

    B. Look for clues that could reveal the MOI.

    C. Stabilize or immobilize the patient's spine.

    D. Pinch the patient to see if he responds.

Answers

1. **B.** As mentioned previously, you shouldn't move a patient until you determine if there is a neck or back injury. Before checking the pulse or determining the NOI or MOI, you should always *determine the patient's mental status*.

2. **C.** Because this patient didn't respond to you or your questions until you invoked pain, his mental status would be *painful*. Because he isn't responding to any of your questions, he cannot be alert or verbal. Because he did respond to pain, he isn't unresponsive.

3. **C.** *The patient's height* shouldn't affect your general impression of the patient's health. A patient's age, gender, race, attitude, appearance, and body position, however, will influence your general impression.

4. **C.** If you're uncertain of the MOI and the patient is unresponsive, you cannot rule out the possibility of a spinal injury; therefore, you should *stabilize or immobilize the spine* before you assess the patient's airway. This ensures that you don't do any further damage to the spine if an injury has already occurred.

C. Physical Exam

The condition of the patient—trauma or medical—will determine the type of focused history and physical examination the patient receives from EMT-Basics. Remember, treating unresponsive patients is very different from treating alert or conscious patients. Although rare, you should always be prepared to treat a completely unresponsive patient. Tests like the EMT-Basic will include multiple questions about completing the focused history and physical exams for both medical and trauma patients.

Tip: If a patient needs oxygen, you may place him or her on a device to assist breathing once the initial assessment is complete and before you begin the physical examination.

1. Responsive Patients

Many medical and trauma patients will be responsive during the physical exam, but the type of examination you perform will vary. The processes of gathering a patient's history, performing the rapid-trauma assessment, and assessing a patient's vital signs will vary depending on the patient you are treating.

a. Medical Patients

Responsive medical patients receive an *objective assessment*. The information for the objective assessment comes from the patient—what he or she verbally tells you combined with what his or her body tells you. You should also complete a *subjective assessment*, which contains information from friends, family, and witnesses.

While gathering focused history from responsive medical patients, ask about the onset, provocation, quality, radiation, severity, and time. Many EMT-Basics use the acronym OPQRST to remember which questions to ask the patient and/or bystanders. After OPQRST, you'll need to gather SAMPLE information. This acronym stands for signs and symptoms, allergies, medications, past medical history, last intake of food or drink, and events leading to the patient's present condition.

As you gather OPQRST and SAMPLE information, you should complete a rapid head-to-toe assessment, spending the most time on the areas related to the patient's chief complaint. Keep in mind that an injury you're assessing today may have occurred days, weeks, or even months ago. Ask your patient if he or she recalls any discomfort in that area in the past. If a patient experiences pain as you press on an area, don't repeat the action.

After you complete the assessment, assess the patient's baseline vital signs. This involves checking the patient's skin, pupils, blood pressure, circulation, and breathing. Administer oxygen to any patient who has trouble breathing. If the patient needs emergency care, you can examine vital signs in the ambulance during transport. If you cannot immediately transport a patient who's having trouble breathing, you should continue administering oxygen and transport the patient as soon as possible.

b. Trauma Patients

Gathering OPQRST and SAMPLE information and performing rapid assessment is more challenging when working with trauma patients because of the high-pressure emergency environment and the injuries to the patient. Trauma patients with simple or serious injuries receive a focused history and a physical examination directed specifically to the injured area. Patients with a high-risk MOI or an unknown MOI receive a rapid head-to-toe trauma assessment regardless of visible injuries. This assessment will expose any hidden or possible internal injuries. High-risk MOIs that involve hidden (internal) injuries often include the following:

- A fall of more than 20 feet
- Ejection from a moving vehicle
- Penetration to the head, chest, or abdomen
- Vehicle rollover
- High-speed vehicle collision
- Motorcycle accident
- Vehicle-pedestrian collision
- Patient with altered mental status

Remember to stabilize or immobilize all trauma patients with suspected neck, back, or head injuries before performing other tasks or attempting to move the patients. Treat these patients as though they have experienced a spinal injury. When performing the rapid-trauma assessment, examine and palpate the patient for injuries using the acronym DCAP-BTLS. These letters stand for deformities, contusions, abrasions, penetrations or punctures, burns, tenderness, lacerations, and swelling. Take a head-to-toe approach with this assessment, starting with the head and working your way down the patient's body.

Tip: If you notice that a previously stable patient's condition is declining, call for immediate transport.

2. Unresponsive Patients

All unresponsive medical patients should receive treatment similar to unresponsive trauma patients. This includes a rapid head-to-toe trauma assessment to reveal any hidden or life-threatening conditions. You should stabilize all unresponsive patients and treat them as though they have a spinal injury. Provide high-flow oxygen using a nonrebreather mask if necessary.

Because the patients cannot answer your questions about their medical history or tell you where they are experiencing pain, you will have to trust family, friends, or witnesses to give you honest answers to your OPQRST and SAMPLE questions. You can obtain this information while your partner performs the physical exam and checks the patient's vital signs. If the patient is alone, you won't be able to complete these questions until the patient becomes responsive.

Additional Topics to Review

- Detailed steps of the OPQRST and SAMPLE
- Evaluating specific body parts, such as the neck, pelvis, and abdomen
- Gathering history from and performing physical exams on children
- Working in a multitiered response system
- Evaluating patients without a specific MOI
- In-depth physical examinations
- Assessing baseline vital signs

Practice

Directions (1–4): Select the best answer for each question or incomplete statement.

1. Which of the following is not a component of the DCAP-BTLS?

    A. abrasions
    B. breathing
    C. lacerations
    D. swelling

2. How would you gather the OPQRST and SAMPLE information on an unresponsive patient?

    A. Wait until the patient is responsive.
    B. Call the patient's next of kin.
    C. Ask a person who is on the scene.
    D. Examine the patient's wallet for receipts.

3. At a construction site, a worker has fallen approximately 30 feet. He is responsive, but only to painful stimuli. He cannot answer your questions and is slipping in and out of consciousness. What should you do first?

    A. Perform a rapid head-to-toe trauma assessment.
    B. Ask witnesses about the fall.
    C. Call for an immediate transport.
    D. Stabilize or immobilize the patient.

4. Which of the following patients most likely has a high-risk MOI with hidden injuries?

    A. a responsive patient who has fallen off a bicycle
    B. a responsive patient who was struck by a car crossing the street
    C. a responsive patient who fell down a set of six steps
    D. a responsive patient who is complaining of chest pain and sweating

Answers

1. **B.** The B in DCAP-BTLS stands for burns, not *breathing*. The acronym stands for deformities, contusions, abrasions, penetrations or punctures, burns, tenderness, lacerations, and swelling. You should assess the patient's breathing before the rapid-trauma assessment.

2. **C.** In this situation, you should ask *a person who is on the scene* to explain what happened. If a friend, family member, or reliable witness is on the scene and knows the patient well, he or she can provide answers to OPQRST and SAMPLE questions. If no one else is on the scene, then you would have to wait for the patient to become responsive.

3. **D.** Because the construction worker fell more than 20 feet, his MOI is considered high risk. Because the patient cannot tell you about his injuries, the first thing you must do is *stabilize or immobilize the patient*. You can't be sure that the patient does not have a spinal injury at this point, so the best thing to do is immobilize him to prevent further injury.

4. **B.** A patient involved in a *vehicle-pedestrian collision* may have a high-risk MOI. Because the patient was struck by a moving vehicle, he or she may have internal injuries that are not easily observed. This type of patient would most likely require immediate transport to a medical facility for further assessment. The patient who fell down the stairs most likely does not have a high-risk MOI because of the distance of the fall, nor does the patient who fell off the bicycle.

D. Ongoing Assessment

Ongoing assessment occurs on the way to the medical facility and includes further examination of and careful attention to the patient. During this time, you should also check on the success or failure of any interventions, such as the use of high-flow nonrebreather masks. Pay close attention to the patient's mental status, vital signs, and blood pressure as you approach the hospital. If the patient becomes unstable, address the situation accordingly and report any changes to the professionals who will take over the care of your patient. Questions about ongoing assessment on exams like the EMT-Basic will appear similar to those about the initial assessment and the physical exam, as the steps are repeated during this process.

1. Components of an Ongoing Assessment

A *stable patient* is one who has endured a simple or specific injury. The condition of these patients remains steady and does not worsen upon further assessment. These patients most likely did not receive a full physical exam, but they should receive ongoing assessment once every 15 minutes. An *unstable patient* is either a medical patient in extreme distress or a trauma patient with a significant MOI. Unstable patients should receive ongoing assessment once every 5 minutes. The components of ongoing assessment include the following steps:

1. Repeat the initial assessment.
2. Determine mental status.
3. Assess airway, breathing rate, and pulse rate.
4. Assess skin color, condition, perfusion, and temperature.
5. Identify priority patients.
6. Record all vital signs.
7. Repeat focused assessments.
8. Check on all interventions.

Although the ideal location to perform an ongoing assessment is on the way to the hospital, sometimes EMS units don't have the ability to transport patients. If you're waiting for transportation, perform the ongoing assessment while you wait.

2. Repeat Initial Assessment

Keep interaction and communication with the patient constant during, or while waiting for, transport. Constant interaction will make reassessing the patient's mental status an easy task and will allow you to take notice of any changes that may occur. Check on the patient's airway and ensure that it is open. Evaluate the patient's breathing and pulse rate using the radial or carotid arteries. Observe the patient's skin color as you interact with him or her. Check on any major bleeding that you attempted to control on the scene while inspecting interventions. If an intervention fails, correct it immediately. If the patient's condition deteriorates, he or she becomes a high-priority patient. In this case, turn on the sirens and lights and maintain a quick, but safe, speed.

3. Repeat Vital Signs and Focused Assessment

You will need to record vital signs for your patient's skin, pupils, blood pressure, circulation, and breathing every 5 to 15 minutes, depending on your patient's stability. Document all vital sign assessments so professionals at the hospital can see how the patient's condition has altered over time. Be sure to complete a focused assessment as often as you check the patient's vital signs. For patients with specific or simple injuries, inspect the site of the injury thoroughly, noting any alterations. If a patient has a life-threatening injury or condition, work with your partner to keep the airway clear and the patient breathing. In these situations, the patient's breathing is your first priority; a formal ongoing assessment may be delayed.

Additional Topics to Review

- Airway, breathing, and pulse assessment
- Emergency intervention plans
- Riding in a moving transport vehicle

Practice

Directions (1–4): Select the best answer for each question or incomplete statement.

1. If a patient has a life-threatening injury, your first priority during transport is to

    A. repeat the initial assessment.
    B. check and record vital signs.
    C. keep the patient breathing.
    D. assess the patient's skin color.

2. One purpose of conducting an ongoing assessment is to

    A. perform a detailed assessment of the patient's abdomen.
    B. determine whether the patient's condition has improved or worsened.
    C. identify conditions that could have caused the patient's injury.
    D. finish incomplete rapid-trauma assessment steps.

3. You are transporting a teenage boy who has sustained injuries to his left ankle and wrist during a high school basketball game. On the way to the hospital, you should repeat your ongoing assessment every

    A. 5 minutes.
    B. 8 minutes.
    C. 12 minutes.
    D. 15 minutes.

4. A stable patient would best be described as a patient whose condition

    A. requires immediate transport.
    B. deteriorates rapidly.
    C. remains steady.
    D. changes every 15 minutes.

Answers

1. **C.** If the patient you are transporting has a life-threatening injury, your first priority is to *keep the patient breathing*. You may informally perform certain parts of the ongoing assessment, but your main concern is the patient's ability to breathe.

2. **B.** One of the main points to conducting an ongoing assessment is to *determine whether the patient's condition has improved or worsened.* All life-threatening conditions should be evaluated during the rapid-trauma assessment, which should be completed before transporting the patient.

3. **D.** The patient in this question is stable; therefore, you should repeat an ongoing assessment every *15 minutes.* If the patient were unstable, you would assess the patient every 5 minutes.

4. **C.** A stable patient is described as a patient whose condition *remains steady* and does not worsen upon further assessment. Although the EMT-Basic should continue to monitor the stable patient, it is unlikely that the patient's condition would deteriorate during transport to the hospital.

E. Documentation and Communication

The EMT-Basic exam will include questions about communicating with patients, bystanders, fellow emergency personnel, and dispatch. You will also encounter questions about written communication, known as documentation. These are two important processes that many experienced EMT-Basics perform with little to no hesitation every day. On the scene of an emergency, EMT-Basics have to communicate effectively and clearly and their notes should be legible and accurate.

1. Procedures for Radio Communication

When you radio dispatch, state the location of your unit, that you have received and understood the call, and that you are responding to the call. Depending on the area, you may need to let other agencies and units know that you are responding to the call. When you arrive on the scene, you need to alert the dispatcher. Contact the dispatcher once again when you reach the patient. You must also notify the dispatcher when you leave the scene with the patient, when you arrive at the hospital, when you leave the hospital, and when you arrive at your station. The dispatcher will record these times and they will be available for you if you need to refer to them when writing your report.

You will also use the radio when communicating with the medical direction physician. Once you have completed your initial assessment of the patient and you have determined that the patient needs immediate medical care, you should radio the medical direction physician with the following information:

- Patient's gender and age
- Patient's chief complaint
- Patient's past medical history
- Patient's mental status
- Your assessment findings and vital signs
- Any emergency care already provided
- Estimated time you'll begin transport
- Estimated time of arrival at the hospital

The medical direction physician will use this information to tell you what you need to do to help your patient. As the physician gives you directions, repeat them to be sure that you understood the instructions completely. Once the task is complete, ask the medical direction physician if he or she can inform the medical facility of your patient's condition. If the physician cannot do this, you will have to update the hospital yourself.

Tip: After pressing the push-to-talk button on your radio, wait a moment before speaking. When you do speak into the radio, hold the microphone approximately 5 to 7 centimeters away from your mouth. This will ensure that your message is transmitted clearly.

2. Minimum Data Sets

Every EMT-Basic is required to obtain two sets of information when responding to a call: patient information and administrative information, as detailed in the following table. Combined, EMT-Basics use these sets to write a prehospital care report (see the next section). All the data in these sets must be accurate, especially the recorded times. Remember to record times using the 24-hour system.

Minimum Data Sets	
Patient Information	**Administrative Information**
Age and gender	Location and type of incident
Chief complaint	Date and time of incident report
Cause of injury and injury description	Date and time of EMS unit notification
Pre-existing conditions	Time of unit response
Signs and symptoms	Time of EMS arrival on scene
Mental status	Time of EMS arrival at patient
Pulse and respiratory rates	Time EMS unit left scene
Systolic blood pressure/skin perfusion	Time of EMS arrival at medical facility
Skin color, condition, and temperature	Time of transfer of patient to facility
Emergency procedures performed by EMS	Time of EMS unit back in service
Medications administered to patient by EMS	Use of lights and sirens
Patient response to treatment/medications	Names of crew members who responded

3. Prehospital Care Report

Because a prehospital care report is a legal document, it is considered confidential; therefore, you should never share information you read or report with anyone else. This report provides information about the patient's status when EMS arrived on the scene, the care that the EMT-Basics provided, and any changes in the patient's condition as he or she was transported to a medical facility. All statements in a prehospital care report should be objective. The patient's nurses, doctors, surgeons, and insurance company agents read the prehospital care report to determine the type of care that a patient needs. Even researchers and medical students may benefit from an accurate and legible prehospital care report. The prehospital care report can also be shared with anyone involved in the patient's ongoing care.

4. Documentation of Patient Refusal

If a patient is competent and is not under the influence of drugs or alcohol, he or she has the right to refuse treatment and transport. Patients who are under the influence of drugs or alcohol are not considered competent, and, therefore, cannot refuse care. EMT-Basics can consult their medical direction physician if they have questions about the patient's competence. Before leaving the scene, try to convince the patient to go to the hospital and inform the patient of the risks of refusing treatment. Offer alternatives to transporting the patient in the ambulance. For example, the patient can ride with a family member in the family's car and the ambulance can follow. If the patient still refuses, call the medical direction physician and ask him or her to speak with the patient. Next, have the patient sign a patient refusal form. Ask a member of your unit to sign the form as a witness. Explain that you will return if the patient changes his or her mind.

Tip: A medical direction physician can help you determine a patient's competency.

Additional Topics to Review

- General radio communications principles
- Communication systems, components, and maintenance
- Trending
- Traditional versus nontraditional prehospital care reports
- Common medical abbreviations
- Correction of documentation errors
- Documentation of special situations including multiple casualty incidents

Practice

Directions (1–4): Select the best answer for each question or incomplete statement.

1. The information collected in minimum data sets is used to complete a

   A. patient refusal form.
   B. prehospital care report.
   C. administrative report.
   D. SAMPLE history.

2. Which of the following pieces of information is NOT necessary to report to the medical direction physician?

   A. the patient's mental status
   B. the patient's age and gender
   C. the presence of the patient's family
   D. the emergency care you've provided the patient

3. After responding to a call concerning a responsive medical patient, you must complete your prehospital care report. You left the scene at 5:43 P.M. Which of the following is the correct way to record this time on your report?

   A. 5:43 P.M.
   B. 6:00 P.M.
   C. 17:43
   D. 17:45

4. After arriving on the scene of a car accident and reaching the patient's side, you perform your initial assessment and splint the patient's leg. When your unit is ready, you load the patient into the ambulance and drive to the nearest hospital. A call to dispatch is NOT necessary after

   A. arriving on the scene.
   B. reaching the patient's side.
   C. splinting the patient's leg.
   D. leaving the scene with the patient.

Answers

1. **B.** The patient information and the administrative information gathered in the minimum data sets are used to complete a *prehospital care report*. This form may be used by doctors, nurses, and surgeons who need to know more about their patients.

2. **C.** The medical direction physician doesn't need to know about *the presence of the patient's family*. He or she is most concerned with treating the patient.

3. **C.** You should always record times using the 24-hour system. This format decreases the chances of confusion caused by a missing "A.M." and "P.M." on a form. You should also never estimate the times you're recording. Always use the most accurate time available.

4. **C.** You don't need to contact dispatch after *splinting the patient's leg*. You do, however, need to contact dispatch when you're moving from one place to another. This includes moving from the scene to the hospital or from the ambulance to the patient.

VIII. Medical Emergencies

The medical emergencies portion of the EMT-Basic exam tests your knowledge of basic pharmacology and quizzes you on the types of situations you'll face during a medical emergency. This chapter covers basic medication information and administration routes, as well as emergencies associated with various body systems, pre-existing conditions and allergies, altered mental status, poisons, and environmental factors.

About 15 percent of the questions on the NREMT cognitive exam are related to medical emergencies. Because this chapter does not cover all the information you may encounter on the EMT-Basic exam, you should examine the "Additional Topics to Review" sections in this chapter.

A. General Pharmacology Lesson

This section of the EMT-Basic exam tests your ability to identify and administer various medications in the field. In this section, you'll review the common medications found on EMS units. You'll also review the various medications that EMT-Basics are permitted to administer, and the medications that EMT-Basics may assist in administering. This section also reviews the various forms of medications, the difference between generic and trade names, indication and contraindication, administration routes, and reassessment of the patient after medication has been administered.

1. Medications on an EMS Unit

EMT-Basics must often administer various medications to patients while working in the field. It's vitally important that you understand what kind of medication a patient needs, how to administer that medication, and when the medication should be administered. EMS units carry a variety of medications for the treatment of patients, including oral glucose, activated charcoal, and oxygen.

2. Medications an EMT-Basic May Administer

There are two types of medications that EMT-Basics will frequently encounter in the field. The first are those medications that EMT-Basics most commonly carry on their unit. Medications such as oral glucose, activated charcoal, and oxygen are simple forms of treatment that EMT-Basics may administer at their own discretion or after receiving permission from the medical direction physician. EMT-Intermediates and EMT-Paramedics carry a much wider variety of medications for more advanced on-scene patient treatment.

3. Medications an EMT-Basic May Assist With

Typically, EMT-Basics will also encounter physician-prescribed medications that patients have in their possession. EMT-Basics can help patients take some medications when they have permission from the medical direction physician. The types of medications that EMT-Basics may assist patients with include nitroglycerin, prescribed inhalers, and epinephrine autoinjectors.

4. Forms of Medication

There are different forms of medication that EMT-Basics use to treat patients. The form of medication an EMT-Basic uses to treat a particular patient can vary based on the onset of action and the ease of administration. The medications that EMT-Basics administer may come in the form of liquids for injection, compressed powders or tablets, gels, fine powder for inhalation, vaporized liquids, sublingual sprays, gases, or suspensions.

5. Difference Between Generic and Trade Names

Most medications have two names: a generic name and a trade name. A medication's *generic name* refers to the name of the medication as listed in the *United States Pharmacopeia*. In most cases, the generic name is a simplified form of the chemical name. A *trade name* is the name given to the medication by the company that sells it. These names are usually copyrighted and will include the copyright symbol. As an example, Nitrostat is one trade name for the medication known generically as nitroglycerin.

6. Indication and Contraindication

One of the most important steps in administering any medication is identifying indications and contraindications. *Indications* are signals that tell you when a medication should be administered. Patient symptoms and medical histories can be potential indications for a particular form of treatment. *Contraindications* are signals that indicate that a medication should not be administered. Under certain conditions, the administration of some medications may have little or no positive effect or may even worsen the patient's condition. Understanding when not to administer a certain medication is an important part of the EMT's job.

7. Administration Routes

An *administration route* refers to the way in which a medication is administered to a patient. There are four primary routes of administration of medications EMT-Basics assist in administering:

- *Oral medications* are swallowed and absorbed into the digestive system. These medications generally require more time to take effect because they must pass through the digestive tract before entering the bloodstream.

> **Tip: Oral medications should only be administered to alert patients.**

- *Sublingual medications* are dissolved under a patient's tongue. When the medication dissolves, it's absorbed into the capillaries under the tongue. Because this method involves direct absorption into the bloodstream, the medication takes effect quickly.
- *Inhaled medications* generally include gases or fine mists. These medications are inhaled directly into the respiratory system, making the onset of action almost immediate.
- *Intramuscular medications* are delivered with an injection into a large muscle. From there, the medication is absorbed into the bloodstream.

8. Reassessment After Medication

Before administering medications, EMTs must take note of the patient's condition prior to receiving any treatment. After any medication is administered, it's important to reassess the patient's condition, noting the time, dose, and route of administration, and any changes that occur in the patient's condition as a result of treatment. You should also take note of any possible side effects of the medication.

Additional Topics to Review

- Medication actions
- Side effects

Practice

Directions (1–5): Select the best answer for each question or incomplete statement.

1. What is the generic name for Ventolin?

   A. oral glucose
   B. metaproterenol
   C. albuterol
   D. nitroglycerin

2. What form of medication is activated charcoal?

   A. a fine powder for inhalation
   B. a vaporized liquid
   C. a sublingual spray
   D. a suspension

3. A patient with a history of cardiac disease is experiencing chest pain. Based on this information, which type of medication should you administer after receiving permission from the medical direction physician?

   A. oxygen
   B. nitroglycerin
   C. albuterol
   D. metaproterenol

4. Which of the following medications may EMT-Basics administer at their own discretion?

   A. epinephrine autoinjectors
   B. nitroglycerin
   C. oral glucose
   D. prescribed inhalers

5. How is a sublingual medication administered?

    A. into a muscle
    B. through the lungs
    C. under the tongue
    D. by mouth

Answers

1. **C.** *Albuterol* is the generic name for Ventolin. Oral glucose is the generic name for Glutose or Insta-glucose. Metaproterenol is the generic name for Alupent. Nitroglycerin is the generic name for Nitrostat or Nitrolingual spray.

2. **D.** Activated charcoal is *a suspension*.

3. **B.** *Nitroglycerin* is typically indicated for patients experiencing chest pain.

4. **C.** EMT-Basics can administer *oral glucose* at their own discretion. Epinephrine autoinjectors, nitroglycerin, and prescribed inhalers all require approval from the medical direction physician.

5. **C.** A sublingual medication is administered *under the tongue*.

B. Respiratory Emergencies

This section of the EMT-Basic exam covers medical emergencies related to the respiratory system. Questions in this section focus on respiratory anatomy and physiology, signs of upper and lower airway obstructions, signs of respiratory distress and failure, emergency respiratory conditions, and the use of inhalers.

1. Asthma and Inhalers

Asthma is a common respiratory illness that EMT-Basics must treat on the job. This chronic disease is characterized by inflammation of the airway and has a two-phase response. In the first phase, a leakage of fluid from the capillaries causes bronchial constriction, which results in reduced expiratory airflow. This phase usually lasts 1 to 2 hours and may be resolved with an inhaled bronchodilator. In the second phase, edema and swelling cause a further reduction in expiratory airflow. This phase usually occurs 6 to 8 hours after the initial onset. Patients at this stage of asthma no longer respond to inhaled bronchodilators and are frequently treated with anti-inflammatory medications such as corticosteroids.

Inhaled bronchodilators, which are administered via inhalers, are the most common form of treatment for asthma. Inhalers deliver bronchodilators into lung tissues and dilate the bronchioles, thus decreasing resistance inside the airways. Some inhalers, known as metered-dose inhalers, are preset to expel a specified dose of medication when activated. Common generic names for inhaler medications include isoetharine, albuterol, and metaproterenol. The trade names for these medications are Ventolin, Proventil, and Bronkometer, respectively.

To assist in the administration of an inhaler, the EMT-Basic must first receive permission from the medical direction physician. The patient must exhibit signs of a respiratory emergency before the EMT-Basic can assist in administering the patient's physician-prescribed inhaler.

Use of a prescribed inhaler may be contraindicated in some cases. Disoriented patients who may not be able to use their inhaler correctly shouldn't be treated with one. Patients should only use inhalers that were prescribed to them. You shouldn't help administer an inhaler without approval from the medical direction physician. Patients who have already met or exceeded the maximum recommended dosage of inhaler medication should not be given any further doses.

Some inhalers are used with a device called a *spacer*, which is an attachment that is situated between the inhaler and the patient. Spacers are used to contain the medication after it has been released from the inhaler, which gives the patient more time to inhale it. These devices are most commonly used by children and patients who have difficulty taking deep breaths.

2. COPD

COPD stands for chronic obstructive pulmonary (lung) disease. This broad category includes three respiratory conditions: asthma (discussed in the previous section), emphysema, and chronic bronchitis.

Emphysema is a degenerative disease that develops as a result of consistent exposure to noxious substances such as cigarette smoke. As emphysema worsens, alveolar surface area decreases. As the alveoli are damaged, the surface area used for gas exchange also decreases. This can cause trapped air, which results in a barrel chest. Patients with emphysema will also have a prolonged expiratory phase and frequently breathe through pursed lips. An increase in red blood cell production also causes pinkish skin coloration. Because of these symptoms, these patients are often referred to as *pink puffers*.

Chronic bronchitis results from the excessive production of mucus in the respiratory tree. In this disease, the alveoli become obstructed by mucus plugs. Patients with chronic bronchitis often become cyanotic, which is why they are often referred to as *blue bloaters*.

On-scene treatment for these conditions usually includes administration of oxygen. For hypoxic patients, oxygen at the highest level of concentration is usually prescribed.

3. Upper Airway Obstruction

Upper airway obstructions are the result of blockage in the upper respiratory tract, which consists of the trachea, voice box, and throat. Common causes of upper airway obstructions include allergic reactions, infections, burns, aspiration of foreign bodies, trauma, or blockage from an unresponsive patient's tongue.

4. Lower Airway Obstruction

Lower airway obstructions are the result of blockage in the lower respiratory tract, which includes the lower end of the trachea and the lungs. Lower airway obstructions are most commonly caused by the buildup of mucus or fluids or by inflammation. These obstructions usually develop as a result of pre-existing respiratory conditions such as emphysema or chronic bronchitis.

5. Respiratory Distress

Respiratory distress occurs when the respiratory system becomes unable to meet the body's demand for oxygen. Difficulty breathing is a primary symptom of respiratory distress. Patients may display poor breathing rates and rhythms, as well as reduced quality or depth of breathing.

A patient who is breathing too quickly or too slowly may not be taking in enough oxygen or not exhaling enough carbon dioxide. Abnormal breathing rhythms often indicate a serious medical emergency and require a doctor's evaluation.

Patients in respiratory distress may also exhibit poor breathing quality. Unequal or diminished breath sounds may indicate that there's not enough air reaching one or both lungs. Unequal chest expansion may also accompany serious respiratory problems.

Patients who are breathing too deeply or too shallowly are experiencing an altered tidal volume, which affects the level of oxygen the body can receive. Some patients in respiratory distress may also experience shortness of breath.

Other signs of respiratory distress include high pulse rate, altered mental status, restlessness, changes in skin color, the use of accessory muscles, chest wall retractions, noisy breathing, and nasal flaring.

Tip: Many patients in respiratory distress will attempt to remain in an upright, seated position. This position is usually the most comfortable for these patients.

6. Respiratory Failure

Respiratory failure occurs when the lungs become unable to function normally and either can't take in enough oxygen or can't expel enough carbon dioxide. Airway blockages, lung damage, or weakened breathing muscles can lead to respiratory failure. Patients in respiratory failure may experience severe respiratory distress. If not treated properly, respiratory failure can be fatal.

Additional Topics to Review

- Respiratory anatomy
- Respiratory physiology
- Artificial ventilation

Practice

Directions (1–5): Select the best answer for each question or incomplete statement.

1. Which of the following signs would indicate an altered tidal volume?

    A. nasal flaring
    B. unequal expansion of chest wall
    C. breathing too shallowly
    D. elevated breathing rate

2. Which position would be most comfortable for a patient experiencing respiratory distress?

   A. sitting upright
   B. lying in the supine position
   C. lying in the fetal position
   D. standing up

3. A patient in respiratory distress is presenting with barrel chest, breathing through pursed lips, and experiencing a prolonged expiratory phase. Which condition does the patient most likely suffer from?

   A. asthma
   B. emphysema
   C. chronic bronchitis
   D. bronchiectasis

4. Which of the following would indicate that a patient should *not* be administered an inhaler?

   A. The patient has a physician's prescription.
   B. The patient has abnormal breathing sounds.
   C. The patient is confused or disoriented.
   D. The patient is taking shallow breaths.

5. The EMT-Basic may only assist in the administration of an inhaler if the

   A. inhaler has a spacer attached.
   B. patient has already exceeded the recommended daily dose.
   C. patient has a lower airway obstruction.
   D. EMT-Basic receives permission from the medical direction physician.

Answers

1. **C.** *Breathing too shallowly* would be an indication of an altered tidal volume. Breathing too deeply would also suggest an altered tidal volume.

2. **A.** Patients experiencing respiratory distress are usually most comfortable *sitting upright*. Other positions, particularly lying face up, may be difficult.

3. **B.** The patient's symptoms suggest *emphysema*. Patients in this state are also commonly referred to as "pink puffers."

4. **C.** Patients who are *confused or disoriented* shouldn't be treated with inhalers because they may not be capable of receiving this treatment properly.

5. **D.** The EMT-Basic should only assist in the administration of an inhaler if he or she *receives permission from the medical direction physician.*

C. Cardiovascular Emergencies

This section of the EMT-Basic exam covers emergency situations related to the heart and cardiovascular system. Possible question topics include signs of angina, heart attack, and ischemia. You may also encounter questions related to OPQRST, ventricular defibrillation, caring for the patient, administering nitroglycerin, and using an automated external defibrillator.

1. Signs of Angina or Heart Attack

Angina is chest pain that occurs when blood flow to the heart muscle is reduced. Angina pain is commonly described as heaviness, tightness, squeezing, or pressure in the chest. There are three forms of angina:

- *Stable angina* is a persistent, recurrent chest pain that is often brought on by exertion. Stable angina can sometimes be relieved by rest or the use of nitroglycerin.
- *Unstable angina*, which is the most dangerous form of angina, is not related to exertion and has an unpredictable pattern. It's often a signal of an impending heart attack.
- *Variant angina* is caused by a coronary artery spasm and usually occurs without exertion. Variant angina often presents with particularly severe symptoms.

Tip: Angina alone doesn't cause damage to the heart muscle.

A *heart attack* occurs as a result of a blood vessel blockage in the heart. The muscle tissue around the blockage loses blood flow and becomes oxygen deprived. This results in physical damage to the heart muscle.

Patients suffering from angina or a heart attack are experiencing cardiac compromise and may exhibit a variety of symptoms that include chest pain, excessive or sudden sweatiness, breathing difficulties, abnormal or irregular pulse rate, abnormal blood pressure, abdominal or epigastric pain, nausea, and vomiting. Patients may also become irritable or anxious.

2. Ischemia

Ischemia is a drop in the supply of blood to tissues, organs, or other body parts. It's frequently caused by blood vessel constriction or obstruction. During cardiac compromise, ischemia occurs when a section of heart muscle is not being supplied with enough oxygen for adequate function. This leads to the onset of angina.

3. OPQRST Questions

As previously discussed in Chapter V, "Preparatory," the OPQRST questions are a series of questions that EMT-Basics commonly use to assess patients experiencing cardiac compromise. OPQRST stands for onset, provocation, quality, radiation, severity, and time.

- *Onset* questions help you determine when the pain began, how long it took for the pain to reach its worst level, and how long the patient has had a cardiac condition.
- *Provocation* questions are used to determine what the patient was doing when the pain started, what causes the pain to improve or worsen, and whether more pain is experienced upon inhalation or expiration.

- *Quality* questions help you to determine exactly what the pain feels like to the patient.
- *Radiation* questions allow EMT-Basics to figure out whether the pain is spreading to other areas of the body outside of the chest.
- *Severity* questions help to determine how bad the pain is. EMT-Basics will usually ask the patient to rate his or her pain on a scale of 0 to 10, with 0 meaning no symptoms are present and 10 indicating that the patient is in severe pain.
- *Time* questions allow you to estimate how long the patient has been experiencing chest pain. These questions will also tell you whether the pain has been consistent or intermittent.

The answers to these questions provide you with vital information about the patient's condition and treatment needs.

4. Defibrillation

Defibrillation is an emergency treatment for patients experiencing a condition called ventricular fibrillation.

Ventricular fibrillation is a form of irregular heartbeat characterized by rapid, electrical impulses. In the event of ventricular fibrillation, heart ventricles quiver helplessly, failing to pump any blood. This causes a severe drop in blood pressure and a loss of blood supply to the organs. This very serious condition can become fatal very quickly.

Defibrillation involves delivering an electrical shock to the heart through the chest wall. This shock temporarily stops the heart and, by extension, the irregular cardiac activity. If successful, this will cause the heart to resume normal function. CPR is also a vital part of the treatment for patients in this condition and is commonly performed along with defibrillation.

5. Automatic External Defibrillator

EMT-Basics may perform defibrillation with an automatic external defibrillator, commonly called an AED. The AED is a computer-controlled defibrillator that requires very little human interaction or decision making. Almost anyone can operate this device. Defibrillation is critical in many cases of cardiac arrest and treatment should be immediate. Because EMT-Basics are not qualified to use a manual defibrillator, the AED makes it possible for EMT-Basics to administer this potentially life-saving treatment even when there are no advanced EMTs on the scene.

There are two types of AEDs: fully automatic and semi-automatic. When using a fully automatic AED, EMT-Basics only need to apply two electrode patches to the patient's chest, connect the leads, and turn on the AED. The AED then analyzes the patient's heart rhythm and, if necessary, delivers a shock.

Semi-automatic AEDs require a little more input from the user. After the patches and leads have been attached and the AED is turned on, the user must push a button to analyze the rhythm. The AED will then suggest the best course of action and, if instructed to do so, the EMT-Basic pushes another button to initiate a shock.

Before using an AED, it's important to be certain that the patient is unresponsive and does not have a carotid pulse. Shocking a patient who has a pulse can lead to ventricular fibrillation or asystole, which is a lack of rhythm that will not respond to further shocks.

6. Administering Oxygen/Positioning Patient

When you confirm that a patient is experiencing cardiac compromise, he or she should be placed in a comfortable position and administered oxygen. Most patients with cardiac or respiratory distress will prefer to sit upright rather than lie down. Once the patient is comfortable, you should administer oxygen. The oxygen should be delivered through a nonrebreather mask at a rate of 15 liters per minute. Because you are attempting to decrease the oxygen demand on the heart with this treatment, the patient should not be allowed to walk or move about.

7. Nitroglycerin

EMT-Basics may administer nitroglycerin tablets or sublingual sprays to patients suffering from chest pain who have a prescription for this drug. Nitroglycerin dilates the blood vessels and decreases the workload of the heart. This may relieve chest pain or discomfort.

Before you administer nitroglycerin, you must determine the patient's normal dosage and find out how many doses the patient took before you arrived. You should also determine how the medication was taken and what effect it had on the patient. If the patient doesn't have a nitroglycerin prescription, you should consult with the medical direction physician and wait for approval before administration. After administration, the patient should be reassessed. If there is no change in the patient's condition, you may administer a second or third dose with approval from the medical direction physician.

Blood pressure should be carefully monitored during nitroglycerin administration. If the patient experiences a sudden drop in blood pressure after nitroglycerin has been administered, you should place the patient in the Trendelenburg position (flat on the back with the feet higher than the head) and reassess his or her vital signs. If systolic blood pressure drops below 100, it's important to look for signs of shock and treat the patient accordingly. An instance of the systolic blood pressure dropping to this is also an indication to cease nitroglycerin administration.

Additional Topics to Review

- Signs of shock
- Cardiovascular anatomy
- Cardiovascular physiology
- CPR

Practice

Directions (1–5): Select the best answer for each question or incomplete statement.

1. A patient on his morning run reports a sudden onset of chest pain. He said that the pain subsided when he stopped running, but it quickly returned when he attempted to start running again. This patient is most likely suffering from

   A. a heart attack.
   B. angina.
   C. ischemia.
   D. ventricular fibrillation.

2. Which type of OPQRST question will help you determine the type of pain the patient is experiencing?

   A. provocation
   B. severity
   C. radiation
   D. quality

3. Which of the following would be a contraindication for administering nitroglycerin?

   A. difficulty breathing
   B. the patient's systolic blood pressure drops below 100
   C. chest pain or discomfort
   D. patient has already taken a dose of nitroglycerin

4. You find an unresponsive cardiac arrest patient with no pulse. Which of the following treatments would be most important to the patient's survival?

   A. the administration of CPR
   B. application of an automated external defibrillator
   C. the use of nitroglycerin
   D. providing the patient with oxygen

5. You are treating an unresponsive patient in cardiac arrest. The patient's pulse is regained while you treat her. Which of the following treatments would be most appropriate?

   A. defibrillation
   B. CPR
   C. immediate transport
   D. nitroglycerin

Answers

1. **B.** This patient is most likely suffering from *angina*. Angina is frequently brought on by physical activity and will often subside when the activity is discontinued.

2. **D.** *Quality* questions encourage the patient to describe what the pain feels like.

3. **B.** Nitroglycerin administration would be contraindicated if *the patient's systolic blood pressure drops below 100*.

4. **B.** *Application of an automated external defibrillator* is the most important treatment for patients in cardiac arrest who are unresponsive and without a pulse.

5. **C.** *Immediate transport* would be the most appropriate treatment in this situation. The patient has a pulse, so defibrillation and CPR should not be administered.

D. Diabetes/Altered Mental State

When a patient's verbal or nonverbal responses indicate that the patient is unaware of the present situation, he or she may be experiencing an altered mental state. Altered mental status can be a symptom of many conditions. In some cases, you may be able to identify the cause of a patient's altered mental status, but treating the patient's symptoms is more important than identifying their cause. Diabetes, seizure, and stroke are common causes of altered mental state.

1. Diabetic Emergency

Altered mental status in a diabetic patient is often an indication of severe illness. When insulin-dependent diabetics miss a meal after taking their insulin or regurgitate their post-insulin meal, they may become *hypoglycemic*, which means that the body's blood sugar is too low. Hypoglycemia can result in an altered mental state in which the patient seems intoxicated. Patients may stagger, exhibit slurred speech, or become totally unresponsive. Patients experiencing this form of diabetic emergency may also have an elevated heart rate and cold, clammy skin. More responsive patients may also complain of hunger.

Patients experiencing altered mental status because of a diabetic emergency may need to be treated with oral glucose, which raises blood sugar and can help reverse the patient's condition. Oral glucose can be administered by EMT-Basics without permission from a medical direction physician in many instances. However, some EMS systems require the EMT-Basic to receive permission from the medical direction physician before administering oral glucose. Oral glucose should not be administered to unresponsive patients or those who are unable to protect their own airway.

2. Seizures

A *seizure* is defined as a convulsive movement or an altered mental state caused by a random discharge of the brain's electrical impulses. There are many different types of seizures with various characteristics, including convulsions and episodes in which the patient stares straight ahead. Common causes of seizures include fever, infection, poisoning, hypoglycemia, head trauma, decreased levels of oxygen, and uncontrolled epilepsy.

Following a seizure, some patients may become unresponsive. This is known as a *postictal state*. This condition occurs after the brain suffers a massive discharge of energy. The postictal state is the body's attempt to recover from this discharge.

EMTs should encourage seizure patients to seek medical evaluation at the emergency department.

3. Stroke

Strokes occur as a result of the blockage or breakage of brain arteries. Strokes can present with altered mental status, as well as other mental and physical symptoms. Stroke victims may have trouble speaking or may seem confused. It is important to check for other signs of stroke in patients with altered mental status so that proper treatment can be administered.

Other signs of a stroke include sudden weakness or numbness on one side of the body, trouble speaking or seeing, headache, and facial droop.

Tip: Other possible causes of altered mental status include intoxication, infection, head trauma, decreased levels of oxygen, and hypothermia or hyperthermia.

4. Emergency Care of Patients with Altered Mental Status

The most important task while treating a patient with an altered mental status is maintaining a patent (open and unobstructed) airway. Cyanotic patients or patients who are having difficulty breathing on their own may require artificial ventilation. Patient assessment should include investigating the scene for clues to the cause of the patient's condition as well as a focused history and physical examination.

Additional Topics to Review

- Other possible causes of altered mental state
- Common diabetic medications
- Administration of oral glucose

Practice

Directions (1–5): Select the best answer for each question or incomplete statement.

1. You are treating an unresponsive patient. You find vomit on the floor and Humulin in the patient's refrigerator. What is the most likely cause of his altered mental state?

   A. stroke
   B. intoxication
   C. poisoning
   D. diabetes

2. A postictal state usually follows a

   A. stroke.
   B. seizure.
   C. diabetic emergency.
   D. heart attack.

3. The most important part of treating a patient with altered mental state is

   A. administering medication.
   B. monitoring vital signs.
   C. maintaining a patent airway.
   D. determining the cause.

4. Altered mental status accompanied by facial droop and slurred speech is most likely caused by

    A. stroke.
    B. seizure.
    C. head trauma.
    D. intoxication.

5. While treating a patient with an altered mental status, you ask the patient's family about her recent medical history. The family indicates that the patient complained of a fever earlier in the day. Based on this information, the patient's altered mental status is most likely the result of

    A. a seizure.
    B. hypothermia.
    C. head trauma.
    D. an infection.

Answers

1. **D.** Vomit and Humulin, which is a type of insulin, would indicate that *diabetes* caused the patient's altered mental state.

2. **B.** A postictal state follows a *seizure*.

3. **C.** *Maintaining a patent airway* is the most important part of treating a patient with an altered mental state.

4. **A.** An altered mental state caused by a *stroke* would likely be accompanied by facial drooping and slurred speech.

5. **D.** Based on the information, the patient's altered mental status is most likely the result of *an infection*. A recent history of a fever is a good indicator of an infection, which can cause patients to become confused.

E. Allergic Reactions

An *allergic reaction* is an exaggerated immune response to a substance. Substances that can cause allergic reactions are called *allergens*. Food, medications, plants, and insect stings and bites are some of the many allergens. Those who come into contact with allergens and suffer an allergic reaction have symptoms ranging from itchy eyes to life-threatening conditions.

1. Causes of Allergic Reactions

Many substances can cause an allergic reaction, but the most common are food, medications, plants, and insect stings and bites. The following lists some of the common allergic reactions that EMT-Basics should look out for in the field:

- Food-based allergic reactions associated with crustaceans and peanuts
- Medical allergies to drugs such as penicillin and sulfa compounds

- Allergic skin reactions caused by some plants, such as poison ivy, or certain materials, such as latex
- Allergic reactions caused by insect bites or stings

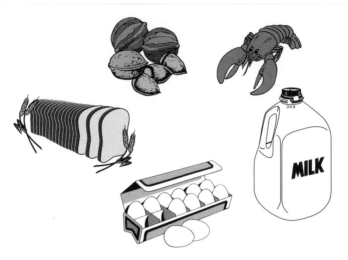

Common food allergens include (clockwise from top left) nuts, shellfish, milk, eggs, and wheat.

2. Signs and Symptoms of Allergic Reactions

Mild allergic reactions present with simple symptoms such as swelling, pain, headache, itchiness, watery eyes, and a runny nose.

Severe allergic reactions, or *anaphylaxis*, may produce life-threatening symptoms. A patient experiencing anaphylaxis may complain of a warm, tingling feeling or numbness in the extremities, mouth, face, and chest. The patient's skin may become flushed and hives may appear. The patient's face and neck may swell, which may lead to respiratory difficulty, so maintaining an open airway is vital.

Severe allergic reactions can also affect the heart. When hypoperfusion occurs, the heart rate increases in an attempt to maintain proper blood pressure. When the patient's blood pressure decreases, the patient may suffer an altered mental status. This is often a key sign of a severe allergic reaction.

3. Emergency Care for Allergic Reactions

When you assess a patient experiencing an allergic reaction, determine the cause of the reaction and the patient's history of allergies and note your general impression of the patient's condition.

If the patient is having an allergic reaction that includes respiratory distress and has a prescribed epinephrine autoinjector, you may administer this medication with permission from the medical direction physician. Also remember to monitor the patient's airway at all times.

Additional Topics to Review

- Epinephrine autoinjectors
- Respiratory distress

Practice

Directions (1–5): Select the best answer for each question or incomplete statement.

1. All of the following are common side effects of epinephrine EXCEPT

   A. chest pain.
   B. pale skin.
   C. decreased heart rate.
   D. nausea.

2. Of the following, the food most likely to cause an allergic reaction is

   A. duck.
   B. monkfish.
   C. crab.
   D. beef.

3. All of the following are common signs of an allergic reaction EXCEPT

   A. wheezing.
   B. stridor.
   C. rapid breathing.
   D. tracheal deviation.

4. The most important task while treating a patient with a severe allergic reaction is

   A. treating the patient's symptoms.
   B. maintaining an open airway.
   C. administering an epinephrine autoinjector.
   D. assessing the patient.

5. You are treating a patient suffering from a severe allergic reaction and she wants you to administer her epinephrine autoinjector. Your first step should be to

   A. make sure the medication belongs to the patient and that she has a prescription.
   B. administer the medication.
   C. contact the medical direction physician for permission.
   D. check for contraindications.

Answers

1. **C.** Epinephrine causes the heart rate to increase; it would not cause *a decreased heart rate*.

2. **C.** Because it is a crustacean, *crab* would be the most likely of these foods to cause an allergic reaction.

3. **D.** *Tracheal deviation* is not a common sign of an allergic reaction.

4. **B.** *Maintaining a patent airway* is the most important part of treating a patient with a severe allergic reaction.

5. **A.** The first step in this scenario would be to *make sure the medication belongs to the patient and that she has a prescription.*

F. Poisoning/Overdose

Poisonings are a common type of medical emergency that occurs when a person accidentally or intentionally ingests or becomes exposed to a toxic substance. *Toxins* are substances that can cause negative effects after entering the body. A poisoning can also result from an overdose of medication.

Remember, it is important for EMTs to take the proper precautions to protect themselves from any toxic substances before assessing and treating the patient.

1. History of Poisoning

When assessing a possible poisoning, it is important to focus on the history of the poisoning. There are several key questions you should ask:

- *What substance was involved?* The most important factor in a poisoning is the type of substance involved. You should look for clues and question family members or other witnesses on the scene for additional information.
- *When was the substance ingested?* The amount of time that the substance has been in the patient's system can have a substantial effect on the patient's condition and on your treatment of the patient.
- *How much of the substance was ingested?* The volume of the ingested substance can also affect the patient's condition and treatment needs.
- *Over what period of time did the poisoning take place?* It is important to determine if the poisoning took place over a long period of time or very quickly.
- *What has happened since the poisoning?* It is important to determine if the patient has attempted to treat himself or herself or if anyone else has attempted treatment.
- *How much does the patient weigh?* Weight is a critical factor in how a poisonous substance affects a patient. It is also important to know the patient's weight if the use of activated charcoal becomes necessary.

2. Types of Toxins

Toxins are classified based on their route of entry. There are four toxin classifications:

- *Ingested toxins* are consumed orally and may result in nausea, vomiting, diarrhea, abdominal pain, or cramps. Some examples include poisonous mushrooms and cleaning products.
- *Inhaled toxins* are taken directly into the respiratory system and may result in coughing, gagging, tightness in the throat, stridor, or hoarseness. A common example of an inhaled toxin is carbon monoxide.

- *Injected toxins* enter the body through skin punctures and may result in dizziness, weakness, nausea, vomiting, chills, and fever. Some examples include snakebites and bee stings.
- *Absorbed toxins* enter the body through the skin and may result in itching, burning, redness, and swelling. Some examples of these toxins are pesticides and dyes.

3. Treatment

Many forms of poisoning affect the airway, so it is important to monitor the patient's airway at all times to ensure patency. In some cases, activated charcoal may be used to treat patients who have been poisoned with an ingested toxin. Activated charcoal can bind to certain poisons and prevent further absorption. Patients must be capable of swallowing in order to take activated charcoal. Be sure to contact the medical direction physician for permission and instruction before administering this substance to a poisoning patient.

Tip: If the patient takes a long time to drink the charcoal, stir or shake the liquid to prevent settling.

Additional Topic to Review

- Administration of activated charcoal

Practice

Directions (1–5): Select the best answer for each question or incomplete statement.

1. Which of the following factors is most important in the history of poisoning?

   A. time of poison exposure
   B. amount of poison involved
   C. type of poison involved
   D. how much the patient weighs

2. A toxin that a person drinks is referred to as an

   A. inhaled toxin.
   B. ingested toxin.
   C. injected toxin.
   D. absorbed toxin.

3. A snakebite would be considered an

   A. inhaled toxin.
   B. injected toxin.
   C. ingested toxin.
   D. absorbed toxin.

4. Activated charcoal can be used to treat an

    A.   inhaled toxin.
    B.   injected toxin.
    C.   ingested toxin.
    D.   absorbed toxin.

5. Which of the following is a possible side effect of activated charcoal?

    A.   diarrhea
    B.   bloody stool
    C.   heartburn
    D.   black stool

Answers

1. **C.** The *type of poison* involved is the most important factor in the patient history.

2. **B.** A toxin that a person drinks is an *ingested toxin*.

3. **B.** A snakebite is an *injected toxin*.

4. **C.** Activated charcoal can be used to treat an *ingested toxin*.

5. **D.** *Black stool* is a possible side effect of activated charcoal.

G. Environmental Emergencies

Environmental emergencies are medical situations that arise from the outdoor environment. These emergencies are often related to weather, water, and bites or stings from various animals. It is important for EMT-Basics to recognize the signs of these emergencies in order to provide adequate prehospital care.

Remember, EMT-Basics responding to environmental emergencies should take the necessary precautions to protect themselves from danger before attempting to assess and treat the patient.

1. Thermoregulatory Emergencies

Thermoregulatory emergencies are situations in which the patient has endured a significant increase or decrease in body temperature. Exposure to excessive cold can lead to hypothermia. *Hypothermia* is a condition in which the body's core temperature falls below 98.6°F (37°C).

Generalized hypothermia affects the whole body. The primary sign of generalized hypothermia is impaired mental status and motor function. As a result of the body's attempt to warm itself, the patient will exhibit elevated heart and breathing rates. As the hypothermia worsens, the patient's vital signs will diminish. Patients with generalized hypothermia should be warmed with blankets and heat packs. Warmed and humidified oxygen can also be administered.

Local cold injuries are specific to certain parts of the body, most commonly the extremities. Examples of these types of injuries include frostbite and frostnip. Local cold injuries are caused by decreased blood flow to or actual freezing of certain body parts. Body parts with local cold injuries should be protected from further injuries and wet or restrictive clothing and jewelry should be removed immediately.

Hyperthermia occurs when a patient's body temperature rises above 98.6°F (37°C). Hyperthermia is most common in hot and humid weather. Dehydration is often a contributing factor of this condition. Symptoms of hyperthermia include muscle cramps; weakness; dizziness; rapid, pounding heartbeat; altered mental state; nausea; vomiting; and abdominal cramps.

EMT-Basics can treat patients suffering from hyperthermia by applying cool packs to the neck, groin, and armpits. It is also important for you to remove the patient from the heat immediately and arrange for transport to the hospital.

2. Drowning and Near-Drowning

Drowning is death that results from immersion in water and *near-drowning* occurs when a patient survives an immersion event. Water rescues can be extremely dangerous. It is important to remember that you should not attempt to rescue a victim from the water unless you have specialized training. In many cases, lifeguards or bystanders may remove the victim from the water before your arrival. At this point, you can begin to assess and treat the patient.

Near-drowning incidents frequently involve spinal injuries caused when the victim strikes an object such as a diving board or the bottom of a body of water. Remember, you should always immobilize the patient's spine if a spinal injury is suspected. A victim of a near-drowning will most likely require fluid removal from the airway. Artificial ventilation may also be necessary and transport to the nearest hospital should be arranged.

3. Bites and Stings

Environmental emergencies may also involve bites or stings from various animals and insects. Patients who suffer animal or insect bites or stings may exhibit a number of symptoms, including rashes, localized pain, redness, swelling, weakness, dizziness, chills, fever, nausea, and vomiting.

In these situations, your most important task is to ensure that the patient's airway is clear. Other important tasks in these situations might involve removing stingers, cleaning bite wounds, and observing the patient for signs of an allergic reaction. When a bite or sting is on an extremity, you should position the bite below the patient's heart.

Tip: If a patient suffers from a bite or sting, remove any jewelry or tight-fitting clothing from the affected area before swelling occurs.

Additional Topics to Review

- Body temperature regulation
- Factors that predispose an individual to hypothermia and hyperthermia
- Allergic reactions to animal or insect bites or stings

Practice

Directions (1–5): Select the best answer for each question or incomplete statement.

1. Which of the following is a sign of late hypothermia?

   A. rapid pulse
   B. high blood pressure
   C. red skin
   D. sluggish pupils

2. Which of the following would NOT be appropriate during treatment of hyperthermia?

   A. applying cool packs to the patient's body
   B. removing the patient from the heat
   C. massaging the extremities
   D. fanning the patient

3. Conduction refers to the

   A. transfer of heat directly from one object to another.
   B. transfer of heat from moving air or liquid.
   C. loss of heat to cooler surroundings.
   D. loss of heat that occurs when a liquid changes into a gas.

4. Which of the following would be an appropriate water temperature in which to immerse the extremity of a patient with a localized cold injury?

   A. 103°F
   B. 100°F
   C. 98.6°F
   D. 105°F

5. Which type of instrument is NOT appropriate for the removal of a stinger?

   A. butter knife
   B. credit card
   C. rigid cardboard
   D. tweezers

Answers

1. **D.** *Sluggish pupils* are a sign of late hypothermia.

2. **C.** *Massaging the extremities* would not be appropriate during the treatment of hyperthermia.

3. **A.** Conduction refers to *the transfer of heat directly from one object to another*.

4. **A.** *103°F* would be an appropriate water temperature in which to immerse the extremity of a patient with a localized cold injury.

5. **D.** *Tweezers* should not be used to remove a stinger because they may squeeze out any remaining venom.

H. Behavioral Emergencies

Behavioral emergencies are situations in which a patient displays unusual or abnormal behavior. Such events can arise from mental illness, abnormal physical conditions, or the use of mind-altering substances, such as illegal drugs, alcohol, or prescription medication.

These situations can be dangerous for EMS personnel. This is why it is important to assess any potential dangers before attempting to treat the patient. If you suspect that the situation is dangerous, call the police before entering the scene.

1. Behavior

Behavior is the way a person acts. Stress, illness, and drugs can all affect behavior. In some cases, patients experiencing a behavioral emergency may be suffering from a psychological crisis. These patients exhibit behavior that suggests a break with reality. Patients who may be at risk of harming themselves or others may display depression and verbalize thoughts of death or suicide.

2. Assessment and Emergency Care

When arriving on the scene of a behavioral emergency, the first task EMTs should accomplish is the scene size-up. When you enter the scene, carefully examine the environment for possible dangers. Be sure to observe the patient's demeanor and check to make sure that he or she is not in possession of any dangerous objects. You should also try to ascertain whether the patient is under the influence of drugs or alcohol. If you think the scene may be dangerous, you should refrain from entering and contact police.

> **Tip:** Stay near a door or an exit if you suspect that the patient's behavior may turn violent. Do not allow the patient to block a potential escape route.

Once you have determined that the scene is safe, you should introduce yourself to the patient and explain why EMS personnel are present. You can then perform a medical assessment. You should ask basic questions to determine the patient's condition and its cause. If you think the patient's condition may be related to a drug overdose, take any drugs or medications you find on-scene with you to the receiving medical facility. In cases involving interpersonal violence, signs or suspicions of physical abuse should be reported to the medical facility.

Try to keep the patient calm by asking questions in a respectful, reassuring manner and make the patient feel comfortable. In situations where you are unable to keep the patient calm, you may need to utilize soft restraints. You may need to restrain the patient in order to provide treatment or initiate transport. You should be aware of the local laws regarding restraining patients, as these may vary in certain states or counties. You may need permission from the medical direction physician or assistance from police in order to apply restraints. Do not use handcuffs or other metal restraints, as these may cause soft tissue damage. If a patient is biting or spitting, you may also apply a surgical or oxygen mask.

3. Medical and Legal Considerations

In most cases, it is the patient's right to refuse treatment and transport to a medical facility. Behavioral emergencies can be particularly difficult because the patient may not be competent enough to make a sound decision regarding treatment. If a patient refuses treatment or transport, you should be careful to follow the local regulations regarding this situation. Beyond that, your decision on whether to treat or transport should be based on the patient's mental state, physical condition, and age. You must contact your medical supervisors before attempting to treat or transport a patient without his or her consent. Police assistance may also be necessary.

When you are confronted with a behavioral emergency, you should never use more than *reasonable force*, which is the basic force required to prevent patients from harming themselves or others. Any additional use of force should only be employed by police.

Finally, it is critically important to document all abnormal behavior the patient may be exhibiting. You should note the patient's position when found, any aggressive or abnormal actions the patient may take, unusual patient statements, detailed assessment findings, any restraining measures you take, and the names of any persons who witness or assist with the patient's treatment or transport.

Additional Topics to Review

- Signs of potential patient violence
- Risk factors for suicide

Practice

Directions (1–5): Select the best answer for each question or incomplete statement.

1. Which of the following symptoms are most commonly associated with bipolar disorder?

   A.   hallucinations
   B.   severe mood swings
   C.   uncontrollable anxiety
   D.   severe memory loss

2. When you arrive on the scene of a behavioral emergency, what is the first thing you should do?

   A.   Assess the patient.
   B.   Determine the cause of the patient's behavior.
   C.   Alert police.
   D.   Assess the scene.

3. Which of the following is NOT a sign of potential patient violence?

   A.   clenched fists
   B.   throwing objects
   C.   yelling or using profanity
   D.   refusal to speak

4. You should never restrain a patient face down on a stretcher because of the risk of

   A. soft tissue damage.
   B. irritation.
   C. suffocation.
   D. escaping from restraints.

5. You believe that a man exhibiting abnormal behavior needs to be taken to a medical facility. However, the patient refuses treatment or transport. What should you do?

   A. Restrain him and initiate transport.
   B. Stop treatment and leave the scene.
   C. Proceed according to local regulations.
   D. Continue treatment on-scene.

Answers

1. **B.** Bipolar disorder is most often characterized by *severe mood swings*. It is also called manic-depressive disorder. During the manic phase, individuals experience euphoria and extreme optimism. The symptoms reverse during the depressive phase, when individuals suffer feelings of hopelessness and extreme sadness.

2. **D.** The first thing you should do when you arrive at a behavioral emergency is *assess the scene*.

3. **D.** *Refusal to speak* is usually a sign that the patient is suffering from depression.

4. **C.** You should never restrain a patient face down on a stretcher because of the risk of *suffocation*.

5. **C.** When you encounter a patient who refuses treatment or transport, you should *proceed according to local regulations*.

I. Obstetrics and Gynecology

This section of the EMT-Basic exam tests your ability to deal with emergencies regarding pregnancy, labor, and the female reproductive system. You will also be tested on how to deliver a child, normal and abnormal delivery, and other gynecological emergencies.

About 16 percent of the questions on the EMT-Basic exam will cover obstetrics and gynecological issues.

1. Parts of the Reproductive System

You should already be familiar with the different parts of the female reproductive system, so this section should serve as an overview of the function of the various organs.

The *fetus*, or unborn baby, develops and grows inside the mother's uterus for about 40 weeks. This amount of time is called the *gestational period*. The *uterus*, also called the womb, is the organ responsible for contracting and expelling the fetus during childbirth. The *cervix*, also called the neck of the uterus, is the organ that widens, or *dilates*, during labor and allows the fetus to pass through. After the fetus passes through the cervix, it makes its way through the birth canal, which is the lower part of the uterus and vagina. The fetus is expelled through the *vagina* when the mother pushes during labor.

During pregnancy, an organ called the *placenta* develops. The placenta is responsible for passing oxygen and nutrients from the mother to the fetus and the passing of waste and carbon dioxide from the fetus to the mother. These exchanges are done through the *umbilical cord,* which attaches the fetus to the placenta. The placenta is expelled during labor and the EMT-Basic cuts the umbilical cord from the newborn.

Inside the uterus, the fetus is surrounded by a bag of fluid called the *amniotic sac,* which contains amniotic fluid that helps cushion and protect the fetus. During labor, this sac breaks and releases the amniotic fluid, which lubricates the birth canal.

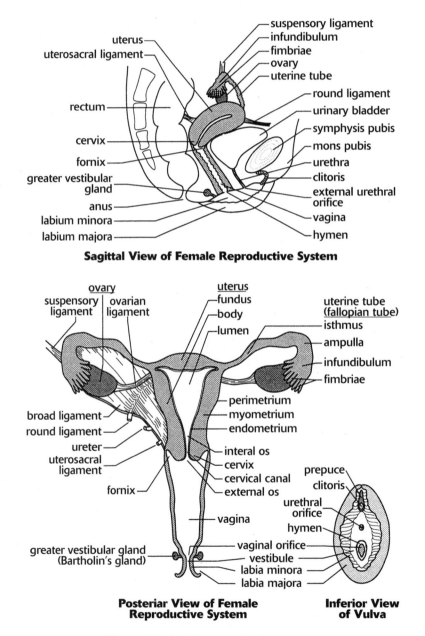

View of the female reproductive system.

2. Labor

Usually when an ambulance is called for a woman in labor, it's the job of EMS personnel to transfer the patient to the hospital for delivery. Sometimes, there's not enough time to make it to the hospital and the EMTs must assist the patient with the delivery. You should be familiar with the contents of the obstetrical kit, which contains a scalpel, clamps, and sterile gloves. Additional items in this kit may include scissors, ties, a bag for the placenta, and a "bunting cap" to keep the baby's head warm.

Labor is the process of giving birth. It is divided into three stages. The first stage of labor begins when the uterus begins to contract, moving the fetus into the birth canal. A woman in this stage of labor may feel strong and sometimes painful contractions. Her cervix dilates to prepare to pass the baby.

After a woman's cervix has dilated to 10 cm, she has entered the second stage of labor. During the second stage, the fetus moves from the birth canal through the vagina. During a normal birth, you will most likely see the baby's head in the vaginal opening. This is called *crowning*. After the baby is born, the mother enters the third stage of labor, in which the mother expels the placenta.

3. Predelivery Problems

Sometimes complications arise before the baby is ready to be born. Problems can be caused by medical conditions or trauma. In certain instances, the cause of these problems remains unknown.

> **Tip:** In a traumatic emergency, a pregnant patient should be treated the same way as other patients with the same signs and symptoms.

a. Miscarriage

A miscarriage occurs when the fetus is delivered before it can survive on its own. This usually occurs during the first three months of pregnancy. Some of the signs of a miscarriage are abdominal cramping and heavy bleeding. The bleeding is usually accompanied by a discharge of clots of tissue. The following steps will help you treat a woman who is experiencing a miscarriage:

1. Treat the woman for signs and symptoms.
2. Call advanced life support (ALS) for assistance.
3. Administer oxygen.
4. Apply external vaginal pads or sanitary pads to reduce the blood flow.
5. Be prepared to treat shock symptoms if they appear.
6. Offer her emotional support, if needed.

b. Seizures

Sometimes a woman will develop medical conditions during pregnancy that cause seizures. *Preeclampsia* is a medical condition that causes a pregnant woman's blood pressure to rise. It also causes weight gain and water retention. If seizures are present with this condition, the woman is experiencing *eclampsia*. This condition usually affects women who have had no prior history of seizures. ALS should be called to assist with these types of EMS calls.

c. Vaginal Bleeding

Many conditions can cause vaginal bleeding late in the pregnancy. This bleeding most often indicates a problem with the placenta, such as *abruption placentae*, a condition in which the placenta detaches from the uterus. Another condition that causes bleeding is called *placenta previa*, a condition in which the placenta implants over the cervix. ALS should be called to assist with these types of EMS calls.

d. Trauma

Sometimes a pregnant woman experiences a trauma that can cause problems for her and her fetus. The following special considerations should be observed when treating a pregnant trauma patient:

- Transport the woman on her left side to relieve the pressure on the vena cava from the weight of the uterus. If spinal injury is suspected, secure the woman on a long backboard, and then tilt the board to the left.
- Administer oxygen.
- Be prepared for vomiting, as digestion slows during pregnancy.
- Be prepared to treat shock symptoms if they appear.
- In the event of the woman's death, continue to administer CPR and transport her to the hospital. Doctors may be able to perform a *cesarean section,* also known as a delivery via surgery, which could save the baby's life.

Tip: If a pregnant trauma patient dies as a result of her injuries, it is important for you to understand the area's policies and protocols involved in this difficult situation.

4. Normal Delivery

Calls concerning pregnancies are not typically emergencies; however, EMT-Basics should always be prepared to perform a delivery when they arrive on the scene. If the woman is not injured or experiencing signs or symptoms of predelivery issues, you should treat the woman as a stable medical patient.

a. Predelivery

When you arrive at the woman's side, you must determine how quickly she will deliver her baby. Ask the patient when the baby is due. Find out how far apart the contractions are and if there is increasing pressure in the vagina. Examine the patient for bleeding or abnormal discharge. Feel the abdomen; if it's hard, your patient is in the later stages of delivery. If you determine that you will not have enough time to transport the patient to a medical facility before she delivers her child, you'll have to assist with the delivery on the scene.

If you must deliver the baby on the scene, the first thing you must do is take the proper body substance isolation precautions to protect yourself from the blood and bodily fluids you will encounter during the delivery. If delivery doesn't occur within 10 minutes of deciding to deliver the child on the scene, call the medical direction physician and request permission to transport your patient to the nearest hospital.

b. Delivery

If you must deliver on the scene, be sure that your patient is lying on her back with her buttocks elevated. As the baby crowns, gently press on the perineum to ensure that the delivery doesn't occur too quickly. A rapid delivery may lead to unsafe conditions for the mother and child. Be sure never to press on the *fontanelles*, the soft spots on the baby's head. When the baby's head appears outside the vaginal opening, ensure that the umbilical cord is not wrapped around the baby's neck. If the cord is around the child's neck, slide it off. If sliding doesn't work, place two clamps on the cord and cut it before removing it from the child's neck.

Next, gently guide the head downward until the first shoulder blade passes the pubic bone. Then, after ensuring you have a secure hold on the infant, guide the infant upward until the second shoulder passes. As your patient delivers the legs and feet, be sure to keep a firm grasp on the baby.

Pass the infant to your partner for evaluation and care while you assist the mother in the final stage of labor, which involves the delivery of the placenta. This process can take up to a half-hour to complete. Once the patient delivers the placenta, place it in a plastic bag and take it to the hospital for physicians to evaluate.

Tip: About 500 ml of blood is lost during a typical childbirth.

c. Care of Newborn

After delivery, EMTs must suction the newborn's mouth and nose to remove fluids and allow for easier breathing. Dry and swaddle the newborn with a towel or blanket. Assess the infant's health 1 minute and 5 minutes after birth using the APGAR scale. Check the newborn's appearance, pulse rate, grimace, activity level, and respirations. Compare the scores from the 1-minute and 5-minute tests.

If the newborn is not breathing, stimulate the infant by massaging the baby's back or flicking the souls of his or her feet. If the newborn doesn't respond to stimulation, take resuscitative measures, as shown in the following figure.

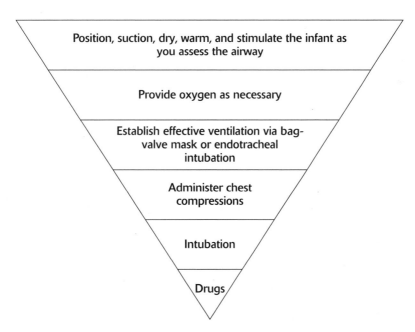

Neonatal resuscitative measures pyramid.

If the newborn is still not breathing, call ALS and transport the infant and mother immediately.

5. Abnormal Delivery

While the majority of deliveries are normal, you must always be prepared to treat a patient experiencing an abnormal pregnancy or delivery. If the baby doesn't appear to be in a *cephalic* (head-first) position, if meconium (fetal stool) is present, or if the delivery is premature, you must attempt to deliver or transport the patient immediately. Call ALS or the medical direction physician if you are unsure of how to proceed at any time.

a. Prolapsed Cord

A *prolapsed cord* is a condition in which the umbilical cord is the first body part out of the vagina during delivery. In this condition, the cord catches between the wall of the birth canal and the baby's head, cutting off the baby's oxygen supply. This condition requires immediate transport.

In the ambulance, elevate the patient's pelvis and place her on high-flow oxygen. Direct her not to push, as the pressure will further cut off oxygen to the baby. Place your fingers into the vagina and gently move the baby's head off the cord. Do not remove your hand until you reach the hospital. If the cord is sticking out of the vagina, dress it to maintain moisture.

> **Tip: In an instance of limb presentation, a leg or an arm may present itself similar to a prolapsed cord. The baby cannot be delivered in this position; therefore, treat the patient as you would for a prolapsed cord and transport her to a hospital immediately.**

b. Breech Presentation

A *breech presentation* occurs when the baby is positioned feet first inside of the womb instead of head first. When a breech baby is delivered in a hospital, a surgical team is present in case the breech position creates complications. You must be prepared to deal with the possibility of a breech presentation. Many times, breech deliveries are similar to cephalic births; once the shoulders are through the birth canal, few complications arise. However, the possibility exists that the baby's head may not deliver as quickly or easily as the rest of the body.

If the head is undelivered, the baby may suffocate, so take immediate action. With your palm up and your index and middle fingers spread apart, place your hand in the vagina between the baby's face and the vaginal wall. Push the vaginal wall away from the baby's face to allow for oxygen flow and deliver the head. If you cannot deliver the baby's head, do not remove your hand and transport the patient to the hospital.

c. Multiple Births

Treat a patient giving birth to multiple babies the same as you would a patient delivering a single child. If you are aware of the multiple births before you arrive on the scene, you may choose to request assistance from a second EMS crew. After the delivery of the first baby, clamp or cut the first umbilical cord. The next baby may deliver before or after the patient delivers the first placenta. As the babies are born, warm them and assess their health. Be aware that multiple births typically produce smaller or premature babies, so you may need to work harder to regulate their body temperatures.

d. Premature Births

If an infant is born less than 37 weeks after being conceived or if the infant weighs less than 5.5 pounds, the infant is considered premature. Babies born early are often not fully developed in terms of their cardiovascular or respiratory systems. Because they cannot regulate their body temperatures and may not be able to breathe on their own, you need to pay close attention to their vital signs. Be sure to keep the infant wrapped in a warm, dry blanket or towel and administer oxygen if necessary. Immediately transport the patient and child to the hospital for emergency neonatal care.

6. Other Gynecological Emergencies

EMT-Basics are often called to the scene of an emergency involving vaginal bleeding, trauma to the external genitalia, or injuries after a sexual assault.

If a woman is experiencing vaginal bleeding not resulting from a trauma, you do not have to examine the genitalia. Obtain the patient's SAMPLE history and ask the patient about the color of the blood, the number of sanitary pads she filled, and if she may be pregnant. Ask her if clots of tissue are present in the blood. While transporting the patient to the hospital, be prepared to treat her for shock.

If there is trauma to the external genitalia, provide treatment on the scene in a professional and efficient manner. As you treat the patient, remember to explain what you are doing and why you are taking such precautions or actions. If the patient is bleeding, apply pressure using a sanitary napkin or dressing. If the genitalia are swollen, apply an icepack wrapped in a towel to the area.

On the scene of a sexual assault, consider the fact that you may be the first person to care for the victim since she reported the crime. Keep your patient calm, reassure her that she is safe, and do not judge her as you gather SAMPLE information. You don't need to examine the patient's genitals if she doesn't report extreme bleeding. If profuse bleeding occurs, it is often more comfortable for the patient if an EMT-Basic of the same sex performs the examination. Because the emergency scene is also a crime scene, work to preserve all evidence, including any on the victim. Do not instruct your patient to shower, urinate, douche, or clean any wounds as doing so might destroy valuable evidence. If you determine any injuries to be life threatening, don't wait for the police to arrive on the scene to transport your patient.

Additional Topics to Review

- Contents of the childbirth kit
- Detailed procedures for normal and abnormal deliveries
- APGAR scoring system
- Resuscitative measures in normal and abnormal deliveries
- Delivery in the presence of meconium

Practice

Directions (1–5): Select the best answer for each question or incomplete statement.

1. What is the term used to describe a delivery that occurs before the fetus can survive outside of the womb and breathe on its own?

    A. breech
    B. predelivery
    C. cephalic
    D. miscarriage

2. When preparing to deliver on the scene, you should wear

    A. a gown, gloves, and a mask.
    B. a gown, gloves, a mask, and eye protection.
    C. a gown, gloves, and foot protection.
    D. gloves, eye protection, and a mask.

3. How much blood does a woman lose during normal childbirth?

    A. 250 ml
    B. 400 ml
    C. 500 ml
    D. 800 ml

4. Your patient is 38 weeks pregnant. She is experiencing painful contractions and her cervix has dilated to 9 cm. You have determined that she is entering the second stage of labor. Which of the following will most likely occur next?

    A. The baby will pass through the birth canal and crown.
    B. You will put on your protective BMI gear and prepare for delivery.
    C. The placenta will pass through the vagina and the umbilical cord will be cut.
    D. You will call ALS or the medical direction physician to report a premature birth.

5. What is the initial action the EMT-Basic should take during a delivery where the umbilical cord presents first?

    A. Elevate the mother's pelvis so that it releases pressure on the umbilical cord.
    B. Transport the mother to the hospital.
    C. Guide the baby's shoulders out of the birth canal.
    D. Insert a gloved hand into the vagina and place your palm facing the baby's face.

Answers

1. **D.** When a delivery occurs before the fetus can survive outside of the womb and breathe on its own, it is called a *miscarriage*. Miscarriages typically occur within the first three months of pregnancy. Abdominal cramping and heavy bleeding are signs of a miscarriage.

2. **B.** Because you will inevitably encounter many bodily fluids during the birthing process, you should wear *a gown, gloves, a mask, and eye protection*. Although a gown is often optional, it is strongly recommended that you wear one during this process.

3. **C.** During a normal childbirth, a woman typically loses *500 ml* of blood. If she loses more than 500 ml, you should locate the cause of the bleeding and perform an immediate intervention. Many times, a uterine massage helps to control or slow the bleeding after delivery.

4. **A.** During the second stage of labor, *the baby will pass through the birth canal and crown*. The placenta is typically delivered after the baby, and you should be wearing your BMI gear before assessing your patient.

5. **A.** The first thing the EMT-Basic should do is to *elevate the mother's pelvis so that it releases pressure on the umbilical cord*. This is important because the umbilical cord provides the baby with oxygen and nutrients while still in the womb.

IX. Trauma

Trauma calls are some of the most difficult situations that EMT-Basics must deal with on the job. Trauma-related injuries often involve bleeding, shock, soft tissue damage, musculoskeletal damage, and injuries to the head and spine. Although every case is different, it is important for EMT-Basics to understand what they might encounter on a trauma call.

About 16 percent of the questions that you encounter on the EMT-Basic exam will test your knowledge of trauma-related injuries and quiz you on how best to handle these situations. Remember, this section does not cover everything that you will see on the exam, so it's important to review what you've already learned about trauma-related situations. Take time to examine the "Additional Topics to Review" sections in this chapter for more information about topics you should study before taking the test.

A. Bleeding and Shock

Bleeding and shock are two of the most common trauma-related injuries you will encounter as an EMT-Basic. In most cases, your initial assessment of the patient will help you determine where the patient is injured and how he or she must be treated. However, internal bleeding can be difficult to recognize, and symptoms of shock are not always clear. Because such injuries can quickly lead to death, it is vital that EMT-Basics understand how to identify and treat these cases.

1. The Cardiovascular System

Before discussing the treatment of blood loss and shock, it is important for you to have a good understanding of the cardiovascular system. As you already know, the cardiovascular system supplies the body's organs with blood and nutrients using a complex network of veins, capillaries, and arteries powered by the heart. Most adults have about 5 to 7 liters of blood in their bodies. Blood performs a task known as *perfusion*. Perfusion is the process by which blood transports oxygen to and removes waste products from bodily organs. Some organs, particularly the brain, require a constant stream of oxygen and nutrients. When the brain's blood supply is impaired, even for a short period of time, changes in mental status may occur.

Blood is pumped through the entire body of an average adult heart at a rate of 60 to 100 beats per minute. At this rate, the body's entire blood volume can be circulated through the whole system in under a minute. When a patient experiences stress or a medical emergency, the heart rate can increase significantly.

One important factor in perfusion is blood pressure. As discussed in Chapter V, "Preparatory," there are two forms of blood pressure. Diastolic blood pressure is the pressure present in the blood vessels when the heart is at rest. Systolic blood pressure refers to the intermittent rise in pressure that occurs when the heart contracts and blood is forced out into the arteries. Healthy blood pressure is a key element of proper perfusion.

2. Shock

An interruption in blood flow can result in cell and organ damage. Severe bleeding depletes the cardiovascular system's blood supply, leading to a decrease in perfusion. A decrease in perfusion causes a condition known as *hypoperfusion*. When hypoperfusion starts to affect the entire body, the patient enters into shock. *Shock* occurs when vital organs are no longer being properly perfused by the cardiovascular system. In cases of shock, organ tissues are damaged by the accumulation of waste products and the lack of oxygen. As damage to the organs progresses, organ failure and death may occur.

Although there are many types of shock, the most common form of shock EMT-Basics will be required to treat in the field is *hypovolemic shock*. This type of shock results from inadequate blood volume and can be caused by problems with the heart, blood, or blood vessels. Other causes include dehydration, vomiting, diarrhea, or severe blood loss.

Your most important responsibilities are to determine what stage of shock the patient is in and the best course of treatment. Recognizing the signs of early shock allows you to transport and treat the patient before the onset of late shock. Most of the signs and symptoms of shock are connected with the body's struggle to maintain perfusion in the event of blood loss. As hypoperfusion sets in, blood flow to the skin is reduced because of blood vessel constriction. This may cause your patient's skin to become pale, cool, and clammy. Vessel constriction also leads to a decrease in peripheral perfusion, which causes weak peripheral pulses.

Elevated heart rate is a critical sign of shock, as the heart rate will rise as the heart attempts to pump the remainder of the body's blood volume faster. In early shock, elevated heart rate and the constriction of blood vessels allow for the maintenance of normal blood pressure. As the blood volume decreases, blood pressure will fall to abnormally low levels. This is a sign of late shock. A patient at this stage is near death. The patient's breathing rate may increase as he or she tries to oxygenate the remaining blood in the cardio-vascular system. When shock worsens, the patient may exhibit shallow, labored, or irregular breathing.

In some cases, a change in mental status due to impaired blood flow to the brain may be a later symptom of shock. Patients may become anxious, restless, or combative. Recognizing changes in mental status is partic-ularly important for patients experiencing shock related to internal bleeding, as these, along with changes in vital signs, may be the only apparent symptoms of this potentially fatal condition.

Tip: Other possible signs of shock may include excessive thirst, nausea, vomiting, sluggishly reactive pupils, or cyanosis of lips, nail beds, and mucous membranes.

The first task in treating a patient in shock is to ensure a patent airway. This is particularly important for trauma patients, who may have various airway obstructions. Once the airway is cleared, you should give the patient high-flow oxygen and ensure adequate ventilation. Then, you should attempt to control any serious bleeding. If there are no injuries that would inhibit moving the patient, you should elevate the legs in order to maximize blood flow to the brain. Also, keep the patient warm to prevent shivering, which would waste energy and oxygen. Next, you must quickly transport the patient to a medical facility where more advanced treatments are available.

3. External Bleeding

The volume of blood loss a patient can withstand before shock develops depends on the patient's size. Smaller patients and children have a naturally lower blood volume and will most likely develop shock quickly if left untreated. Elderly patients are also at risk of an earlier onset of shock because their hearts may not be capable of meeting an increased demand. The severity of blood loss can be measured based on the patient's signs and symptoms.

When an injury causes blood loss, the body tries to stop the blood flow with vessel constriction and blood clotting. Some injuries may cause excessively forceful bleeding that the body can't stop on its own. This uncontrolled bleeding can lead to shock.

There are three type of bleeding:

- *Arterial bleeding* occurs after damage to an artery. Highly pressurized blood may spurt out of a wound. Blood loss from this type of injury is rapid and shock may begin very quickly. External arterial bleeding will produce bright red, oxygen-rich blood. The high pressure of arterial blood makes this type of bleeding the most difficult to control.
- *Venous bleeding* originates from a vein and produces dark red blood that flows steadily from the wound. The lower pressure of venous blood makes this type of bleeding easier to control.
- *Capillary bleeding* results from scrapes and abrasions and will produce dark red, oozing blood. This type of bleeding is easily treatable and usually clots on its own.

All forms of bleeding require the same basic treatments. Because most bleeding is localized to one main artery or vein, the best way to control blood loss is with *concentrated direct pressure*. Use your fingertip to press directly on the bleeding point with sterile gauze. Try not to remove the gauze frequently, as this may break up clots that have started to form.

For large injuries or situations where bleeding is occurring at more than one location, *diffuse direct pressure* may be applied. When using this method, place sterile gauze pads on the injury and apply pressure using the entire hand. This decreases blood flow to the injury site. In the event that blood starts seeping though the gauze, add more layers on top. Don't remove the initial layer of gauze at any time.

In cases where the patient shows no signs of swelling, pain, or deformity, you may raise the affected extremity above the level of the heart. This helps to reduce blood flow to the injury site.

You can also slow bleeding by utilizing pressure points. A *pressure point* is a place in an extremity where a major artery lies close to the bone. Applying pressure on these areas can reduce blood flow to that extremity. These are the same locations where you are able to palpate the patient's pulse.

Splints may be used to help control bleeding caused by skeletal injuries. When you immobilize a bone injury with a splint, you decrease the movement of broken bone ends that can cause damage to blood vessels and tissues. Immobilization of the lower extremities can be accomplished with the use of pneumatic antishock garments. These devices are placed on the lower extremities and inflated with air. This diffuse pressure immobilizes limbs and helps control bleeding.

Tourniquets have traditionally been used as a last-resort option for controlling bleeding because of the risk of permanent damage to muscles, nerves, and blood vessels. Extensive damage to an extremity can lead to the need for amputation, so tourniquets should only be used in situations where there is clearly a life threat. However, if the patient is already in shock and you are unable to control hemorrhage from an extremity with direct pressure, a tourniquet should be immediately applied to prevent the patient from further deterioration.

Blood loss from certain areas of the body may require different forms of treatment. Bleeding from the ears or nose may indicate a skull fracture. In this instance, the ears and nose should be lightly covered with sterile gauze. Facial bleeding caused by trauma can usually be treated with direct pressure. A bloody nose, or *epistaxis*, can be caused by blunt force to the nose or digital trauma, such as finger insertion. As long as no spinal injuries are present, you can treat a nosebleed by placing the patient in a seated, forward-leaning position and pinching the fleshy part of the nostrils together.

4. Internal Bleeding

Compared to external bleeding, internal bleeding can be more difficult to recognize and harder to control. *Internal bleeding* is bleeding inside the body. Internal blood loss can result in a rapid onset of shock and cannot be treated in the field. The goal of an EMT-Basic is to recognize the signs of internal bleeding and transport the patient to a medical facility capable of surgical intervention as quickly as possible.

When internal organs are damaged, they may bleed into the thoracic and abdominal cavities. Skeletal trauma may cause damage to blood vessels and blood loss into the extremity. Because there may not be any apparent signs of internal bleeding, this diagnosis is generally based on the mechanism of injury and the patient's other symptoms. In many cases, the only sign of internal bleeding is the onset of shock.

One important possible indication of internal bleeding is bleeding from the mouth, rectum, or genitals. Even when these types of external blood loss appear minor, the internal bleeding causing it may be severe. Additional signs and symptoms of internal bleeding may include swelling, discoloration of the skin, and pain.

In some cases, internal bleeding may occur inside the gastrointestinal tract. The specific characterizations of blood that exits the gastrointestinal tract can indicate the exact location of the bleeding and when it started. Blood in the stomach is very irritating to its lining and frequently causes vomiting. This may produce vomit tinged with bright red blood. If vomiting is delayed for a period of time, it can become mixed with digestive fluids, and, when regurgitated, appears dark brown in color with a consistency similar to coffee grounds.

Blood in the intestinal tract that is partially digested usually results in dark, tarry stool. Undigested blood that originates in the lower intestinal tract usually results in stool with bright red blood.

Damaged abdominal cavity blood vessels can cause massive, hard-to-control internal bleeding. Blood that is trapped in the abdominal cavity can cause distention, rigidity, and tenderness.

On-scene treatment of internal bleeding is generally limited to maintaining a patent airway, supplemental oxygen, and rapid transport. When internal bleeding is caused by an injury to an extremity, you can reduce bleeding with direct pressure and splinting. The use of a pneumatic antishock garment may be necessary when a patient shows signs of shock, has abdominal tenderness, or has a pelvic injury.

Additional Topics to Review

- Cardiovascular anatomy and physiology
- Specific types of shock

Practice

Directions (1–5): Select the best answer for each question or incomplete statement.

1. The process of delivering oxygen to and removing waste products from organs is called

   A. diffusion.
   B. perfusion.
   C. hypoperfusion.
   D. shock.

2. _____ is a type of shock that can result from a severe bacterial infection.

   A. Cardiogenic shock
   B. Septic shock
   C. Anaphylactic shock
   D. Neurogenic shock

3. Assessing capillary refill would be a reliable indication of shock in patients who are

   A. experiencing severe bleeding.
   B. unable to breathe deeply.
   C. taking medication.
   D. under 6 years of age.

4. Which of the following symptoms would indicate the onset of late shock?

   A. sluggish pupils
   B. cyanotic lips
   C. rapid, weak pulse
   D. lowered blood pressure

5. A patient in shock has low blood pressure, a pulse of 130 beats per minute, and a respiratory rate of 35 breaths per minute. The patient is confused and anxious. Based on these signs, approximately how much blood has the patient lost?

   A. 1,500–2,000 ml
   B. 600–700 ml
   C. up to 750 ml
   D. more than 2,000 ml

Answers

1. **B.** The process of delivering oxygen to and removing waste products from organs is called *perfusion*.

2. **B.** *Septic shock* is a type of shock that can result from a severe bacterial infection.

3. **D.** Assessing capillary refill would be a reliable indication of shock in patients who are *under 6 years of age*.

4. **D.** *Lowered blood pressure* would indicate the onset of shock.

5. **A.** The patient's signs indicate he has lost approximately *1,500–2,000 ml* of blood.

B. Soft Tissue Damage

EMT-Basics may encounter a variety of soft tissue injuries in the field. *Soft tissue injuries* can include open and closed injuries and burns. In most cases, these injuries look worse than they actually are and necessitate only minor emergency care.

1. The Skin

In order to properly recognize and treat soft tissue damage, you must have a sound understanding of the skin. The largest organ in the human body, the skin covers the entire surface area of the body and acts as a protective barrier. The skin guards the body against the environment, viruses, bacteria, and other potentially harmful organisms. The skin also acts as the body's insulation, regulating body temperature by opening and closing pores and releasing or retaining heat. Nerves in the skin allow us to feel heat, cold, touch, pressure, and pain.

The skin has three layers:

- The *epidermis*, which is the skin's outermost layer, is a very thin layer of dead skin cells and pores. The majority of superficial injuries occur here. In most cases, epidermal injuries will not result in pain or bleeding.

- The next layer is the *dermis*, which consists of sweat and subcutaneous glands, hair follicles, small blood vessels, and nerve endings. Injuries to the dermis often result in pain and bleeding.

- The deepest layer of skin is the *subcutaneous layer*. Subcutaneous skin injuries can cause significant pain and bleeding. Severe subcutaneous skin injuries may include exposure of bones, muscles, or other tissues.

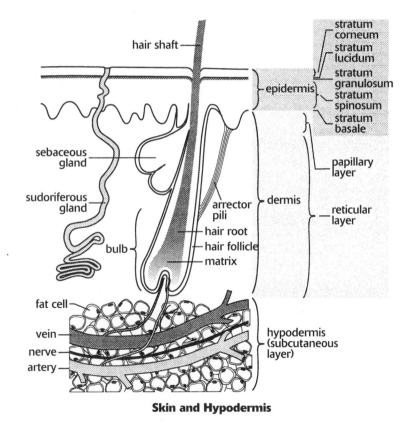

Skin and Hypodermis

A section of skin with various accessory organs.

2. Closed Injuries

Patients with closed soft tissue injuries will present with fully intact skin and no external bleeding. Because there are no open wounds with these injuries, EMT-Basics do not have to clean or cover the site of the injury.

There are three basic types of closed soft tissue injuries:

- *Contusions*, also known as bruises, are closed injuries characterized by damaged skin cells and torn blood vessels in the dermis. The site of the injury will become discolored due to internal blood accumulation. Contusions are sometimes accompanied by swelling or pain.
- *Hematomas* are a more severe form of contusions. Hematomas occur with injuries to larger blood vessels. These injuries lead to a much greater accumulation of blood under the skin. Particularly large hematomas may lead to hypoperfusion, so it is important to assess the patient for symptoms of the early onset of shock.
- *Closed crush injuries* result from force applied to an area of the body with a blunt instrument. Closed crush injuries in the vicinity of an organ may be an indication of damage to that organ and internal bleeding as a result.

3. Open Injuries

Open soft tissue injuries involve breakage of the skin and, in most cases, external bleeding. Open wounds are at risk of infection and should be cleaned and covered with sterile dressings.

Abrasions are simple scrapes that damage only the epidermis. Pain, oozing blood, and redness are common symptoms of abrasions.

Lacerations are cuts or breaks in the skin of various depths. Lacerations can be *linear* (regular) or *stellate* (irregular) and sometimes occur in connection with other soft tissue injuries. In most cases, lacerations are caused by a forceful impact with sharp objects, like knives or shards of broken glass. Severe bleeding may be present based on the location of the wound.

A patient suffers an *avulsion* when a section of skin or soft tissue is torn partially or fully off the body. These types of injuries can be found anywhere on the body.

Penetration or puncture wounds occur when an object, most commonly a knife or a bullet, is forced into the body. The object may still be in the wound, or it may have exited the body at another area.

An *amputation* occurs when a limb or appendage is completely severed from the body. Amputations may be accompanied by massive bleeding.

In some cases, crush injuries can cause open soft tissue injuries, along with internal organ damage. Most open crush injuries result in pain, swelling, and deformity. The severity of blood loss may vary in these cases.

4. Treatment of Open and Closed Soft Tissue Injuries

As with most medical emergencies, the first objective in treating a patient with an open or closed soft tissue injury is to ensure a patent airway. Check for spinal injuries and immobilize, if necessary. Because severe bleeding may occur with open injuries, you should carefully monitor the patient for signs of shock and treat accordingly. When attempting to control bleeding, the wound should be exposed and covered with dry sterile dressings.

If the patient is deemed stable and no life threats are found, you should splint any injured extremities before transport. Patients in shock should be transported immediately and splinted en route.

Some wounds require special treatment. For example, penetrating chest wounds require sealed occlusive dressings that don't allow air to enter or exit the wound. In the event of a sucking chest wound (an injury in which an object penetrates the skin and lung cavity), the dressing should only be sealed on three sides. This allows air to exit but not re-enter the wound.

In some cases, an abdominal injury will result in part of an organ protruding from the skin. This is known as an *evisceration*. The exposed organ should be covered with a sterile dressing that has been moistened with water or saline. An occlusive dressing should then be applied to prevent the wound from drying.

When you find a patient with a foreign object still in a wound, you should not, in most cases, attempt to remove it. Generally, the only situations in which you should attempt removal are when the object interferes with the airway or your ability to administer chest compressions.

In the event of an amputation, it is important to attend to the severed appendage. If the amputated part is salvageable, wrap it in plastic and keep it cool.

Tip: Never place an amputated body part directly on ice, as this will damage the tissue.

Another injury that requires special consideration is an open neck injury. Open neck injuries should be covered with a sterile occlusive dressing. The carotid artery should not be compressed unless required for control of bleeding, and only one side should be compressed at a time.

When you encounter soft tissue injuries of the face or head, it is important to check for skull or spinal injuries before proceeding with treatment. If there are no skull fractures, dressings and bandages should be applied with direct pressure. If a skull fracture is present, don't apply direct pressure.

Eye injuries may require flushing. If the patient has an object embedded in the eye, don't attempt to remove it. Stabilize the object and cover both eyes in order to minimize eye movement as you transport the patient.

Oral injuries may result in airway obstructions due to blood or broken teeth. Secure the airway and use dressings to control bleeding before transport.

5. Burns

Burns are very painful injuries that can cause permanent disfigurement or disability. While burns themselves may not be fatal, the damage they may cause to the airway, respiratory system, and circulatory system can be extremely dangerous. Because burns can result in severe damage to the protective layers of skin, they can also lead to fluid loss, hypothermia, and infection.

The classification of burns is based on the depth of the injury. Burn severity is measured by the depth and location of the burn, the percentage of the body that is burned, pre-existing conditions, and age.

There are three burn classifications:

- *Superficial burns* affect only the epidermis and result in redness and minor pain. The most common form of superficial burn is sunburn.
- *Partial-thickness burns* affect both the epidermis and the dermis and are characterized by severe pain and blistering. You may also find moist or mottled skin that ranges from white to red in color.
- *Full-thickness burns* affect the epidermis, dermis, and the underlying tissues. These burns may be deep enough to involve bones or organs, as well. Full-thickness burns will produce dry, leathery skin that feels hard to the touch and may appear white, dark brown, or charred. Pain may be isolated to the edges of the burn because of nerve damage.

The "rule of nines" is the common method used to determine the percentage of body area that has been burned. In adults, the front and back of the head and neck make up 9 percent of the body, the front and back of each arm is 9 percent, each side of the trunk is 18 percent, the front and back of each leg is 18 percent, and the genitalia represent 1 percent. Total percentage can be determined by adding each burned area. These percentages are different in children and infants.

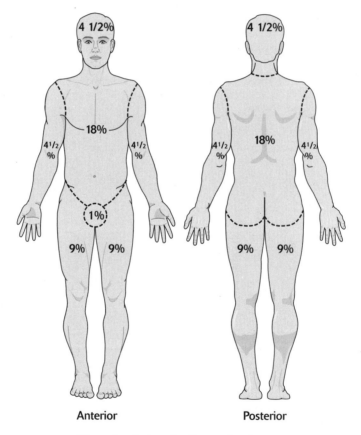

Anterior   Posterior

The rule of nines in diagnosing burns.

Critical burns are those affecting the face, hands, feet, or genitalia or those involving respiratory injuries or illness. Full-thickness burns covering more than 10 percent of the body or partial-thickness burns covering more than 30 percent of the body are also considered critical. Burns to a painful, swollen, or deformed extremity or those that encircle an extremity are also critical. Some burns that would be considered moderate in an adult may be critical in children or infants. Ensuring a clear airway and initiating immediate transport to the nearest burn center are the most important early treatments for critical burns.

Moderate burns occur away from critical areas. Moderate full-thickness burns may cover between 2 and 10 percent of the body. Moderate partial-thickness burns may cover up to 30 percent of the body. In turn, moderate superficial burns, such as sunburns, may cover up to 50 percent of the body.

Minor full-thickness burns may cover less than 2 percent of the body and minor partial-thickness burns may cover less than 15 percent of the body.

When treating a burn victim, you should be sure that the patient is kept warm, as burned skin may be unable to properly control body temperature. Because children and infants have a greater surface area in relation to their total body size, they may be particularly susceptible to increased loss of heat and fluids, shock, airway difficulties, and hypothermia.

Never attempt to treat a burn with cold water or ice. Small burns may be cooled with cool water. Larger burns should not be cooled due to the risk of hypothermia.

Certain types of burns require special attention. Airway burns are often the result of inhaling superheated air or chemicals related to combustion. Airway burns may result in swelling, which leads to respiratory difficulty. Patients with airway burns may decline rapidly, requiring advanced airway maneuvers. Indications of airway burns may include facial burns, singed facial hair, burns around the mouth or nose, oral burns or swelling, and a hoarse voice. These types of injuries are most common in patients who have recently been inside a burning building.

Chemical burns may require the use of special protective equipment. Most chemical burns should be cleaned and flushed with water. Dry powder chemicals should be carefully brushed away from the affected area. Exact treatment protocol will depend on the chemical involved.

Tip: When treating a chemical burn, remember to take the necessary body substance isolation (BSI) precautions to protect yourself before treating the patient.

Before treating the victim of an electrical burn, be sure that the patient has been removed from the source. Once the scene is safe, carefully and continually check for signs of respiratory or cardiac arrest. Look for entrance and exit wounds. Injuries resulting from electrical burns may be more severe than they appear, so you should be aware of the possibility of internal damage and cardiac injury. It is also important to look for early signs of shock in these patients.

Additional Topics to Review

- Dermatology
- Dressings and bandages
- Shock

Practice

Directions (1–5): Select the best answer for each question or incomplete statement.

1. An injury in which the epidermis is damaged by a scraping force is called

   A.   an avulsion.
   B.   a laceration.
   C.   an abrasion.
   D.   a contusion.

2. Which of the following describes an avulsion?

   A.   a wound caused by a gunshot
   B.   a piece of skin torn from the body
   C.   a deep cut caused by broken glass
   D.   a massive accumulation of blood under the skin

3. Which of the following injuries would require the application of a partially sealed occlusive dressing?

   A.   a sucking chest wound
   B.   an evisceration
   C.   a penetrating chest injury
   D.   an avulsion

4. Which of the following would indicate a critical burn?

   A.   a superficial burn covering 9 percent of a child's body
   B.   a partial-thickness burn covering 25 percent of an adult's body
   C.   a full-thickness burn covering 20 percent of a child's body
   D.   a superficial burn covering 50 percent of an adult's body

5. Which of the following is not a sign of a partial-thickness burn?

   A.   blisters
   B.   dark brown skin
   C.   mottled skin
   D.   moist, white skin

Answers

1. **C.** An injury in which the epidermis is damaged by a scraping force is called *an abrasion.*

2. **B.** An avulsion is described as *a piece of skin torn from the body.*

3. **A.** *A sucking chest wound* would indicate the application of a partially sealed occlusive dressing.

4. **C.** *A full-thickness burn covering 20 percent of a child's body* would be considered a critical burn because any moderate burn is critical for children.

5. **B.** *Dark brown skin* would be a sign of a full-thickness burn, not a partial-thickness burn.

C. Musculoskeletal Care

Musculoskeletal injuries are very common in emergency medical care. The majority of musculoskeletal injuries are relatively simple and do not require advanced treatment. Most of these injuries will only need assessment, splinting, and transport to a medical facility. Some severe musculoskeletal injuries, however, may be life threatening and can necessitate emergency treatment.

1. The Muscular and Skeletal Systems

The musculatory system has three chief duties. Muscles give us shape, protect our internal organs, and allow us to move. There are three kinds of muscles in the body:

- *Voluntary muscles*, or skeletal muscles, are connected to bones and account for most of the body's muscle mass. These muscles are commanded by the nervous system and can be voluntarily contracted or relaxed.

- *Involuntary muscles*, also called smooth muscles, are located in the walls of the gastrointestinal tract, urinary system, blood vessels, and bronchi. These muscles are responsible for automatic tasks such as the flow of blood and bodily fluids and cannot be consciously controlled. Involuntary muscles respond independently to stimuli like external temperature and the stretching that occurs when an organ is full.

- *Cardiac muscles* are exclusive to the heart and can contract entirely on their own, a property known as automaticity. These involuntary muscles have their own blood supply delivered through the coronary artery system and can only withstand an interruption in this supply for a very brief period.

The skeletal system is composed of the bones of the skull, face, spinal column, thorax, pelvis, and the upper and lower extremities. The purpose of the skeletal system is similar to that of the muscular system in that it also provides body shape, protection for internal organs, and assistance with movement. Muscles and bones, along with various connective tissues, work in conjunction to make movement possible. Movement of the extremities occurs at the *joints*, the points where bones connect to other bones. The two most common types of joints are *ball-and-socket joints*, such as the hip; and *hinge joints*, such as the knees.

2. Injuries to Bones and Joints

In order to effectively treat bone and joint injuries, you must understand the forces that cause these injuries. The greater the force of an injury, the more likely that severe bodily damage will result. These forces are known as the *mechanism of injury*. You can often use the mechanism of injury to predict the most likely injury, but only a physical examination can determine the severity of a musculoskeletal injury.

Elderly patients are at higher risk of skeletal injuries than other patients because of conditions like *osteoporosis*, which causes brittle, weakened bones. Arthritis can make immobilization of these patients difficult because they may have angulations that you cannot straighten, such as a spinal curvature. Children, on the other hand, usually have much more flexible and resilient bones. Because of this, the bones may flex instead of fracture, allowing the force to be applied to internal structures. In this way, children can receive internal injuries without sustaining any bone damage at all.

Most musculoskeletal injuries occur as the result of a force applied to a particular part of the body. These injuries are called *direct injuries*. An example of a direct injury would be someone being hit by projectile, such as a baseball.

Indirect injuries occur away from the point of impact. An example of this type of injury would be a dislocated hip that results from a patient falling from a height and landing on his feet. The bones of the leg are very strong. When force is applied along the leg's axis, the force is transmitted up the bones of the leg to the hip, which may fracture or dislocate.

Twisting injuries occur when an extremity is pulled and turned beyond its typical range of motion. A typical twisting injury is a sprained ankle.

A musculoskeletal injury can be either open or closed. Open injuries involve a break in the skin and may present with external bleeding. Open injuries also carry a risk of infection. Closed injuries do not include any breaks in the skin, but may be accompanied by internal bleeding.

There are a number of common signs of bone and joint injuries. The injury site may be deformed, angulated, or tender. The patient may experience pain when movement is attempted. In cases where bone ends are separated, you may hear or feel *crepitation*, or grating, which occurs when the bone ends rub together. Swelling and discoloration are also common. In the event of open bone injuries, the broken end of an injured bone may protrude from the skin. In some cases, the bone may retract back under the skin after protrusion, leaving an open flesh wound with no visible bone. Joint injuries can sometimes result in the affected joint becoming locked and unmovable.

A common type of musculoskeletal injury is a *fracture*. Fractures result when bones are actually broken or cracked. In addition to fractures, you may encounter dislocations, sprains, and strains. *Dislocations* occur when the bone ends become separated at the joint. *Sprains* are partial ligament tears, and *strains* are tendon injuries. It is generally impossible to differentiate between these injuries in the field and all should be treated as if they were fractures.

3. Emergency Care of Bone and Joint Injuries

If you encounter a bone or joint injury, you should begin, as always, by ensuring a patent airway. When the airway is secure, you should determine if the injury needs to be splinted. Splinting helps protect the patient against further injury from bone ends or fragments. Broken bones or bone fragments can damage muscles, nerves, and blood vessels. Splinting reduces the risk of these injuries. Splinting can also stop a closed injury from becoming an open injury. A splint may reduce the pain associated with a bone injury. The risk of paralysis can also be reduced by splinting.

When applying a splint to an extremity, it is important to note the patient's pulse, motor function, and sensation distal to the injury before and after the splint is applied. This will help to ensure that the splint has been applied properly and is not interfering with circulation. Before applying the splint, cut away clothing to increase the splint's effectiveness and properly dress and bandage any open injuries.

Tip: Remember to include the bones and joints above and below the injury site in the splint. This helps to minimize the movement of muscles around the injury site.

In cases where there is severe deformity or when the distal extremity has no pulse, you should align the injury with gentle traction only as far as is necessary to restore circulation. If you feel resistance, it is best to splint the extremity in the position you found it. If distal pulse does not return, rapid transport is indicated to prevent the loss of the limb.

If the patient has an open injury with the bone protruding from the skin, you shouldn't attempt to replace the bone. In some cases, these bones will move back into place by themselves when the splint is in place. When you apply a splint to a hand or a foot, you should immobilize it in the position of function, which is the relaxed position of the extremity where there is minimal movement or stretching of the muscles.

Lifesaving interventions, including transporting the patient, should never be delayed to apply a splint. In many cases, a patient can be immobilized to a long backboard, which can be used to quickly splint multiple fractures and still allow for rapid transport.

Tip: You may not always be able to tell if an extremity is fractured. Be safe and splint the injury in case a fracture is present.

There are various types of splints used for immobilization.

Rigid splints are nonformable splints that support an injured extremity and immobilize the surrounding joints and bones.

Traction splints are used specifically for femur injuries when there are no accompanying joint or lower-leg injuries. Traction splints should not be used if the injury is near or includes the knee or ankle, there are bone ends protruding from the skin, or there are partial amputations or avulsions.

Pneumatic splints are flexible, conforming splints that are often used with angulated injuries. Some examples of pneumatic splints are air splints, pneumatic antishock garments, and vacuum splints. These types of splints are applied and then filled with or emptied of air.

When using an *air splint*, you should first cover all wounds with clean dressings. Next, place the extremity inside the splint and inflate with air. Inflation may be achieved by pumping or by blowing into a valve.

Pneumatic antishock garments are often used to immobilize the lower extremities in the event of pelvic instability or injuries to the long bones of the legs that result in shock. In most cases, the garment is placed on the backboard and the patient is rolled or moved on top of it. The necessary compartments can then be inflated. There are various techniques for using pneumatic antishock garments based on the type and location of injury.

Vacuum splints work in the opposite fashion of pneumatic antishock garments and air splints. An already-inflated splint is placed on the injured extremity and a vacuum removes the air, allowing the splint to conform to the area.

There are also a variety of possible improvised splints. Pillows can be used as splints for joint injuries, particularly ankle injuries. A pillow can be wrapped entirely around the ankle and secured. Remember to leave the toes accessible so that you can continue to assess pulse, motor function, and sensation. The sling-and-swathe technique is commonly used for shoulder injuries. The patient's arm is placed into the sling and the swathe is then wrapped around the arm and body to immobilize the arm and shoulder.

Improper use or application of splints can lead to further injury. Splints can cause the compression of nerves, tissues, and blood vessels. A splint that is applied too tightly or incorrectly can cause a reduction in distal circulation, increased bleeding, or tissue damage. A poorly applied splint can also cause a closed injury to open.

With the splint properly in place, you are ready to begin transport. While transport is in progress, you may apply cold packs to reduce swelling and pain. Unless other injuries or pain prevent it, you should elevate injured extremities to decrease blood flow.

Additional Topics to Review

- Skeletal anatomy
- Muscular anatomy
- Types of fractures

Practice

Directions (1–5): Select the best answer for each question or incomplete statement.

1. Which of the following bones would NOT be found in the lower extremities?

    A.   tibia
    B.   femur
    C.   cuboids
    D.   metacarpals

2. Which of the following actions should NOT be done while applying a splint?

    A.   Cut away clothing.
    B.   Cover open wounds.
    C.   Replace protruding bones.
    D.   Align the extremity with gentle traction.

3. What kind of fracture is caused by repeated pressure on a bone?

    A.   greenstick
    B.   stress
    C.   spiral
    D.   comminuted

4. Which type of splint is commonly used for a painful, swollen, closed femoral injury?

    A.   traction splint
    B.   rigid splint
    C.   air splint
    D.   vacuum splint

5. Which of the following is NOT an example of a rigid splint?

   A.   Hare splint
   B.   cardboard splint
   C.   padded-board splint
   D.   ladder splint

Answers

1. **D.** *Metacarpals* would be found in the upper extremities.

2. **C.** You should not *replace protruding bones* while applying a splint.

3. **B.** Fracture caused by repeated pressure on a bone is a *stress* fracture.

4. **A.** A *traction splint* is commonly used for a painful, swollen, closed femoral injury.

5. **A.** A *Hare splint* is a type of traction splint.

D. Injuries to the Head and Spine

Head and spinal injuries can be very dangerous and require extremely careful assessment and immobilization on the scene. Because of the potential consequences of head and spinal injuries, rapid transport to a medical facility is of the utmost importance. EMT-Basics use an array of devices to ensure proper immobilization of patients with head and spine injuries.

1. The Nervous and Skeletal Systems

The nervous system is responsible for all the body's voluntary and involuntary actions. It consists of two distinct systems: the central nervous system and the peripheral nervous system. The *central nervous system* is composed of the brain and spinal cord. The brain is situated inside the cranium and the spinal cord is located inside the spinal column, which runs between the brain and the lumbar vertebrae. A substance called cerebrospinal fluid surrounds and protects both the brain and the spinal cord. The *peripheral nervous system* is a network of sensory and motor nerves. Sensory nerves send information from the body to the spinal cord and on to the brain. Motor nerves send information from the brain and spinal cord to the rest of the body.

The skeletal system has three basic functions: providing body shape, protecting the internal organs, and assisting with body movement. The skull provides the brain with protective housing. The structure of the face and skull consists of an array of fused bones. These bones include the orbital bones of the eye, nasal bones, the maxilla, the mandible, and the zygomatic bones (or cheekbones).

The spinal column runs the length of the trunk and neck and includes 33 vertebrae. Among these vertebrae are 7 cervical, 12 thoracic, 5 lumbar, 5 sacral, and 4 coccygeal vertebrae. The spinal column encases and protects the spinal cord. Twelve pairs of ribs connect to the thoracic vertebra. The first ten ribs are also attached anteriorly to the sternum. The eleventh and twelfth ribs don't connect to the sternum and are commonly called floating ribs.

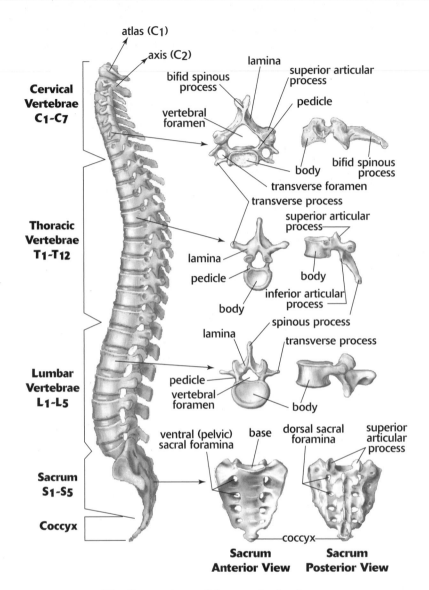

The four regions of the vertebral column.

2. Devices for Immobilization

Any patient who may have suffered a head and/or spinal injury must be immobilized in order to reduce the risk of further injury. Full-body immobilization is indicated even when trauma is localized to one small part of the spinal column.

The most commonly used immobilization device is the *cervical spine immobilization device*. Also known as a cervical collar, this device is used with any suspected spinal injury. Cervical spine immobilization devices should always be used in conjunction with short or long backboards. These backboards are made of a rigid material. The anterior portion is built to firmly fit the chin and rest on the chest. When the cervical spine immobilization device is properly applied, patients shouldn't be able to move their heads up and down.

Cervical spine immobilization devices must be properly fitted before being applied. The sizing may vary depending on the type and design of the specific device. Using an improperly sized device can lead to further injury. A device that is too tight can restrict the patient's airway and cause the head to bend forward.

Before placing a cervical collar, be sure that the patient's head is in a neutral position. In the event that you can't put the head in a neutral position or you don't have a collar that fits the patient, you may use rolled-up blankets or towels as an alternative means of immobilization.

Other important immobilization tools are the short and long backboards. *Short backboards* are used to immobilize the head, neck, and torso of a patient in the seated position. *Long backboards* are used for immobilizing the entire body when the patient is lying or standing. Long backboards are commonly used in conjunction with short backboards, cervical collars, or other head immobilization devices.

It is very important to ensure that all immobilization devices are used properly. This will prevent the patient from suffering further injury.

3. Injuries to the Spine

The first step in assessing a spinal injury is to size up the scene and determine the mechanism of injury. The mechanism of injury can help you determine the type of injury and the severity of the injury.

There several types of spinal injury. *Compression injuries* occur when the head is pushed downward, compressing the spine. These injuries are often found in victims of car accidents, diving accidents, and falls. Spinal injuries also occur as a result of extreme flexion, extension, rotation, or lateral bending of the spine. The most common causes of these spinal injuries are car accidents in which the victim experiences *whiplash*, a rapid backward, and then forward flexion of the neck.

Distraction spinal injuries occur when the spine is pulled apart. Spinal separation often results when the head is pulled away from the spine. Distractions are most commonly seen in hanging victims.

Assessment and treatment of spinal injury patients should begin with airway management and bleeding control. Victims of spinal injuries will often experience tenderness around the injury site or pain related to movement. Patients may sometimes feel pain without movement or palpation along the spinal column or extremities. Be sure that the patient doesn't move at any time.

When assessing a spinal injury, you may find soft tissue injuries or spinal deformity. Other injuries may indicate which part of the spine has been injured. Head and neck injuries may indicate a cervical spine injury. Thoracic or lumbar spine injuries are often accompanied by shoulder, back, or abdominal injuries. Soft tissue injuries found on the lower extremities may indicate a lumbar or sacral spine injury.

Spinal injuries that damage the spinal cord may result in numbness, weakness, tingling, or paralysis below the injury site. These patients may also experience a loss of bowel control.

If the patient is responsive, use the DCAP-BTLS method to assess the injuries. Have the patient grasp your hands or push your hands with his or her feet to determine if strength is equal on both sides of the body. You should acquire and record important information from responsive patients quickly, as they may become unresponsive at any time.

When assessing unresponsive patients, check the scene for the mechanism of injury and report your findings to the receiving medical facility. The patient should be assessed and immobilized with a long backboard. After treating any life-threatening injuries, quickly assess the patient using the DCAP-BTLS method and ask bystanders or other witnesses for more information regarding the mechanism of injury and the patient's mental status prior to your arrival.

Spinal injuries can have many complications, including inadequate breathing or paralysis. It is extremely important to limit movement of the patient during immobilization. You should reassess the patient's condition after each intervention. With combative patients, you should also reassess their condition after any movements they make.

Spinal cord injuries involving the nerves that control diaphragm movement or the accessory muscles may lead to respiratory difficulty. These patients should be monitored very closely and artificially ventilated, if necessary. Some patients may vomit after immobilization, so be sure the patient's airway remains clear at all times.

Treatment of spinal injuries should begin with manual in-line cervical spinal immobilization, which should continue until the patient is fully immobilized with a long spine board, straps or tape, a cervical immobilization device, and head blocks or towel rolls. You should complete the initial assessment and provide airway control and artificial ventilation, when needed. Check for pulse and motor and sensory function in all of the patient's extremities.

Lying patients can be moved onto a long backboard with a technique known as a *log roll*. The log roll is designed to keep the spinal column aligned while transferring the patient with the least amount of movement possible. While executing the log roll, you can assess the patient's posterior side for DCAP-BTLS.

Patients who are found in a seated position should first be immobilized in that position with a short backboard and then transferred to a long backboard.

4. Injuries to the Brain and Skull

Injuries to the head and brain are often accompanied by spinal cord injuries, so patients with suspected head injuries should be fully immobilized. Head injuries frequently present with scalp or brain injuries. Scalp wounds may appear more severe than they actually are because of the presence of numerous capillary beds in this area. Skull injuries may lead to damaged brain tissue or bleeding inside the skull. This bleeding causes increased pressure inside the skull and may lead to an altered mental state.

As always, you should begin assessment and treatment by securing the airway. If the patient requires artificial ventilation, be sure to ventilate the patient at a normal rate, as rapid ventilation may result in the constriction of brain blood vessels in victims of head trauma.

Initial and focused assessments and immobilization should be carried out before you begin transport. Once you are en route to the receiving medical facility, you may perform a more detailed physical examination.

Tip: Remember to monitor the patient's airway, breathing, pulse, and mental status for signs of deterioration.

Bleeding should be controlled, but direct pressure should not be applied to open or depressed skull injuries. You should be prepared to administer suction in the event that the patient vomits. Roll the patient to the left side for the most effective airway control. Once the patient is secure, immediate transport is necessary.

In certain instances, you may not be able to fully stabilize a patient with a skull or spine injury. When the scene is unsafe or the patient is unstable, you may need to perform rapid extrication, which is the immediate removal of the patient from the scene. Because this technique is performed without any form of immobilization, it should not be attempted unless absolutely necessary. If rapid extrication is indicated, align the patient's body, lower the patient onto a long backboard, and extract the patient while providing manual stabilization.

In some cases, you may encounter a patient who is wearing a helmet. You may or may not have to remove the helmet, depending on several factors. The need for removal is based on the fit of the helmet, the patient's head movement inside the helmet, and the access the helmet allows to the patient's airway. Helmets with open anterior portions allow for easy access to the patient's airway and do not usually need to be removed. Helmets with closed anterior portions, like motorcycle helmets, often obstruct your access to the patient's airway, and will likely need to be removed in the event of respiratory difficulty. If the helmet immobilizes the patient's head it can be kept on, but helmets that allow too much movement must be removed. You should also remove the helmet if it is impeding proper spinal immobilization, or if the patient is in cardiac arrest.

Children and infants should be immobilized on a rigid board that is appropriate for their size. Because children and infants have larger heads than adults do, you may need to provide extra padding from the shoulders to the heels in order to keep young patients in a neutral position. Children may also be immobilized by adding pads and tape to their car seats if this adequately limits movement.

As with adults, it is important to ensure that the cervical spinal immobilization device fits the child properly. If you don't have a cervical collar small enough to fit a young patient, you should pad under the patient's neck, torso, and legs. You must also maintain manual stabilization of the patient in a neutral position while carrying out this task. Children are often more likely to resist immobilization and may be comforted by the use of a snug, whole-body immobilization device. Tape or loose straps may result in further problems because the child may become frightened and attempt to escape from these restraints.

Immobilizing elderly patients may be complicated by arthritis. The patient may be unable to fully straighten or move some joints. Patients with osteoporosis may have spinal curvature that prevents normal immobilization. You may need to add extra padding between the patient and the immobilization device to ensure proper support.

Additional Topics to Review

- Soft tissue damage to the head
- Musculoskeletal injuries

Practice

Directions (1–5): Select the best answer for each question or incomplete statement.

1. Which of the following mechanisms of injury would indicate a spinal distraction?

   A. motorcycle accident
   B. diving accident
   C. blunt head trauma
   D. hanging

2. Head and neck injuries most frequently indicate which type of spinal injury?

    A. lumbar spine injury

    B. thoracic spine injury

    C. cervical spine injury

    D. sacral spine injury

3. You encounter a patient with a suspected spinal injury sitting in the passenger seat of a car. There is no immediate danger on the scene. How should you proceed with immobilization?

    A. Extricate the patient immediately.

    B. Apply a short backboard, and then transfer the patient to a long backboard.

    C. Perform a scene size-up.

    D. Apply a long backboard, and then extricate the patient from the vehicle.

4. Which of the following conditions would indicate the removal of a helmet from the victim of a motor-cycle crash?

    A. patient with no signs of respiratory distress

    B. patient wearing a custom-fitted helmet

    C. patient wearing a helmet with an open anterior portion

    D. patient experiencing cardiac arrest

5. Patients with head injuries requiring artificial ventilation should be ventilated at a rate of

    A. 12–14 breaths per minute.

    B. 8–10 breaths per minute.

    C. 15–20 breaths per minute.

    D. 20–30 breaths per minute.

Answers

1. **D.** Spinal distraction would be indicated by a *hanging*.

2. **C.** Head and neck injuries most frequently indicate a *cervical spine injury*.

3. **B.** In this scenario, the appropriate choice would be to *apply a short backboard, and then transfer the patient to a long backboard*.

4. **D.** You should remove any type of helmet in the event of a *patient experiencing cardiac arrest*.

5. **A.** Patients with head injuries should be ventilated at a normal rate of *12–14 breaths per minute*.

X. Infants and Children

Infants and children differ significantly from adults on both a physical and an emotional level. As an EMT-Basic, it's your job to understand the anatomical, physiological, and even psychological differences between adults and children in order to administer proper care.

About 16 percent of the NREMT cognitive exam will feature questions about pediatric care. Remember to take a look at the "Additional Topics to Review" sections in this chapter for more information on some of the subjects you may encounter on the test.

A. Developmental Differences in Infants and Children

Children go through several developmental stages in which their bodies and minds undergo significant changes; they are learning and growing all the time. Treating very young children is challenging because they often can't communicate their needs in the ways that adults do. As an EMT, it is your job to recognize the common signs and symptoms that will help you identify injuries or illnesses in young children, even when they cannot tell you what is wrong.

The following sections describe the various stages of childhood development. You will most likely need to modify the way in which you treat patients based on where they fall on this developmental scale.

1. Newborns and Infants

Babies who are less than 1 month old are called *newborns*, while babies under 12 months of age are *infants*. Children this young are generally easier to assess and treat if their parents are present; however, they don't necessarily fear strangers, so brief separation may not affect them negatively.

Newborns and infants struggle to maintain their body temperature, so EMT-Basics should attempt to keep the surrounding environment warm. When infants lose body heat, their circulation slows and they use more oxygen in an attempt to raise their body temperature.

As you examine newborns and infants, it is important to note the following vital signs:

- Respiratory rate
- Skin color
- Activity level
- Interest level in environment
- Interaction with parents/EMT-Basics
- Use of accessory muscles when breathing

2. Toddlers

Children between 1 to 3 years of age are referred to as *toddlers*. Toddlers don't like to be touched, and they especially don't like removing their clothing when they are uncomfortable. If you must remove the child's clothing during the examination, ask the child's parents or family members to assist you. Move the clothing aside and replace it quickly. This will make the child more comfortable as you perform the examination.

Remember to assess toddlers on their level by kneeling or sitting beside them; this will make them feel less frightened. Let them know what you're doing just before you perform the action. For example, if you must use a needle on a toddler, be honest and explain that it might hurt for a moment. Don't wait too long before performing the procedure, otherwise the child may grow afraid or upset during the process.

Use simple words when speaking with toddlers. Reassure them that they aren't in trouble and that they aren't being punished. Examine the heart and lungs first, showing the child the tools you are using as you go, and then move to the trunk and head. Always be prepared to deal with uncooperative, upset, and scared children. The best thing to do when dealing with uncooperative or scared children is to be patient with them, use a gentle tone of voice, and do your best to comfort them.

3. Preschool Children

A child between the ages of 3 and 5 years old is a *preschool child*. These children respond negatively to being separated from their parents, having their clothing removed, or having oxygen masks placed on them. Portable suction units may also scare preschool children who don't understand exactly what is going on around them. As with toddlers, if removing the clothing becomes necessary, do so quickly and ask a trusted family member for help if the child is uncomfortable.

Preschool children may understand that pain and injuries are typically "bad." They may have also developed a fear of blood at this age. If fear is evident, clean the area quickly or cover the area so they cannot see it.

When speaking to preschool children, ask them simple questions about what happened to them or how they are feeling. Don't hesitate to ask them to perform easy tasks or follow simple directions. Explain the steps you are taking to ensure their health and safety and show them the tools you use as you work. Inspect your young patient's most painful areas at the end of your assessment. By this point in the exam, you will have gained the patient's trust and he or she will be more likely to cooperate with you.

4. School-Age Children

Children between the ages of 6 and 12 years old are considered *school-age children*. While they embrace their independence, they also rely on their parents for guidance and support, especially in emergencies. Most are afraid of blood and pain and may be embarrassed during the physical examination. Respect their modesty; replace clothing shortly after you have moved it to inspect an area.

Most school-age children will respond to direct questions and follow directions well. If you tell them that you need their help, they will perform tasks to the best of their abilities. If you need to perform a task such as administering an IV or a needle, have the child count down to the needle prick. This allows the child to feel as though he or she is in control. If you abide by the patient's countdown, he or she will grow to trust you.

5. Adolescents

Children 12 to 18 years of age are *adolescents*. These children should be treated as adults and may choose to be examined away from their parents. Respecting adolescents' privacy and modesty helps build trust between the EMT-Basic and the patient. Adolescents are often concerned with permanent disfigurement, scarring, loss of function, and death. Be straightforward and honest with adolescent patients about their injuries or illness.

Additional Topics to Review

- Using oxygen masks on newborns, infants, and toddlers
- Anatomical and physiological concerns regarding children's airways
- Performing modified jaw thrusts on children
- Using portable or onboard suction units on children
- Inserting an oral or nasopharyngeal airway

Practice

Directions (1–3): Select the best answer for each question or incomplete statement.

1. While treating a 7-year-old female patient, you notice that she is struggling to breathe. Upon evaluating her condition, you find that her airway is blocked by a large amount of fluid. After placing the child in the supine position, you insert the tube of your portable suction unit into her mouth and turn on the unit. You should remove the tube after

   A. 5 to 10 seconds.
   B. 10 to 15 seconds.
   C. 15 to 20 seconds.
   D. 20 to 25 seconds.

2. A 3-year-old male on the scene of a motor vehicle accident is crying and wheezing. He is in his mother's lap and she is attempting to calm him. You ask the child's mother to lift his clothing so you can look for bumps, bruises, and cuts. The child continues to cry. What should you do to help calm the child as you perform the assessment?

   A. Ask the mother to step away from the child.
   B. Remove all the child's clothing so you can get a closer look.
   C. Kneel down beside the child and speak to him in a soft voice.
   D. Give the child your stethoscope to play with while you perform the assessment.

3. The presence of blood may *not* frighten

   A. toddlers.
   B. preschool children.
   C. school-age children.
   D. adolescents.

Answers

1. **B.** You should remove the tube after *10 to 15 seconds* of suction. You should take care never to have a portable or onboard suction unit turned on for more than 10 to 15 seconds at a time. If you need suction again after the first round, replace the catheter in the patient's mouth and turn the device back on.

2. **C.** Children may be more cooperative and calm if you approach them on their level. In this scenario, you should *kneel down beside the child and speak to him in a soft voice* in an attempt to calm him as you perform the assessment.

3. **A.** *Toddlers* may not be affected by the presence of blood. Preschool and school-age children often learn to associate blood with injuries and negative images or events, but the majority of toddlers may not recognize the presence of blood as frightening.

B. Assessing Infants and Children

Once you have determined that the scene is safe, you can begin your initial assessment. Because many children don't like to be touched, you may want to form your general impression as you approach them. Determining whether a child is healthy, sick, or injured is typically not challenging if you know what to look for. As you approach children, note their involvement with the surrounding environment. Is the child interacting with people or objects? Is the child quiet, listless, or disinterested? Is the child displaying appropriate emotions for his or her age and the emergency setting? Does the child recognize his or her parents? An experienced EMT-Basic with knowledge of the developmental stages of children can spot a healthy or sick child in seconds.

Once you have formed your general impression, assess the child's mental status using AVPU distinctions—this acronym stands for *alert*, responds to *voice*, responds to *pain*, and *unresponsive*. The parents play an important role in determining a young patient's mental status. Have the parents speak to the child to see if he or she recognizes or responds to vocal stimuli. Also instruct the parents to tell you immediately if they notice a change in the child's behavior; a parent knows what is "normal" for the child and will notice if something is wrong.

Next, open the airway, if necessary, and assess the patient's breathing. Look for the following signals as you continue your assessment:

- Nasal flaring
- Use of accessory muscles
- Retractions
- Airway noises
- Quality of crying or speaking
- Presence or absence of breath sounds
- Equal bilateral expansion of the chest
- Wheezing or stridor

While you assess the patient's respiratory system, note any changes in skin color. If a child needs oxygen, he or she will not automatically become cyanotic. Instead, the child's skin will look patchy or mottled at first.

In infants specifically, use the brachial and femoral pulses to assess circulation. While checking a child's heart rate, compare the rates of both pulses to determine both quality and equality. If the rates differ, the infant may be suffering from poor circulation. If the patient is too young to assess blood pressure, assess the *capillary refill*. The EMT-Basic performs this action by applying and releasing pressure on the nail bed. If perfusion is adequate, the capillary refill should only take about 2 seconds. A capillary refill of more than 2 seconds could indicate shock.

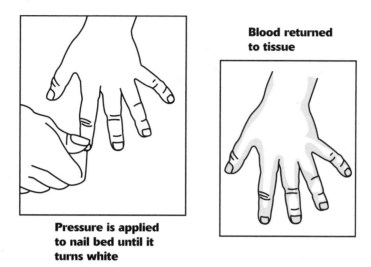

Pressure is applied to nail bed until it turns white

Blood returned to tissue

Capillary refill is used to assess the circulation of children under the age of 6.

After completing your initial assessment, decide if your patient is a priority patient. Young patients experiencing an altered mental status, respiratory distress, and poor circulation are priority patients and should be transported and treated immediately.

As you gather a focused history from the child (if he or she is old enough) and the parents, perform the physical examination starting with the heart and lungs. Then assess the patient's lower half before moving to the child's head. Save any painful areas for the end of your assessment. This approach is called *trunk-to-head*. The process of assessing for DCAP-BTLS allows you to gather key information from the parent and the patient while simultaneously building the patient's trust.

Additional Topics to Review

- Determining mental status (AVPU)
- Working with emotional parents
- Opening a newborn's or infant's airway
- Oxygen administration techniques
- Performing a physical exam (DCAP-BTLS)

Practice

Directions (1–6): Select the best answer for each question or incomplete statement.

1. On the scene of an emergency, you are assessing a 5-year-old female with an altered mental status. Her airway appears clear, but the pulse at two different points is not equal. You check her capillary refill in an attempt to assess her circulation. If her circulation is healthy, her capillaries should refill within

   A. 1 second.
   B. 2 seconds.
   C. 4 seconds.
   D. 5 seconds.

2. When evaluating an 8-month-old's pulse, you should use the

   A. brachial pulse.
   B. carotid pulse.
   C. brachial and femoral pulses.
   D. femoral and radial pulses.

3. On the scene of a house fire, you approach a mother and her 3-year-old daughter. They are seated on the back of a fire truck and the child is crying. Which of the following assessment steps can you complete as you approach them?

   A. Determine the child's mental status.
   B. Listen for issues with the child's respiratory system.
   C. Note the child's skin color and temperature.
   D. Form a general impression of the child's health.

4. You should assess blood pressure in patients who are

   A. 1 year of age.
   B. 2 years of age.
   C. 3 years of age.
   D. 6 years of age.

5. Where should EMT-Basics begin their assessments of infants and young children?

   A. the head
   B. the heart and lungs
   C. the abdomen and pelvis
   D. the legs and feet

6. Which of the following procedures should you perform when evaluating the circulation of infants and children under the age of 6?

A. capillary refill
B. rescue breathing
C. blood pressure reading
D. chest compressions

Answers

1. **B.** In children under 6 years of age, the capillaries under the fingernails should refill within *2 seconds*. If capillary refill takes longer than 2 seconds, your patient may have a problem with perfusion.

2. **C.** When assessing an infant's pulse, you should locate and measure the *brachial and femoral pulses*. The brachial pulse is located inside of the infant's elbow, while the femoral artery is in the infant's thigh. Compare these rates to determine if the infant is experiencing circulation problems.

3. **D.** You can *form a general impression of the child's health* before you actually reach your patient. From afar, you can determine if the child is acting appropriately for the situation and if the child is aware of his or her surroundings.

4. **C.** If you have time, assess your patient's blood pressure if he or she is *3 years of age* or older. Be sure not to waste time evaluating the patient's blood pressure. Locate any life-threatening injuries and perform all interventions and treatments first.

5. **B.** You should begin your assessment of infants and young children with *the heart and lungs*. You should then move on to the abdomen and pelvis, then the legs and feet, and finish with the head.

6. **A.** You should perform a *capillary refill* to check the circulation of a patient under the age of 6. Pressing gently on the nail bed and observing how quickly the capillaries refill allows you to gauge the strength of a young patient's circulation. This method is most commonly used in emergencies when you may not have time to find a pulse or take a child's blood pressure.

C. Common Problems in Infants and Children

Many children all over the world experience medical and health emergencies every day. Depending on their age, they may engage in behaviors that cause injury or illness. For example, many young children put small toys in their mouths and choke. They may also occasionally eat things off the ground like dirt, wild mushrooms, or bugs. These events can lead to serious injury or illness, so it's best to be prepared for anything when you arrive on a call involving a sick or injured child.

The EMT-Basic exam will test your knowledge of how to treat some of the most common pediatric problems you'll encounter in the field. These include emergencies such as airway obstructions, seizures, and poisonings.

1. Airway Obstructions

You must be familiar with the signs of a *partial airway obstruction* and a *complete airway obstruction*, as treating a partial airway obstruction incorrectly could lead to a life-threatening full obstruction. The following table features key symptoms and signs that will help you differentiate between partial and complete airway obstructions in children.

Partial vs. Complete Airway Obstruction Symptoms		
	Partial	**Complete**
Appearance	Healthy to slightly sick, awake, agitated, and distressed	Obviously ill, altered mental status including possible unresponsiveness
Color	Normal skin color to pale	Pale skin, mottled, or cyanotic
Breathing	Increased breathing rate, loud breath sounds	Gasping breaths or no effort to breathe
Sounds	Stridor, rough/barking cough, hoarse voice	Silence, unable to speak or make sounds

a. Partial Airway Obstruction

As seen in the table, you may recognize partial airway obstructions by loud coughing, a hoarse voice, and an increased breathing rate. Children with partial airway obstructions are typically awake and will struggle to remove the obstruction on their own. Reassure them and encourage them to cough. Keep their parents nearby at all times. Do not perform a detailed examination on a child if he or she is agitated, afraid, or upset. A physical exam may further upset a child, which will affect his or her breathing rate, possibly leading to further obstruction. Transport the child in an upright position and do not allow the child to lie down, as this may also lead to further obstruction. Unless the child's mental status or skin color changes, allow physicians at the hospital to remove the obstruction.

b. Complete Airway Obstruction

A complete airway obstruction is considered life threatening and requires EMT-Basics to take immediate action. As seen in the table, children with completely obstructed airways may have skin that appears mottled, pale, or blue. These patients are often unable to speak or cough if they are responsive. Treatment for patients with completely obstructed airways differs according to the patient's mental status and age.

It is important that you are familiar with the anatomy of a child's respiratory system (shown in the following figure) and abdominal muscles before performing CPR, ventilation, or finger sweeps for obstructed objects.

Responsive infants have often placed a small object, known as a *foreign body*, in their mouths and attempted to swallow it. Follow these steps to remove a foreign body from an infant:

1. Position the infant so he or she is face down and the head is lower than the trunk.
2. Deliver no more than five back blows between the infant's shoulder blades.
3. Turn the infant so he or she is face up, supporting the head and neck.
4. Deliver no more than five chest thrusts over the lower half of the sternum.
5. Repeat steps 1 through 4 until the airway is unobstructed or the infant becomes unresponsive.

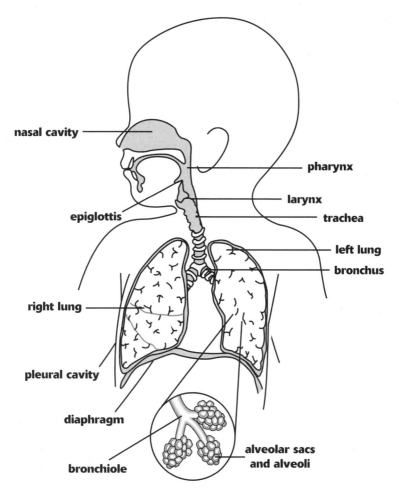

EMT-Basics should be familiar with the unique structure of children's respiratory system in order to provide them with proper care.

If you believe an infant is unresponsive, confirm this condition by tapping the soles of the infant's feet or gently rubbing the infant's chest or back. If the infant doesn't respond, open the airway. The following steps will help you treat an unresponsive infant with a complete airway obstruction:

1. Look, feel, and listen for signs of breathing.
2. If the infant is not breathing, position the head appropriately, cover the infant's nose and mouth, and deliver two breaths.
3. If the infant is still not breathing, deliver two more breaths and begin CPR.
4. Deliver chest compressions.
5. Check the infant's airway. If you can see the foreign body, use a finger sweep to remove the object.
6. If you are unable to remove the obstruction, repeat steps 2 through 5.

After an obstruction has been removed, transport the patient to the hospital. At the hospital, physicians will evaluate the airway to determine if permanent damage has occurred.

Because toddlers, preschool, and school-age children are bigger than newborns and infants, EMT-Basics perform a different set of actions when they treat these children for a complete airway obstruction. EMT-Basics should not perform back blows or chest thrusts on these children. Children of this age typically choke on large pieces of food or candy.

If you have determined that the airway is completely obstructed and the child is responsive, coughing may help move the object. If coughing does not help or if the child is unable to cough, perform the following steps to remove the obstruction:

1. Have the child stand upright.
2. Kneel or stand behind the child and place your arms around the child's waist.
3. Make a fist, cover it with your other hand, and place it on the abdomen.
4. Deliver quick, upward abdominal thrusts until the object is dislodged or the child becomes unresponsive.

If you have determined that a child is unresponsive and suffering from a complete airway obstruction, follow these steps to remove the obstruction:

1. Place the child in a supine position.
2. Perform a tongue jaw lift and look for the obstructed object.
3. If you spot the object, use a finger sweep to remove it.
4. Open the airway and listen, feel, or look for signs of breathing.
5. If the child is not breathing, attempt ventilation.
6. Reposition the child's head and attempt ventilation again.
7. Start chest compressions.
8. Once again, check for the foreign body.
9. Repeat steps 4 through 8 as necessary.

If you are unable to remove the foreign body from an infant or small child with a complete airway obstruction, follow your local protocol as you transport your patient to the hospital. Call the medical direction physician if you are unsure of how to handle the situation.

2. Respiratory Emergencies

Recognition and the proper treatment of respiratory distress, failure, and arrest by EMS crews save thousands of young lives every year. Approximately 80 percent of all infants and children who experience cardiac arrest experience respiratory arrest first. Understanding the symptoms of respiratory distress will help you to prevent the occurrence of respiratory failure and arrest.

A patient is experiencing *respiratory distress* if he or she finds it difficult to breathe. If the child does not receive a high volume of oxygen, the condition may escalate rapidly. Signs of respiratory distress include

- Increased breathing rates
- Retractions
- Nasal flaring
- Splotchy or mottled skin

- Overuse of abdominal muscles
- Stridor
- Grunting
- Wheezing

Respiratory distress can lead to *respiratory failure* if it is not treated immediately. Infants and children in respiratory failure struggle to breathe and often become tired very quickly. Signs of respiratory failure include

- Severe retractions
- Decreased muscle tone
- Severe overuse of abdominal muscles
- Breathing rate of more than 60 breaths per minute or fewer than 20 breaths per minute
- Fatigue

To treat respiratory failure, you must ventilate the child using the highest concentration of oxygen available. During transport, ensure that the child is comfortable and in the supine position. Explain your actions to the child and his or her parents as you place the mask over the child's nose and mouth and seal it.

Respiratory failure often leads to cyanosis, decreased peripheral perfusion, and decreased mental status. If untreated, it may also cause a child to enter *respiratory arrest*. In respiratory arrest, a child's entire respiratory system will shut down. Symptoms of respiratory arrest include

- Breathing rate of fewer than 10 breaths per minute
- Slow or absent heart rate
- Weak or absent pulse
- Limp muscles
- Unresponsiveness
- Irregular breathing patterns and/or gasping

Respiratory arrest is one of the leading causes of cardiac arrest in children. Young patients suffering from respiratory arrest should be carefully assessed and immediately transported and treated. Using a bag-valve mask, ventilate the child, paying close attention to his or her respiratory rates. Ensure that the airway is open and unobstructed. If you are treating an infant who goes into respiratory arrest with a heart rate of fewer than 60 beats per minute, start chest compressions and call ALS.

3. Seizures

When responding to calls that report a seizing child, remember that children who experience seizures may be ill, injured, or suffering from chronic seizures. After a seizure, children may experience difficulty breathing and a change in mental status. Seizures can result from the following:

- Decreased levels of oxygen
- Head injury
- Low blood sugar
- Chronic medical conditions

- Fever
- Infection
- Poisoning

Although you should be familiar with the causes of seizures, you don't need to determine what specifically led to your patient's seizure. Instead, you are responsible for watching your patient's vital signs and taking note of the events (multiple seizures, convulsions) that occur during transport. This information will be useful to physicians who continue to care for the patient at the hospital. During seizures, keep the child safe from injury and be prepared to suction or remove foreign bodies from the airway. You should also immobilize the patient if any injury to the spine is suspected.

> **Tip: Remember to ask the child or the parents about any medications the patient is taking when you collect information about the patient's history.**

4. Altered Mental Status

In the midst of numerous types of emergencies, an infant or child's mental status may worsen. Parents or EMT-Basics may notice a change in mental status if the child does not respond appropriately to his or her environment, if the child is no longer interested in the people or objects around him or her, or if the child no longer recognizes his or her parents by appearance or voice.

Causes of altered mental status include

- Infection
- Poisoning
- Head trauma
- Decreased oxygen levels
- Diabetic emergencies
- Shock
- Seizure

Attain the patient's focused history from his or her parents, but do not waste time determining the cause of the change. Make sure the airway remains open during transport and ventilate using an oxygen mask if necessary.

5. Poisoning

The age of the child often determines how he or she was poisoned and how much of a substance he or she ingested. When responding to a call in which an infant was poisoned, suspect unintentional poisoning or abuse by the parent or caregiver. If a preschool or school-age patient is poisoned, assume that the child innocently placed the toxic substance in his or her mouth. These children typically only ingest small amounts of substances found on floors or toys. Adolescents who are poisoned typically administer and ingest toxic substances intentionally in hopes of achieving psychological side effects or relief from emotional stress or depression.

At the scene, always perform a scene size-up and employ proper BSI. Some poisons are airborne and may poison you if you inhale or physically encounter the toxin. Look for any bottles or containers that contain the substance in question. Ask the child and his or her parents about the patient's history with toxins and if any poisonous liquids or powders are available inside the home.

Be prepared to administer suction, artificial ventilation, and high-flow oxygen. A child who ingested a poison may vomit, seize, or become unresponsive. Keep the airway clear and assess for signs of injury. Complete ongoing assessments until you reach the hospital. If you are uncertain about how to proceed, call the medical direction physician, ALS, or your local poison control center.

6. Fever

A child has a *fever* if his or her body temperature is above 100.4°F (38°C). Although fevers alone are not usually life threatening, the factors that may cause fevers can be extremely dangerous. For example, fever is a symptom of bacterial meningitis, a serious and often life-threatening illness.

Look for, and obtain information about, the following while performing a trunk-to-head examination and focused history:

- Mental status
- Motor activity
- Irritability
- History of illness
- Vomiting or diarrhea
- Rash

After ensuring an open airway, adequate breathing, and adequate circulation, treatment should begin with attempts to prevent the child's body temperature from rising. Ask the child's parent to remove articles of clothing, being careful not to produce shivering. The muscular contractions during shivering will raise the body temperature. If this occurs, replace the clothing. Do not bathe or splash the patient with cold or ice water, as this will almost surely cause shivering. Arrange for immediate transport to the nearest medical care facility. Perform ongoing assessments during transport and be prepared to provide emergency care if the patient begins to seize.

7. Shock

Hypoperfusion, also known as *shock*, occurs when the cardiovascular system fails to supply vital organs with oxygenated blood. If shock is not treated immediately, it can cause irreversible damage or death. Causes of shock in infants and children include

- Blood loss
- Infection
- Vomiting
- Diarrhea
- Dehydration
- Trauma

Tip: Although cardiac problems rarely cause shock in young children, the possibility does exist.

Children in shock may breathe rapidly and their skin may become pale and clammy. Their pulse may also become weak or absent. Use capillary refill to assess blood pressure for children under the age of 6. If in shock, capillary refill time will occur slowly. A child in shock may also become unresponsive or may be unable to output urine or form tears due to dehydration.

If ALS is unable to respond to an emergency in which a child is in shock, transport the child to a hospital immediately. The focused history and physical examination can be performed while in transit, as shock patients should be transferred as soon as the scene is secure and they are immobilized. During transport, keep the child warm and elevate the legs. If you suspect an injury has occurred, stabilize the child's spine.

8. Near-Drowning

If a child dies from suffocation within 24 hours of being underwater, he or she has *drowned*. If a child survives an underwater event beyond 24 hours, then he or she has suffered from a *near-drowning*. Drowning is one of the most common causes of death in children under the age of 14.

Infants, toddlers, and preschool children typically drown after falling into pools, lakes, or ponds. These children are often unsupervised and may not know how to swim or float. Adolescents often drown due to an inability to react after consuming drugs or alcohol. Drowning may also be a direct result of a head or spinal injury after diving into shallow water. If exposed to cold air or water temperatures a child may become hypothermic and die.

Many times, a patient in need of a water rescue is removed from the water before EMS arrives on the scene. If the child is still in the water, however, only attempt to rescue the child if you have had adequate training in water rescues. Remember that your safety comes first in these instances.

Once the patient is pulled from the water, open the airway, provide oxygen and suction, ventilate, and start chest compressions if needed. Immobilize the spine if an injury is suspected. If a patient has been submerged in cold water for a prolonged period, check his or her pulse for a full minute before beginning resuscitation efforts. Transport near-drowning victims to the hospital. Here, the patient will be monitored for *secondary drowning*, or the deterioration of the respiratory system within 96 hours of being underwater.

9. Sudden Infant Death Syndrome

When an infant dies unexpectedly and there is no information in the child's history or autopsy that points to a cause of death, medical examiners often label the child as a victim of *sudden infant death syndrome*, or SIDS. Usually, SIDS affects children between the ages of 1 month to 1 year.

When you respond to a call for an unresponsive infant, be prepared to examine the child for rigor mortis. If rigor has not yet set in, attempt to resuscitate the child and transport him or her to a hospital. While on the scene, pay careful attention to your surroundings and document anything that raises a question or appears suspicious. Doctors often misdiagnose infants who are victims of abuse with SIDS. Even if you suspect abuse, never place blame on the parents. Instead, offer them your support.

> Tip: Cases in which children die can severely affect the emotional health of EMT-Basics. If you are emotionally affected after responding to an incident that results in the death of a child, request a critical incident stress debriefing (CISD). See Chapter V, "Preparatory," for more information.

Additional Topics to Review

- Performing CPR in adolescents and adults
- Recognizing signs of lower airway obstructions due to illness
- Locating the xiphoid process
- Ventilating infants and small children
- Administering charcoal in poison emergencies

Practice

Directions (1–10): Select the best answer for each question or incomplete statement.

1. Which of the following is NOT a sign or symptom of respiratory distress in children?

    A. nasal flaring
    B. delayed capillary refill
    C. retractions
    D. grunting

2. You are treating a 14-year-old male who appears to be in shock. He was hit by a car and may have suffered a head injury. As you assess him, you confirm that the airway is open and that he is breathing adequately on this own. His wounds are not bleeding profusely. What should you do first?

    A. Check the patient's heart rate.
    B. Place the patient on 100 percent oxygen.
    C. Check the patient's airway for obstructions.
    D. Place the patient on a stretcher.

3. Which of the following can be both a symptom of an illness and a condition by itself?

    A. poisoning
    B. altered mental status
    C. partial airway obstruction
    D. fever

4. Reports of unresponsive infants who are later labeled as victims of sudden infant death syndrome are usually made during the

    A. early morning hours.
    B. middle of the afternoon.
    C. early evening hours.
    D. middle of the night.

5. Which of the following steps should you perform first when responding to a call in which an infant is unresponsive?

   A. Tap the soles of the infant's feet.
   B. Look for signs of breathing.
   C. Check the infant's airway.
   D. Deliver two small breaths.

6. Your partner is treating a 7-year-old boy who is suffering from shock as you attempt to comfort the boy's mother. You overhear your partner discussing the boy's condition with another EMS professional as they prepare for transport. You hear your partner say that the conditions that led to the child's shock are rare. Your partner is most likely suggesting that the boy's shock was caused by

   A. infection.
   B. cardiac complications.
   C. dehydration.
   D. blood loss.

7. When performing emergency care for a responsive child with an airway obstructed by a foreign object, make a fist with one hand and use the other hand to locate the

   A. right lumbar and left lumbar.
   B. umbilicus and xiphoid process.
   C. G.I. tract and abdominal wall.
   D. inguinal and epigastrium.

8. Which of the following water temperatures puts a submerged child at risk of hypothermia?

   A. 87.5°F
   B. 98.6°F
   C. 99.3°F
   D. 100.4°F

9. Which of the following symptoms is NOT indicative of a partial airway obstruction?

   A. irritation
   B. loud breath sounds
   C. mottled skin
   D. barking cough

10. Which of the following breathing rates would NOT necessarily indicate respiratory failure in a child?

   A. 4 breaths per minute
   B. 10 breaths per minute
   C. 35 breaths per minute
   D. 70 breaths per minute

Answers

1. **B.** *Delayed capillary refill* is a sign of poor circulation, not a respiratory problem.

2. **B.** Because your patient's wounds are not bleeding profusely, your first step should be to *place the patient on 100 percent oxygen*. Then, you should begin preparing the patient for rapid transport with spinal precautions.

3. **D.** Often, *fevers* are not life threatening on their own. They may be indicators of bigger, more serious conditions such as meningitis or infection.

4. **A.** Reports of unresponsive infants later diagnosed with SIDS are typically reported in the *early morning hours*. Many times, SIDS victims die in their sleep and are not discovered until the parents check on them in the morning.

5. **A.** In this situation, you must first confirm that the patient is unresponsive. Do this by *tapping the soles of the infant's feet* or gently rubbing the infant's chest or back.

6. **B.** Although *cardiac complications* rarely occur in children, they may cause a child to experience shock. Infections, dehydration, vomiting, diarrhea, trauma, and blood loss are all common causes of shock in children.

7. **B.** When performing emergency care on a responsive child with a partial airway obstruction, make a fist with one hand and locate the *umbilicus and xiphoid process* with the other. Then position your fist between these two abdomen landmarks and thrust upward.

8. **A.** Hypothermia occurs when a child has been exposed to air or water temperatures below 98.6°F. If a child was submerged in water that was *87.5°F*, he or she would be at risk of experiencing hypothermia.

9. **C.** *Mottled skin* is not a symptom of partial airway obstruction. Mottled, spotted, or blue-tinted skin typically indicates a complete airway obstruction.

10. **C.** Children in respiratory failure have a breathing rate of fewer than 20 breaths per minute or more than 60 breaths per minute. Based on this, a breathing rate of 4, 10, or 70 breaths per minute would indicate a problem. Choice C is correct because a breathing rate of *35 breaths per minute* would not necessarily indicate respiratory failure in a child.

D. Treating Children with Special Needs

As an EMT, you will occasionally travel to a home in which a child with special needs has been injured or is ill. These children are often dependent on an array of medical technology, including instruments that help them breathe and eat or machines that administer medication. These machines may fail, requiring assistance from EMS. Questions about responding to calls involving children with special needs will most likely appear on the EMT-Basic exam, so be sure to review what you already know about tracheostomy tubes, ventilators, and shunts.

1. Ventilators

Children who cannot breathe completely independently are often placed on mechanical *ventilators* for assistance. Parents typically understand the operation of ventilators, so the most common call EMS crews receive involving these machines concerns their failure or malfunction.

In the instance of a home ventilator failure, use a bag-valve mask to ventilate and transport the child to a medical care facility. If the child has a tracheostomy, connect the bag-valve mask directly to the tube.

2. Tracheostomy Tubes

A common intervention for children with respiratory issues is the insertion of a *tracheostomy tube*. During surgery, a physician cuts an opening into the trachea and inserts a plastic or metal tube to help the child breathe. If the tube falls out or becomes obstructed, the child's life may be in danger.

If you are called to a scene where the tube has fallen out and cannot be safely reinserted, ventilate the child using a bag-valve mask. Transportation to a hospital is necessary in these instances, as specialists are needed to replace the tube. First attempts at ventilation should be made over the mouth and nose. Be sure to cover the stoma. If this doesn't appear to assist the child in his or her breathing, use a smaller mask and place it directly over the entrance to the trachea and direct the patient to keep his or her mouth closed.

3. Gastrostomy Tubes

Similar to tracheostomy tubes, *gastrostomy tubes* are inserted into a child's abdomen to assist with the consumption of food. EMT-Basics are often called when a gastrostomy tube has been dislodged and parents cannot reinsert it. In this case, assess the patient as you would any other infant or child, paying close attention to the patient's mental status. Ask the patient or the parents if the child is diabetic. If so, test for low blood sugar while transporting the patient to the hospital.

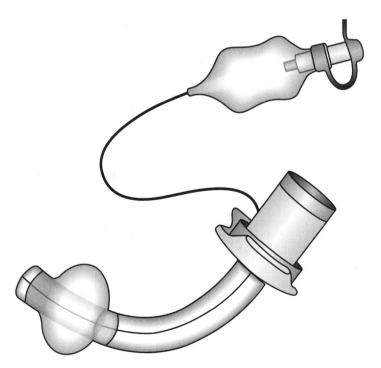

A tracheostomy tube is a small tube that is placed directly in the patient's windpipe to assist in breathing.

4. Central Lines

Specialists often insert *central lines* into the veins of a child's neck, chest, or groin to administer fluids or medications or to monitor central venous pressure. If a line is cracked or broken or the entrance to the line becomes infected or starts to bleed, parents often call EMS. You can manage the bleeding as you would any other wound, using a sterile dressing and applying pressure to the entrance of the line. This emergency requires transportation to the hospital to reinsert the central line and assess for further complications or damage.

5. Shunts

If you are responding to a child with a *shunt* (a tube), the illness or injury may be unrelated to the shunt entirely. You must still be aware of its presence, however. The most common shunt found in infants and children runs from the brain to the abdomen and works to drain excess fluid. These shunts are called *central nervous system shunts*.

Treat children with shunts similar to other children with medical problems or injuries and always be aware of their mental status. You may have to take special precautions when immobilizing these patients as you don't want to damage the shunt in any way. Patients with shunts are also prone to respiratory arrest, so you should be prepared to administer ventilation at all times.

Additional Topics to Review

- Treating premature newborns with special needs
- Assessing children with neurological disorders
- Evaluating children with chronic diseases
- Responding to calls regarding children with altered functions
- Recognizing child abuse and neglect in children with special needs

Practice

Directions (1–5): Select the best answer for each question or incomplete statement.

1. Which of the following should you look for if you are told that a child with a gastrostomy tube has missed a feeding?

   A. vomiting or diarrhea
   B. bleeding
   C. altered mental status
   D. seizures

2. Your patient is an 8-year-old male who is on a mechanical ventilator at home. You notice that the ventilator is off. What should you do first?

   A. Transport the patient to a medical facility.
   B. Attempt to restart the ventilator.
   C. Ventilate the patient using a bag-valve mask.
   D. Assess the patient's mental status.

3. When a shunt is positioned between the base of a child's skull and the child's abdomen, it is most likely draining

    A. peritoneal fluid.
    B. cerebrospinal fluid.
    C. cerumen buildup.
    D. sebum buildup.

4. When called to the home of a 10-year-old female with a central line, you see that blood surrounds the entrance of the line. Which of the following should not be done to manage the bleeding?

    A. Remove the central line.
    B. Use sterile dressings.
    C. Apply pressure.
    D. Assess for clotting.

5. When ventilating a patient with a tracheostomy tube, it's best to use a

    A. nonrebreather mask.
    B. pocket mask.
    C. bag-valve mask.
    D. flow-restricted mask.

Answers

1. **C.** Children who miss feedings on a gastrostomy tube often experience *altered mental status*. If a patient is diabetic, his or her blood sugar may be low. These children may be distracted, disinterested, or unaware of their surroundings.

2. **C.** Because the mechanical ventilator is assisting in the child's breathing, it is important that you continue to help the child breathe when the machine fails. You should first *ventilate the patient using a bag-valve mask*. Once the patient is breathing adequately, assist the parents in restarting the ventilator. If it doesn't work, transport the patient to the hospital.

3. **B.** Shunts positioned between the base of the skull and the abdomen drain *cerebrospinal fluid*. Peritoneal fluid is found in the abdomen, but doesn't originate in the skull. Cerumen is another name for earwax, and sebum is oil found on the skin.

4. **A.** You should never *remove the central line* when managing bleeding near the entrance of the line. You should assess for clotting, apply direct pressure, and use sterile dressings, but never attempt to remove an intact or damaged central line. Instead, transport the patient to a hospital where professionals with adequate training can further assess and treat the patient.

5. **C.** When administering oxygen to a child who has a tracheostomy tube, position a *bag-valve mask* over his or her nose and mouth and manually cover the stoma. If this does not work, place a smaller bag-valve mask directly over the stoma and instruct the child to keep his or her mouth closed.

XI. Operations

Operational skills, which do not involve the treatment of a patient, are a vital part of every EMT-Basic's job. They involve skills such as taking inventory of ambulance supplies, preparing to gain access to a patient in the event of an emergency, and the management of major incidents, such as hazardous materials situations. Although cleaning and taking inventory are often tedious tasks, remember that these are important parts of the EMT-Basic's job.

This chapter covers ambulance operations, rescue operations, special operations, tactical emergency support, and weapons of mass destruction. It is important for you to familiarize yourself with and review these skills to prepare for the EMT-Basic exam. Approximately 16 percent of the questions that you will encounter on the NREMT cognitive exam are related to operational skills.

Because this chapter doesn't include all of the material that you may encounter on the exam, take a few moments to examine the subjects listed in the "Additional Topics to Review" sections.

A. Ambulance Operations

This section will help you understand all of the phases of an ambulance call as well as your responsibilities when preparing a patient for air medical transport.

1. Phases of an Ambulance Call

There are nine steps in a typical ambulance call: preparation for the call, dispatch, en route to the scene, arrival at the scene, transferring the patient to the ambulance, en route to the receiving facility, arrival at the receiving facility, en route to the station, and the postrun phase. Although it may seem difficult to distinguish between these phases in the middle of a call, you should understand your responsibilities during each phase.

a. Preparation for the Call

During this phase, EMT-Basics prepare for calls by ensuring that they have everything they need to respond to an emergency situation. One of the most important parts of this phase is to make sure that you are mentally and physically prepared for a call. EMT-Basics who are physically or emotionally stressed could put themselves, their partners, and their patients at risk. As discussed in Chapter 5, "Preparatory," eating well, getting enough sleep, and exercising are important to the physical and emotional well-being of the EMT-Basic. Taking care of yourself will enable you to perform your job in an effective and efficient manner.

You can also prepare yourself for the challenges of the day by arriving at the station about 15 to 20 minutes before your shift starts. Arriving early provides sufficient time to organize your thoughts and inspect your EMS unit. As an EMT-Basic, you need to ensure that your vehicle is in good working condition before you take it out on a call. Check that the vehicle has fuel, motor oil, and engine coolant. Examine the tires for signs of wear and tear. The driver should also test all lights and sirens at the beginning of the shift before going out on a call.

Taking inventory of your vehicle's supplies is another important part of preparing for a call. Your vehicle should be equipped to handle most medical emergencies. Your specific EMS agency, along with state and local regulations, will determine the medical supplies that your ambulance must carry at all times.

Ambulances also carry safety equipment to protect the EMT-Basics and patients. This includes body substance isolation (BSI) gear such as gowns, gloves, masks, and protective eyewear. Additional safety equipment may include helmets, bunker pants, tarps and blankets, and leather gloves. Other important supplies found on most ambulances include local maps, preplanned routes, and report forms. Check to ensure that your unit has all the necessary supplies before responding to a call.

b. Dispatch

Dispatch centers have a general access number, usually 911, which people can contact in an emergency. Employees at the dispatch center often provide friends, family, or witnesses with medical instructions that allow them to start treating the patient before EMT-Basics arrive on the scene.

In most cases, the dispatcher will provide the EMS unit with information regarding the nature of the emergency and the location of the incident, as well as a brief description of the patient, including age and gender. Additional information may become available while en route to the emergency. Make sure that you understand all information provided by dispatch. Repeat any confusing information back to the dispatcher and request clarification.

c. En Route to the Scene

Remember, you can't help anyone if you don't arrive at the scene safely. Always wear your safety belt when riding to an emergency. When you're leaving the station, notify dispatch that you are responding to the call and record the time.

If you are acting as the ambulance operator, it is important that you use caution when driving the vehicle. Ambulances can roll over easily, so drive quickly but carefully to the scene of any emergency. Ambulance operators must consider a number of factors when traveling to a scene. Traffic, weather, and road conditions will affect the route you take and the speed at which you travel.

> **Tip: Some states and EMS agencies require EMT-Basics to take a special course on operating emergency vehicles.**

As the driver of an emergency response vehicle, it's your responsibility to know and follow all state and local regulations when using sirens or flashing lights. Not every call is necessarily a true emergency. Use the information you've received from dispatch to determine if the use of such devices is necessary.

When driving an ambulance, it is important to have due regard for other drivers and pedestrians while en route to the scene. *Due regard* describes the way that a responsible person would act in a similar situation. For instance, if you see a red light ahead, due regard calls for you to make a complete stop at the light. You must always provide other drivers with sufficient notice of your approach to avoid an accident. When operating an ambulance, follow state and local regulations concerning potentially dangerous situations, such as maneuvering through traffic and stopping at red lights.

Calls that require the response of multiple emergency vehicles can be particularly dangerous. To avoid an accident and protect the safety of other drivers, radio other units to notify them of your approach at points where your vehicles might converge. Communication between all responders will ensure that everyone arrives at the scene safely.

If you aren't driving the ambulance, you can contact dispatch for additional information about the emergency. This will help you determine what equipment will be necessary at the scene and if additional support from other EMS units is needed.

Once you get closer to the scene, help your partner determine the best place to position the vehicle. Park the ambulance in a safe place that will allow an easy departure from the scene. Careful positioning is especially important at the scene of a car accident where traffic may still be moving.

d. Arrival at the Scene

When you arrive at the scene, notify dispatch and record the time of your arrival. Remember, you need to size up the scene before attempting to assess or treat the patient. If the scene seems dangerous, wait for police to arrive. Before approaching, you must outfit yourself with the proper BSI gear for the situation. You must also determine if any patients should be removed from the scene to avoid further injury.

When you determine that the scene is safe, take note of the mechanism of injury or the nature of illness if possible. If there is only one patient, you can begin your assessment. If there is more than one patient, you may need to call dispatch for additional support. You must also alert dispatch when you arrive at the patient's side, noting the time.

Finally, you should provide all necessary care for the situation and arrange for transport to the nearest medical facility. Ensure that all dressings or splints are secure before transferring the patient to the ambulance.

e. Transferring the Patient to the Ambulance

The patient's safety is of upmost importance, especially during transfer to the ambulance. When using a stretcher, make sure that the patient is secure before moving him or her to the ambulance. Use a blanket or tarp to protect the patient from inclement weather.

Patients' family members will sometimes ask to ride in the ambulance. Consult your EMS agency's policies regarding this situation. Ensure that all passengers are wearing their seat belts before leaving the scene.

f. En Route to the Receiving Facility

After all passengers are secure in the ambulance, the driver should inform dispatch of your departure from the scene, noting the time of departure and your destination. The severity of the patient's condition will determine the mode of transport to the hospital.

During transport, the EMT-Basic treating the patient will continue assessing the patient and evaluating any interventions that were performed in the field. This person should also keep a constant record of the patient's vital signs, noting any changes in the patient's condition. If the patient is stable, the EMT-Basic may also begin the prehospital care report.

g. At the Receiving Facility

Notify dispatch as soon as you arrive at the receiving facility, noting the time of your arrival. Transfer the patient to the appropriate department and provide the staff with a brief report on the patient's condition, noting all pertinent information that could aid in the patient's treatment.

All crew members should wash their hands and take any other additional infection prevention measures at this time. After this, the prehospital care report should be completed. Leave a copy of this report with the receiving facility staff as a part of the patient's permanent medical record.

Before notifying dispatch of your ability to take another call, you must clean and disinfect the vehicle and restock the ambulance with necessary supplies. One person can focus on restocking while the other decontaminates the vehicle. *Decontamination* is the use of chemical agents to destroy blood-borne pathogens that could potentially transmit disease or infection. It is important to decontaminate all equipment used on the previous call.

Sterilization, which is the destruction of microorganisms, is used on instruments that penetrate skin and on devices that come in contact with normally sterile parts of the body. It is important for you to follow the cleaning and disinfecting policies established by your EMS agency.

h. En Route to the Station

Once your vehicle is cleaned and disinfected, notify dispatch of your departure from the receiving facility. As you travel, discuss the previous call with your coworkers. Think about what went well and consider areas that could use improvement. In a positive manner, discuss the steps you and the crew can take to help the next call run more smoothly.

i. Postrun

When you arrive back at the station, you should inspect the vehicle once again. Make sure that the ambulance has enough fuel and oil. Restock any supplies that weren't available at the receiving facility. At this time, you should also complete any paperwork that is required by your agency. Additional disinfection procedures that could not be completed at the receiving facility should be taken care of at this time.

Once these tasks are complete, take a moment to prepare yourself for the challenges you may face on the next call.

2. Air Medical Transport

In certain emergencies, air medical transport is necessary to ensure the survival of the patient. Air medical transport is often considered in cases of severe trauma or when the patient needs to be transported to a care facility, such as a neonatal unit or a burn center. Some situations that may necessitate air medical transport include a vehicle rollover in which the passengers were unrestrained, motorcycle accidents, ejection of the patient from a vehicle, and a fall of more than 15 feet. Other considerations include the length of time ground transportation will take, the amount of time it takes to extricate the patient, and the severity of the patient's injuries or illness. Air medical transport may also be necessary if local EMS resources are limited.

Tip: Remember, air medical transport may not always be available when it is needed. It is important to have a backup plan when air medical transport is unavailable.

a. When to Request Air Medical Transport

Certain EMS agencies will provide guidelines for requesting air medical transport. EMT-Basics always consider the specific circumstances of a situation before placing a call to air medical transport. Many EMT-Basics also consult with medical direction before calling in a request for air medical transport.

b. Establishing a Landing Zone

After calling for air medical transport, you must establish a safe landing zone for the helicopter. Designate one person to handle communications with the air medical transport dispatcher. This communications officer, who is not involved in the care of the patient, will provide the dispatcher with pertinent information, including the number of aircraft needed, the location of the emergency, and any local landmarks that will help the pilot locate the scene.

Choose another person who is not involved in the patient's care to establish a safe landing zone. Ideally, the landing zone should measure 100 feet by 100 feet. If this space is unavailable, a minimum area of 60 feet by 60 feet is needed for safe landing. The landing zone should also be clear of trees, power lines, fences, buildings, and other objects. Mark each corner of the landing zone with secured cones, flares, or light sticks.

The communications officer should listen carefully for the sound of the helicopter. When the helicopter can be heard, the communications officer should supply the pilot with any pertinent landmark information. After this, the communications officer should provide a brief, detailed description of the landing zone and note any nearby hazards, such as buildings, towers, poles, and power lines.

Tip: When providing the helicopter pilot with information, remember that the pilot is always facing the 12 o'clock position.

c. Safety

Safety is a primary concern when the helicopter is preparing to land. Use a common sense approach to protecting yourself, your partner, and the patient. Shield your eyes from any debris that may be kicked up during landing. Ensure that everyone maintains a safe distance from the helicopter as it lands and while the blades are still turning.

Tip: Always avoid the tail section of the helicopter. The tail rotor is very difficult to see and it may still be turning even after the blades have stopped spinning.

Once the blades have stopped turning, keep bystanders at least 100 feet away from the helicopter. Wait for directions from the pilot or flight crew before approaching the helicopter. After the crew gives you directions, approach the helicopter from the 9 o'clock to 3 o'clock positions, which keep you in the pilot's field of vision. Always keep low when approaching the helicopter. Don't carry equipment over your head as you approach the helicopter. Loose hats and clothing should also be avoided.

Air medical transport helicopter.

If the pilot lands on a hill, always approach from the downhill side. The main rotor blade will be closer to the ground on the uphill side, so it is best to avoid this area.

Follow the flight crew's directions when departing the landing zone. Ensure that all crew members and equipment are out of the landing zone before the pilot prepares for departure.

Your EMS agency can provide additional information on safety procedures to follow when preparing for air medical transport.

Additional Topics to Review

- Emergency medical equipment basic supplies
- Factors contributing to emergency vehicle crashes
- Levels of decontamination

Practice

Directions (1–5): Select the best answer for each question or incomplete statement.

1. The use of an escort vehicle is considered acceptable when

    A. the ambulance operator is unfamiliar with the way to the hospital.
    B. the ambulance operator is trying to avoid traffic.
    C. the patient's condition is severe.
    D. weather conditions are severe.

2. Which piece of information from dispatch is most important in order to respond to a call?

    A. the age of the patient
    B. the patient's condition
    C. the patient's phone number
    D. the location of the incident

3. In which of the following situations would air medical transport most likely be necessary?

   A. a case involving a teenage who has broken his leg
   B. a child who has fallen from a height of 8 feet
   C. a vehicle rollover in which all of the occupants were wearing safety belts
   D. a pedestrian who has been hit by a car traveling at 50 miles per hour

4. Which ratio of chlorine bleach to water is used for intermediate-level disinfection of surfaces that come into contact with exposed skin?

   A. 1:20
   B. 1:100
   C. 1:200
   D. 1:1000

5. Your unit is one of several responding to a multi-vehicle accident. As you approach a busy intersection, you notice another EMS unit in front of you. What should you do?

   A. Use the same siren as the unit in front of you.
   B. Follow behind the other unit as closely as possible.
   C. Use an alternate route to avoid a collision with the other unit.
   D. Follow the other unit at a safe distance that allows motorists to see both vehicles.

Answers

1. **A.** The only situation in which an escort vehicle is appropriate is *when the ambulance driver is unfamiliar with the way to the hospital.*

2. **D.** The most important piece of information you need from dispatch is *the location of the incident.*

3. **D.** Air medical transport would most likely be necessary in an incident involving *a pedestrian who has been hit by a car traveling at 50 miles per hour.*

4. **B.** The proper ratio of chlorine bleach to water used for intermediate-level disinfection of surfaces that come into contact with skin is *1:100.*

5. **D.** In this situation, you should *follow the other unit at a safe distance that allows motorists to see both vehicles.*

B. Rescue Operations

As an EMT-Basic, you may **respond to** calls in which the patient may be trapped. This type of situation is most common in motor vehicle **collisions**. In these situations, your personal safety is paramount. Remember, you cannot help anyone if you are injured and your injuries may need to be treated by EMS personnel, thereby taking vital resources away from the patients on the scene.

In many cases, rescue operations are handled by firefighters, police officers, or special rescue personnel. Some EMS agencies require EMT-Basics to take a special course in rescue operation techniques so they can assist rescue personnel with certain emergencies.

This section will review the basics of patient extrication, the safety equipment used in rescue operations, and the techniques used to access and remove patients from dangerous situations.

1. Basics of Extrication

Extrication is the process of removing a patient from a motor vehicle or other dangerous situation. In some situations, you must remove debris or other objects to safely access the patient in a process called *disentanglement*. This often involves the use of specialized equipment. EMT-Basics with additional education or certifications may utilize this equipment to help extricate the patient, or the extrication process may be handled by firefighters or specialized rescue crewmembers before you arrive. Regardless of your role in the rescue of the patient, all extrication efforts must be coordinated to ensure the safety of the emergency responders and the patient.

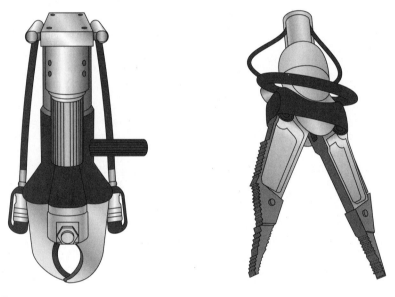

Hydraulic extrication tools.

In some areas, an incident commander will coordinate the efforts of the rescue and medical personnel. This person is also often responsible for coordinating transport in incidents involving multiple victims.

Remember, critical care must be provided before and during patient extrication. Because this could put you in a dangerous situation, it is important to ensure that you have all the necessary equipment to protect yourself as you treat the patient. This may include wearing protective gear, such as a helmet or goggles.

Work with the rescue crew to ensure that the patient is removed in a way that doesn't cause further injury. When you reach the patient, begin immediate care. In trauma situations, this will most likely involve implementing c-spine precautions, managing the airway, controlling bleeding, and supplying the patient with oxygen.

Tip: Critical care precedes extrication in most cases. However, extrication may be necessary if the patient is in immediate danger.

2. Safety and Equipment

In rescue operations, safety should be your primary concern. You also need to ensure the safety of your partner, the patient, and any bystanders. To do this effectively, you need to ensure that you take the proper precautions before attempting to assess or treat any patients.

a. Your Safety

One of the easiest ways to ensure your personal safety is to wear protective gear that is suitable for each emergency. This may include a helmet, protective eyewear, and leather gloves. Some EMT-Basics also wear puncture-resistant clothing and steel-toed boots in certain situations.

Check to make sure that you and your partner are wearing the appropriate protective gear before entering the scene.

b. The Patient's Safety

After you have considered your safety needs, you must focus on safely removing the patient from harm's way. In some cases, rescue personnel will use special equipment to remove the patient from the vehicle or structure. The removal process may create sparks or break glass. In this situation, you should protect the patient from glass, metal, and other dangerous debris. Use a blanket or a tarp to cover the patient. This will also protect the patient from the elements.

It is also important to explain the extrication process to the patient. Inform the patient of the sounds that he or she may hear during the process. This will help keep the patient calm.

Remember to keep witnesses and other onlookers away from the scene. This will reduce the risk of additional injuries and allow the rescue workers and medical professionals to focus on helping the patient.

c. Other Safety Concerns

Motor vehicle accidents present rescue workers with a number of challenges. You should always be aware of the risk of fire at the scene of a motor vehicle accident. Ensure that the vehicle's engine is turned off to reduce the risk of fire. Don't attempt to extinguish a vehicle fire unless you have the knowledge and equipment to do so. If you are not equipped to deal with this situation, wait for firefighters to secure the scene.

Another hazard when dealing with a patient trapped inside a car is the stability of the motor vehicle. Before entering the vehicle and caring for the patient, work with other rescue responders to secure the vehicle.

The risk of electric shock is another hazard you may encounter on the job. Downed power lines should only be handled by utility or rescue workers who have special training. Don't attempt to approach or treat a patient if downed power lines are in your way. Wait for the appropriate authorities to secure the scene before attempting to treat the patient.

Hazardous materials also present a unique danger to both rescue workers and patients. The steps for handling emergencies that involve hazardous materials are explained later in this chapter.

In some situations, it may be helpful to appoint a safety officer to oversee the entire operation. This person should not be involved in the rescue or treatment of the patient. The safety officer observes the scene and notes any potential hazards that medical and rescue personnel might not notice during the emergency.

3. Accessing the Patient

Simple access of a patient doesn't require any special equipment or training. However, accessing the patient is sometimes difficult, particularly in motor vehicle accidents. Remember to always wear protective clothing, even when accessing the patient is simple.

Don't attempt to access the patient on your own when the extrication process is particularly complex. Call dispatch for further assistance if you think that accessing the patient might be difficult or dangerous. Follow the directions of rescue workers to access the patient in a safe and timely manner. If you are unable to assist in the extrication, do your best to reassure the patient during the process.

Tip: Check with your EMS agency to see if additional training is available to become a rescue technician.

4. Removing the Patient

Once you are able to gain access to the patient, you should begin critical care before and during the process of extrication. In cases where a spinal injury is suspected, you should always stabilize the spine before moving the patient. The only instance in which you should move the patient without spinal stabilization is when there is an immediate danger to the patient or rescue workers.

Ensure that you have the proper personnel to safely remove the patient from the vehicle or structure. Choose a pathway that will protect the patient from further injury as you leave the scene of the accident.

Additional Topic to Review

- Recommended minimum personal protective equipment for vehicle rescue

Practice

Directions (1–5): Select the best answer for each question or incomplete statement.

1. You are responding to a motor vehicle accident in which patients are trapped inside the vehicle. What is the best way to access the patients?

   A. the windshield
   B. a window
   C. a sunroof
   D. the door

2. You are on the scene of a motor vehicle accident in which rescue workers are using cutters and spreaders to access a trapped patient. After gaining access to the patient, what is the first thing you should do?

   A. extricate the patient
   B. manage any bleeding
   C. stabilize the patient's spine
   D. provide the patient with oxygen

3. You arrive at a scene where there are downed power lines blocking your access to the patient. What should you do?

   A. request the assistance of trained utility workers
   B. move the power lines away from the patient
   C. remove the patient from the scene
   D. begin treatment of the patient

4. What is your first priority when you arrive on the scene of a rescue operation?

   A. personal safety
   B. patient safety
   C. extrication of the patient
   D. treatment of the patient

5. Of the following, who is responsible for coordination of rescue teams at the scene of an emergency?

   A. a firefighter
   B. a police officer
   C. an EMT
   D. an incident commander

Answers

1. **D.** In the event of an emergency, the best way to access the patients is through *the door*.

2. **C.** Before removing the patient from the vehicle, you should always *stabilize the patient's spine*. Once the patient is stabilized, extricate the patient, administer oxygen, and manage any bleeding. The only time emergency personnel should extricate a patient before immobilizing the spine is if the patient is in immediate danger.

3. **A.** If you cannot access a patient due to downed power lines, *request the assistance of trained utility workers*. Never attempt to access a patient if a threat to your life, or the patient's life, is present. Wait for trained workers to secure the scene before accessing the patient.

4. **A.** In every emergency situation, your *personal safety* should be your first priority. If you are injured during an attempt to rescue, assess, or treat a patient, then your patient faces a higher risk of further injury or illness. Once the scene has been determined safe, then you may help the patient.

5. **D.** Depending on the area, *an incident commander* may be responsible for the coordination of rescue and medical teams at the scene of an emergency. The incident commander doesn't attempt to help with the rescue; instead, he or she assigns responsibilities and tasks to emergency personnel and continues to patrol the scene for safety.

C. Special Operations

As you already know, you need additional training if you hope to serve on a special response team. The more educated you are in the area of disaster planning and response, the more prepared you will be for mass-casualty situations and emergencies involving life-threatening and hazardous materials. Although not every person taking the EMT-Basic exam may have an interest in joining a specialized team, general questions about special operations will appear on the test.

1. Hazardous Material

Most EMT-Basics are required to complete a First Responder Awareness Level education program before they can respond to situations involving hazardous materials. Hazardous materials pose a serious threat to the lives of patients, emergency personnel, and bystanders. As an EMT, you may come in contact with hazardous materials during a motor vehicle accident or a situation involving weapons of mass destruction, which are discussed later in this chapter. Completing a First Responder Awareness Level education program will ensure that you

- Understand your role in an emergency response plan.
- Recognize the presence of hazardous materials and their risks.
- Understand the various outcomes of hazardous material situations.

a. Safely Approaching the Scene

As always, your safety and the safety of the patient and other personnel is paramount when responding to a situation involving hazardous materials. These situations may also involve the safety of bystanders, witnesses, and the surrounding community. Before arriving on the scene of a hazardous materials situation, gather as much information about the incident as possible. If you suspect or are told that hazardous materials are on the scene, approach with extreme caution. Never enter any situation that could compromise your safety or the safety of others. Based on the information you receive, make sure you're wearing the appropriate protective gear for the situation.

As you approach the scene, be sure to isolate and avoid the area where the hazardous material is located. As an EMT, you should recognize any sounds, odors, or clouds that may indicate the presence of hazardous materials. Report anything unusual to dispatch.

b. Sources of Information

One of the most valuable pieces of information you can obtain during a hazardous materials situation is the name of the chemical(s) involved. Knowing which chemicals you are dealing with will help determine how you proceed. The easiest way to identify a hazardous material is to locate the container. The size, shape, and the placard on the container will provide you with information about the toxin in question.

Hazardous materials symbols and placards.

The placard will you tell if the chemical is corrosive, flammable, or radioactive. In some cases, the placard will also tell you if the chemical is a liquid, a solid, or a gas.

If you can't locate the container, there are other ways to identify the agent. If a vehicle is involved in the situation, the driver should be in possession of shipping papers that list all of the materials being transported. When a hazardous material emergency occurs at a power plant, in a lab, or at a factory, ask the supervisor for the Material Safety Data Sheets (MSDS). The United States Department of Labor requires companies, laboratories, and farms to keep public records of the chemicals they use. This information will be listed on the MSDS.

Once you are aware of the hazardous materials you're working with, you may be instructed to call the Chemical Transportation Emergency Center, also known as CHEMTREC. This service operates 24 hours a day, 7 days a week. Operators can provide immediate assistance or advice on how to treat a patient who may have been exposed to a hazardous material.

Tip: If you have completed the First Responder Awareness Level education program and have the appropriate protective equipment, you may be able to act or intervene before other emergency teams arrive on the scene.

c. Emergency Procedures

Every hazardous materials situation is different; therefore, it is important to be prepared for any type of situation. Many EMS crews refer to the most updated version of *Emergency Response Guidebook: A Guidebook for First Responders during the Initial Phase of a Dangerous Goods/Hazardous Materials Incident*. If you haven't received specialized training in working with hazardous materials, this book, which may be purchased from most major booksellers, will provide information on preserving your safety and securing the scene.

In general, no matter the contaminant, you should always complete the following procedures:

- Use caution while approaching the scene.
- Identify all hazardous materials and their sources.
- Make sure you're wearing the proper protective gear for the situation.
- Follow the guidelines outlined in the *Emergency Response Guidebook*.
- Don't allow anyone to enter the contaminated zone.
- Isolate all patients who have been in contact with or contaminated by the toxin.
- Call CHEMTREC or radio your medical direction physician for information on treating patients.
- Don't walk through any puddles or clouds and don't touch any spilled materials.
- Don't inhale any questionable vapors, smoke, or fumes.

Remember that some toxins may be odorless or colorless. Don't assume you're safe simply because you don't notice anything unusual. Use extreme caution if you suspect that a hazardous material might be present.

2. Incident Management Systems

State or local agencies create and organize *incident management systems* to ensure efficient and effective responses by fire departments, police departments, and EMS crews. Such systems help every member of every crew understand their individual responsibilities. This eliminates confusion and guarantees that no one overlooks or forgets to complete a task. Communication is a key component of a successful incident management system.

Incident management systems are often used in situations involving hazardous materials or multiple extrications. They are also used when an incident requires specific resources or equipment, such as the use of air medical transport.

a. Sectors

Once a major incident has been declared, an incident commander is chosen. The incident commander then establishes sectors. Some of the most common sectors you'll encounter on the job include the following:

- *Staging sector*—This sector is responsible for the movement of all transportation vehicles that arrive at and depart from the scene. This team also handles communications with the media and international aid agencies such as the Red Cross and Salvation Army.
- *Transportation sector*—This sector involves the use of ambulances and helicopters to transport patients, personnel, and equipment to and from hospitals. This team coordinates its efforts with the staging sector and the support/supply sector.
- *Support/supply sector*—This sector records all requests for and receipts of supplies and support services. Members of this team track the use of all additional personnel, resources, and equipment. They coordinate with the transportation center frequently.
- *Extrication sector*—This sector is responsible for removing trapped or entangled patients. If the rescued patient is in critical condition, members of this team will perform an initial assessment and provide treatment. If the patient is stable, members of this sector will transport the patient to the treatment sector.

- *Treatment sector*—This sector receives patients from the triage and extrication sectors. Members of this team perform initial assessments, obtain focused histories, and complete physical examinations. They also prioritize patients for transport.
- *Triage sector*—This sector is responsible for continued reassessment and further treatment of patients. In most incidents, this sector is combined with the treatment sector.

The incident commander appoints a leader to each sector who coordinates the members of his or her team by assigning specific tasks and responsibilities. EMT-Basics with disaster training are often designated sector leaders. Sectors are often marked on scene using colored flags. In most situations, sector leaders will stay off the radio to keep the airways clear for the incident commander to give instructions to and maintain contact with other agencies.

b. Role of EMT-Basics

Within an incident management system, EMT-Basics must consult with their sector leader or incident commander before making any decisions. EMT-Basics' responsibilities are often assigned according to the time that they arrive on the scene. The incident commander and triage sector leader are chosen from the first crew to arrive on scene. As more help arrives, other sectors are established. If you arrive on scene after the incident management system is completely functional, you will most likely be directed to the staging sector for an assignment. Once you complete your assignment, return to the staging sector and request another task.

3. Mass-Casualty Situations

Rarely will you arrive on the scene of a mass-casualty situation and find that an incident management system is not in place. Dispatchers will often notify EMS crews of mass-casualty situations before first responders even arrive on the scene. During such incidents, confusion can arise quickly. Having an incident management system organizes the chaos and helps emergency workers understand their individual responsibilities. Some examples of mass-casualty situations include bus and train collisions, bombings or explosions, building or bridge collapses, and earthquakes.

a. Patient Prioritizing

During mass-casualty situations, an EMT's most important task is performing patient triage. *Triage* is a method of categorizing patients according to the severity of their injuries. Emergency responders use a tagging system to indicate which patients require immediate treatment and transport. These color-coded or numbered tags indicate one of the following conditions:

- Life-threatening, requiring immediate transport
- Moderate, requiring transport as soon as possible
- Minor, requiring delayed transport
- Not injured, no transport necessary
- Deceased, no transport necessary

Some tags may also include information about the patient's vital signs, the treatment he or she received from EMT-Basics, or the location of his or her injuries. The highest priority is given to patients who have airway obstructions, severe bleeding, altered mental status, symptoms of shock, severe burns, or multiple bone or joint injuries. Other high-priority patients include those who are experiencing a serious medical issue, such as cardiac or respiratory arrest.

b. Procedures

As in many other incident management systems, those that are created for mass-casualty situations require that an incident commander and a triage sector leader be appointed when the first crew arrives on scene. The most knowledgeable and capable member signs on as incident commander and then quickly appoints a triage sector leader. While sizing up the scene, help from additional crews and agencies should be requested.

The triage sector leader performs quick assessments of all patients, but he or she will only provide treatment if a life-threatening condition exists. If no life-threatening conditions are discovered, the incident commander will tag each individual and assign other EMT-Basics to move the patients to the treatment sector. After the patients receive additional assessment and treatment from the treatment sector, EMT-Basics move the patients to the transportation sector, where they will await transport according to their priority level.

Additional Topics to Review

- Hazardous material placards and labels
- First Responder Awareness and Operations Programs
- Hazardous Materials Technician Programs
- Hazardous Materials Specialist Programs
- On-Scene Incident Commander training

Practice

Directions (1–8): Select the best answer for each question or incomplete statement.

1. Before participating in a hazardous materials emergency, most states require all EMT-Basics to complete a program called

   A. Medical Threat Assessment.
   B. First Responder Awareness Level.
   C. Tactical Emergency Medical Support.
   D. Basic Life Support.

2. Within an incident management system, the transportation sector frequently coordinates its efforts with the

   A. trauma sector.
   B. extrication sector.
   C. triage and treatment sectors.
   D. staging and support/supply sectors.

3. Which piece of information would you most likely find on a hazardous materials placard?

    A. information about treating people who come in contact with the material

    B. information about handling the material in a safe manner

    C. information about how the material is used

    D. warnings about the material's flammability

4. Your crew arrives first on the scene of a train derailment. The incident commander assigns you to the position of triage sector leader. The first patient you assess is able to breathe on his own, but he is also experiencing severe bleeding and signs of shock. How should you tag this patient?

    A. life-threatening, requiring immediate transport

    B. moderate, requiring transport as soon as possible

    C. not injured, no transport necessary

    D. minor injuries, requiring delayed transport

5. If you are on the scene of a hazardous materials situation at a local factory and you are placing a call to CHEMTREC, you have most likely

    A. identified the material in question.

    B. obtained the MSDS.

    C. both A and B.

    D. none of the above

6. Your EMS unit is the third crew to arrive on the scene of a collapsed building. The dispatcher declared the scene a mass-casualty situation before any crews had responded. Where should your EMS crew report?

    A. incident commander

    B. staging sector

    C. triage or treatment sector

    D. extrication or transportation sector

7. If you are in the hot zone of a hazardous materials emergency, you are in an area where

    A. a perpetrator may be able to spot you or the patient.

    B. it is safe to perform life-saving medical interventions, such as CPR.

    C. there is sufficient cover from life-threatening conditions.

    D. both contamination and life-threatening conditions exist.

8. You arrive on the scene of a motor vehicle crash involving an overturned tanker truck that was transporting hazardous substances. You approach the scene cautiously, but you don't notice any spills, clouds, or vapors. The driver of the tanker truck is still trapped inside the vehicle. You should

    A. extricate the patient trapped in the tanker truck.

    B. approach the tanker truck to see if the driver is conscious.

    C. wait for a specialized team to declare the scene safe.

    D. put on the appropriate body substance isolation gear.

Answers

1. **B.** The majority of EMT-Basics across the country must complete the *First Responder Awareness Level* program before they are allowed to respond to calls involving hazardous materials. In this program, EMT-Basics are taught how to recognize hazardous materials and treat patients who have been contaminated by these chemicals.

2. **D.** Within an incident management system, the transportation sector coordinates regularly with the *staging and support/supply sectors*. The transportation sector is responsible for keeping records of all personnel, resources, and equipment that enter the scene. Members of this team are also responsible for keeping records of the transportation of patients to medical care facilities.

3. **D.** A hazardous material placard doesn't provide information about treating someone who is contaminated by the material. The placard also does not provide information about how the material is used or how to handle the material safely. The placard will, however, provide *warnings about the material's flammability*.

4. **A.** All patients who experience symptoms or signs of shock, especially those who are bleeding severely, are of the highest priority. In this situation, the patient's tag would read *life-threatening, requiring immediate transport*. Although the patient may be breathing on his own, his other injuries may cause his condition to deteriorate rapidly.

5. **C.** The correct answer is Choice C, *both A and B*. When responding to hazardous material situations at facilities such as factories, you should request the MSDS, which will help you identify the materials on the scene. You would call CHEMTREC after completing the actions described in Choices A and B.

6. **B.** Because the scene has been declared a mass-casualty situation, you can assume that an incident management system is in place. Two other crews have arrived before you; therefore, an incident commander and sector leaders have most likely been appointed. Because the system is functional, you would report to the *staging sector* to receive your orders.

7. **D.** In this situation, the hot zone is an area where *both contamination and life-threatening conditions exist*. The warm zone of a hazardous materials situation is the area where people may be contaminated, but life-threatening conditions do not exist. The cold zone, which is another name for the safe zone, presents no life-threatening conditions or risks of contamination.

8. **C.** Although you may not see any spills, vapors, or clouds, this doesn't mean that the area is safe. Hazardous materials may be odorless and colorless; therefore, you should *wait for a specialized team to declare the scene safe* before you attempt to rescue the trapped patient. Your personal safety always comes first in these situations. Remember, you can't help anyone if you become injured or contaminated.

D. Tactical Emergency Medical Support

In extremely dangerous or violent emergencies, a *tactical emergency medical support* (TEMS) team may be called in to deal directly with anyone involved in the threat. TEMS crews are comprised of specially trained EMS workers who are responsible for the care of patients during a traumatic event. Even if you never serve on a TEMS team, it's important for you to understand the duties that individual crew members perform. In addition, you may encounter some questions regarding TEMS teams on the EMT-Basic exam.

1. TEMS Responsibilities

A TEMS team may be called on in a variety of dangerous situations. Their support is often requested during hostage negotiations and raids on drug laboratories. Members of the TEMS squad are responsible for assessing and treating anyone who is injured or becomes ill during the operation. In the field, TEMS members commonly encounter and treat the following conditions:

- Gunshot wounds
- Penetrating trauma (stab wounds)
- Pepper spray or tear gas exposure
- Premature pregnancy
- Cardiac or respiratory arrest
- Heat stroke
- Hypothermia
- Hazardous material exposure
- Explosion injuries or burns

As always, this specialized team is led by a knowledgeable and dependable EMS worker. This person, called the tactical leader, is responsible for performing a medical threat assessment (MTA) before other units arrive on the scene. An MTA prepares the EMS crews for the scene and ensures that they know what medications, equipment, and protective gear to bring with them. In some situations, firearms or other weapons may be necessary. Remember, you should never handle a firearm or any other weapon unless you have specialized training. Once EMS crews arrive, the tactical leader will schedule team deployment, rotations, and hydration breaks.

Tip: Preparation for TEMS calls begins before an event takes place. Team members should always be physically and mentally prepared to deal with the stress of the emergency.

2. Field Care and Triage

The tactical leader, along with his or her team members, creates three zones at the scene: *the cold zone*, *the warm zone*, and *the hot zone*. The cold zone is an area where EMS workers and patients are safe from any threats. The warm zone is the outer perimeter of the scene. In this area, contact with perpetrators is unlikely, but injury is still possible. The hot zone, or inner perimeter, is where a persistent or unknown threat still exists. Before establishing these zones, TEMS providers and basic life support (BLS) providers must size up the scene.

a. Scene Assessment

The mnemonic device ACE helps TEMS providers remember how to assess a scene in a tactical environment. ACE stands for assessment, cover and concealment, and evacuation.

As TEMS providers perform their scene assessment, they must always consider the risk of injury or illness to themselves, their team members, bystanders, and patients. These risks include environmental conditions such as extreme heat or cold, scene-specific risks such as stray bullets from a gunman, or any uncommon problems or issues at the scene.

While searching for risks, TEMS providers need to simultaneously determine the boundaries of the hot, warm, and cold zones. These zones must be selected according to the safety they will provide patients and emergency personnel. Ideal zones will provide both concealment, which keeps TEMS providers and patients hidden from perpetrators, and cover, which protects both parties from attack using some kind of physical barrier. TEMS providers use their specialized training to spot protected locations for these zones.

As part of the MTA, the tactical leader will identify locations for helicopter landing zones and EMS contact points before anyone steps foot on the scene. Knowing where these points are is vital and reaching them is challenging. Moving patients from the hot zone to the warm zone and then into the cold zone is called *evacuating*. In case an evacuation route is blocked or compromised, you must be aware of alternate routes. Once in the cold zone, you may begin advanced medical interventions.

b. Medical Care

In a tactical emergency, the level of care you can provide a patient with depends on the zone in which you are working. The hot zone is constructed along the innermost perimeter of the scene and the safety level is either unknown or nonexistent. In this zone, the perpetrator or threat may still be nearby. To ensure the safety of the emergency personnel and the patients, very few medical interventions are performed in the hot zone. Performing an intervention such as CPR could draw the attention of a perpetrator, putting the responders and the patients in great danger. In certain situations, tactical leaders may direct TEMS providers who have specialized BLS training to treat life-threatening conditions in the hot zone.

Occasionally, TEMS providers may need to treat injured coworkers in the hot zone. When approaching a TEMS provider who has been injured, follow these steps:

1. Identify yourself as an EMT-Basic or TEMS provider and verbalize your intent to help.
2. If you're under fire and have the proper training, return fire and allow your patient to return fire. If you're not under fire, disarm the patient.
3. If the patient is hemorrhaging, attempt to intervene using a tourniquet or direct compressive dressings.
4. Evacuate the patient to the warm zone for further care using a fireman's carry, one-person drag, or one-to-two person lift, depending on your patient's injuries. If the patient can walk, help support his or her weight.

Remember to communicate with your patient throughout your approach, treatment, and evacuation. If you approach a patient who appears deceased, don't attempt rescue until the area is declared safe. Doing so would only put your life, and possibly the lives of your coworkers, at risk.

Although the warm zone is usually a safe distance from the threat, workers in this zone must always be aware of their surroundings. The risk of injury from explosions and hazardous materials still exists in this zone. Workers in the warm zone are able to provide a higher level of patient care because there is a lower risk of injury. If a threat from an assailant with a dangerous weapon is verified, workers must follow noise and light restrictions to avoid attracting additional attention to themselves and their patients. Workers may need to treat or assess patients in nontraditional and uncomfortable positions to avoid giving away their position.

When a patient comes to you for medical assistance in a warm zone, follow these steps:

1. If patient has a weapon, disarm him or her and confiscate all secondary weapons.
2. Assess the patient's airway, breathing rate, and circulation.
3. Place the patient in the recovery position.
4. Inspect the patient for additional injuries, including those from contact with hazardous materials.
5. Splint any fractures.

Continue communicating with the patient as you move, paying close attention to any changes in mental status. Patients who are confused, unresponsive, in shock, or who have sustained a life-threatening wound should be evacuated to the cold zone as soon as possible.

Tip: Never perform CPR on your patient in the warm zone; your actions may give away your position.

The cold zone is an area located far enough away from the event that all workers and patients are no longer at risk of injury or contamination. Regular standards and rules regarding trauma, triage, and transport apply in the cold zone. Advanced life support (ALS) and advanced trauma life support (ATLS) providers are positioned in this zone and will tend to any serious injuries before transport.

Minor injuries such as contact with pepper spray or tasers should be treated in the cold zone. Before patients can be transferred, the emergency responders must disarm them, determine their priority, and decontaminate them. If the patient is a member of an emergency response team, it is recommended that a TEMS provider accompanies the patient to the hospital. This allows the TEMS provider to communicate any changes in the patient's condition to the team onsite.

Additional Topics to Review

- Basic principles of tactical field care and triage
- Working with BLS providers, ALS providers, and other support teams
- Lifts/carries used during evacuations or extrications
- Performing rapid circulatory assessments
- START method

Practice

Directions (1–5): Select the best answer for each question or incomplete statement.

1. Which medical intervention would you most likely perform in a hot zone?
   A. immobilization of the spine
   B. CPR
   C. hemorrhage control
   D. oxygen administration

2. What is the first step the tactical leader should take after learning of an emergency?

   A. Schedule hydration breaks.
   B. Perform a medical threat assessment.
   C. Request necessary medical equipment.
   D. Determine the boundaries for necessary zones.

3. You have reached the side of a patient who has been shot in the leg by a sniper. In the prone position, you disarm your patient and assess his vital signs. You then place the patient in the recovery position and inspect the patient for additional injuries. A line of blood on the ground that stretches around the corner tells you that the patient moved away from the location where he was shot. You are most likely in the

   A. zeroed position.
   B. cold zone.
   C. warm zone.
   D. incident location.

4. Which of the following teams frequently assist TEMS providers on the scene?

   A. HAZMAT
   B. DMAT
   C. USAR
   D. all of the above

5. When approaching the hot zone, you notice that a patient is lying on the ground with his gun at his side. You signal to him that you're approaching, but don't receive a response. As you move closer, you identify yourself and express your intention to help him. He doesn't yell back and he has yet to move in your presence. What should you do?

   A. Approach the patient slowly and assess his vital signs.
   B. Toss an object at the patient and see if he responds.
   C. Wait until the scene is declared safe before approaching the patient.
   D. Grab the patient under the arms and drag him into the warm zone.

Answers

1. **C.** The only interventions you should perform in the hot zone are simple airway maneuvers and *hemorrhage control*. You should never perform CPR in a hot or warm zone, as it may attract the attention of nearby perpetrators. You will also most likely not have time to immobilize the patient or administer oxygen in the hot zone.

2. **B.** Before a tactical leader can schedule hydration breaks, determine boundaries of zones, and request necessary medical equipment, he or she must *perform a medical threat assessment*, or MTA. After completing the MTA, the tactical leader can determine boundaries, establish teams, and schedule breaks and rotations.

3. **C.** The actions you are completing signal that you are in a *warm zone*, a concealed and covered zone that provides you with enough freedom to inspect the patient for additional wounds while simultaneously inspecting your surroundings for threats. If the patient had not moved himself away from where he was shot, you would have been in the zeroed position.

4. **D.** The correct answer is Choice D, *all of the above.* HAZMAT (hazardous material), DMAT (disaster medical assistance teams), and USAR (urban search and rescue) teams often assist TEMS providers on the scene of an emergency.

5. **C.** If a patient is unresponsive, you should *wait until the scene is declared safe before approaching the patient.* If the patient is in the hot zone and is unconscious or unresponsive, he cannot assist you in his rescue, which puts both of you at serious risk of injury.

E. Weapons of Mass Destruction

Weapons of mass destruction (WMD) present unique challenges for EMS workers. These threats come from three distinct sources: international terrorists, domestic issue terrorists, and lone terrorists.

EMS crews are often the first people to respond to an incident involving a WMD. The WMDs you may encounter in the field include chemical, biological, and radiological threats. Understanding your role in an incident involving WMDs is critical to protecting yourself and your patients. Although these situations are uncommon in the field, you will encounter questions about WMD incidents on the EMT-Basic exam.

1. Agents of Terrorism

The effects of chemical, biological, and radiological weapons can cause significant damage if the signs and symptoms are not recognized and treated immediately. Because it is often difficult to determine the sources of chemical, biological, and radiological weapons, the best way to identify an agent of terrorism is to become familiar with the common symptoms of exposure to such weapons.

a. Chemical

The most common agents used in chemical attacks are nerve agents, including tabun, sarin, soman, VX, and novichok. These agents produce a toxic condition called *cholinergic crisis.* EMT-Basics use the acronym SLUDGE to remember the symptoms of cholinergic crisis. SLUDGE stands for

- Salivation
- Lacrimation
- Urinary incontinence
- Defecation incontinence
- Generalized weakness
- Emesis

Nerve agents are especially dangerous because residue can cling to the victim's clothing, skin, and possessions for days after the initial exposure. Because the risk of contamination is high, EMT-Basics must take the proper BSI precautions before assessing or treating the patient. EMT-Basics should always wear rubber gloves and chemical-resistant clothing with an air filtration system while treating victims of a chemical attack.

Treatment of victims who have been exposed to nerve agents often involves the administration of atropine and pralidoxime autoinjectors. After such drugs are administered, immediate transport to a specialized facility is usually required.

Terrorists also use *vesicants*, or blister agents, as chemical weapons. Vesicants, which include mustard and lewisite, have the capability to kill growing cells in bone marrow and the gastrointestinal tract. They also cause blisters within the airway and on the skin. Up to 24 hours may pass between the patient's initial exposure to the chemical and the onset of painful symptoms. This makes it difficult to discover where and when the patient was infected. If not treated, vesicants can cause immune system failure, which can lead to death. If blisters have formed in the patient's throat, you must ensure that a patent airway is maintained at all times. This may require you to intubate the patient before transport to the hospital.

Like nerve agents, vesicants leave residue on the patient's skin and clothes, which can infect EMS workers. The contents of the blisters are not toxic, but EMT-Basics should avoid touching the area unless barrier protection is available.

Chemical asphyxiants (including the gases carbon monoxide, cyanide, and hydrogen sulfide) are another form of chemical warfare commonly employed by terrorists. These chemicals affect the patient's breathing, which may lead to unconsciousness or death if left untreated. Carbon monoxide is extremely difficult for humans to detect because it is colorless and odorless. Specialized equipment can sometimes assist EMS workers in determining if carbon monoxide gas is present. Cyanide gas, however, sometimes gives off a bitter almond scent. Hydrogen sulfide may produce a smell similar to rotten eggs.

Symptoms of chemical asphyxiant poisoning include headaches, nausea, restlessness, and a decrease in the person's attention span. Long-term exposure to these chemicals can result in unconsciousness, which can quickly lead to death if the patient doesn't receive immediate treatment.

EMT-Basics may suspect chemical asphyxiant poisoning if they treat multiple patients with similar symptoms. In most cases, these symptoms are treated by removing the infected patient from the scene of exposure. In cases of cyanide poisoning, EMT-Basics may need to use a cyanide antidote kit under the supervision of medical direction. When responding to an incident that may involve chemical asphyxiants, EMT-Basics must outfit themselves with the proper respiratory protection.

Terrorist groups may also utilize lung irritants (such as chlorine, ammonia, and phosgene) in an attack on the population. Lung irritants often produce a strong odor. Once inhaled, they create an irritating sensation in the nose and lungs, which may produce fits of violent coughing.

It's important to note that these chemicals are also used by various industries across the country. Every day, trucks and trains transport these chemicals to labs, factories, farms, and research facilities. An accident involving these vehicles could release lung irritants into the environment. Once released, these chemicals often form low-hanging clouds that are easily transported by the wind. Fortunately, these clouds help EMS workers establish a safe zone away from the scene of the initial incident. In these cases, you may be responsible for evacuating people from the area. Always take the proper BSI precautions before attempting an evacuation. Never drive your vehicle through one of these low-hanging clouds during an evacuation. Find an alternate route that doesn't put you at risk of exposure.

Exposure to lung irritants may lead to damaged cells in the lungs, adult respiratory distress syndrome, or the formation of noncardiogenic pulmonary edema. There are no antidotes for lung irritants, so EMT-Basics should remove infected patients from the area and provide them with high-flow oxygen.

Further treatment often involves lots of rest. Constant movement and heavy breathing will only spread the irritant throughout the lungs and into other areas of the body.

b. Biological

Terrorists use biological weapons to spread illness and disease throughout a designated area. The most common biological weapons are microbes (bacteria or viruses) and toxins (chemicals derived from microbes). Both are often extremely contagious. If you're responding to a call that may involve biological weapons, it's important to wear the appropriate BSI gear. Because many illnesses are airborne, you must protect yourself by wearing gear with either an air filtration system or an independent air supply.

EMS workers are often the first to recognize the spread of a biological illness. After treating multiple patients with the same symptoms over a period of hours or days, EMS workers should report their suspicions of a biological illness to dispatch, local hospitals, or medical direction.

Symptoms of illnesses caused by biological weapons are similar to pneumonia, which can be life threatening to young children and the elderly. As time passes, physicians or scientists may confirm the presence of a bioterrorism agent. Common bioterrorism agents include

- Influenza
- Tularemia
- Brucella spp.
- Plague
- T-2 mycotoxin
- Staphylococcus enterotoxin B
- Ricin
- Anthrax

Often, neurological conditions are indicators of bioterrorism. Those infected may experience paralysis, loss of function in their extremities, and numbness. Although neurological conditions may support the presence of bioterrorism, physicians must first rule out more common causes of these symptoms, such as consumption of expired foods or improper handling of raw foods. EMT-Basics who respond to calls where multiple patients are experiencing neurological symptoms may be in the presence of one of the following bioterrorism agents:

- Botulism
- Venoms from snakes
- Venezuelan equine encephalitis
- Maitotoxin
- Ciguatoxin
- Tetrodotoxin

Another rare but serious biological weapon you may encounter as an EMT-Basic is hemorrhagic viral disease. Patients suffering from a hemorrhagic viral disease experience abnormal bleeding and fever. Symptoms of the disease include bleeding from the gums or rectum, vomiting blood, and easy and excessive bruising.

Emergency personnel can test for hemorrhagic viral diseases on the scene by fixing a standard venous tourniquet. If small spots appear under the skin or excessive bruising forms near the tourniquet, then the EMT-Basic should call medical direction and the hospital to warn them of a possible case of hemorrhagic viral disease.

Other diseases contracted after exposure to bioterrorist agents include

- Rift Valley fever
- Congo-Crimean hemorrhagic fever
- Ebola virus infection
- Korean hemorrhagic fever
- Smallpox

All of these diseases are extremely dangerous. Be sure to outfit yourself with the proper BSI gear if you suspect that your patient may be suffering from one of these illnesses. Remember that signs and symptoms of infection may take days or weeks to manifest, so it is important to monitor your health carefully if you've been exposed to one of these biological agents.

The course of treatment for exposure to bioterrorist microbes, toxins, or diseases will largely depend on which agent the patient has been exposed to and, in some cases, the length of exposure. This is why it is important to try to identify the agent and then contact the closest medical care facility to alert it of the issue before initiating transportation. EMT-Basics should also contact their medical direction physicians for advice on interventions that could help stabilize the patient or provide pain relief.

c. Radiological Devices

Radiological threats differ from biological and chemical threats in that they can be detected and measured using specialized equipment. At any time, a device can be used to test for the level of radiation in a given location. Luckily, the human body is resistant to many forms of low-level radiation as long as these substances are not ingested or inhaled.

This type of terrorism often involves hiding a small piece of radioactive material in a crowded area. People who pass by the material are unknowingly exposed to radiation. Over time, hundreds of thousands of people could be exposed to radiation. Terrorists may also contaminate the food or water supply with radioactive materials.

When responding to a call that could involve a radiological device, EMT-Basics use a Geiger counter to measure the level of radiation in the area. Crews who don't have access to a Geiger counter may have to obtain one from other emergency response teams. If the Geiger counter indicates that radiation is present, patients are transported to the hospital where they receive a series of tests. If a person has been exposed to enough radiation over an extended period, he or she may develop *radiation syndrome*, which can cause serious damage to the immune system.

In situations involving radiological devices, EMT-Basics are responsible for decontaminating the patients and transporting them to the hospital. Decontamination can involve many forms, but the basic principles involve washing off any external contaminants with soap and water. Sand and clays may also be used for liquid contamination. During this process, EMT-Basics should protect themselves from cross-contamination by wearing, goggles, gloves, and gowns. After the decontamination is complete, more testing is often necessary before a course of treatment can be determined for these patients.

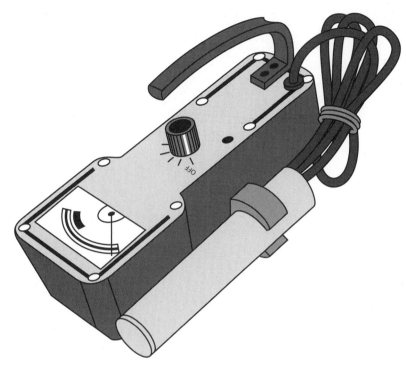

Geiger counter.

2. Response Strategies

Recognizing that an emergency may involve a WMD is both critical and difficult. If you're responding to an emergency at a highly publicized political or social event, be suspicious of the cause of injuries or illnesses. Other clues that might signal a terrorist attack include a drastic increase in the number of people suffering from a rare illness or a certain section of the population (designated by age, race, sex, or religion) suddenly becoming extremely ill.

If you suspect a terrorist attack, contact medical direction, the hospital, and law enforcement officials before transporting the patient. Once transport is complete, your vehicle and your crew must be decontaminated before responding to another call.

Additional Topics to Review

- Treating patients exposed to nerve agents
- Treating patients exposed to chemical asphyxiants
- Using a cyanide antidote kit
- Treating patients exposed to riot control agents
- Managing blast injuries
- Methods of decontamination
- Maintaining infection control

Practice

Directions (1–4): Select the best answer for each question or incomplete statement.

1. Which of the following is NOT a common nerve agent used in chemical weapons?

   A. novichok
   B. soman
   C. atropine
   D. tabun

2. You are treating a 32-year-old female for severe bleeding. She has a fever and you've noticed that her skin bruises easily. Which of the following diagnoses is most likely correct?

   A. Venezuelan equine encephalitis
   B. hydrogen sulfide poisoning
   C. T-2 mycotoxin exposure
   D. Ebola virus

3. After arriving at the scene of an emergency, you're asked to determine if radiation is present. What should you do first?

   A. Assess the area using a Geiger counter.
   B. Transport the patients from the area.
   C. Put on the proper respiratory protection.
   D. Contact medical direction for further instructions.

4. The acronym used to remember the symptoms of cholinergic crisis is

   A. MUCK.
   B. SLUDGE.
   C. GRIME.
   D. SLUSH.

Answers

1. **C.** *Atropine* is an autoinjector used to treat nerve agents such as tabun, soman, and novichok, along with sarin and VX. It is included in a Mark I kit along with pralidoxime.

2. **D.** The patient's abnormal bleeding, excessive bruising, and fever point to the presence of a hemorrhagic viral disease, such as the *Ebola virus*.

3. **C.** You can assess the area using a Geiger counter and transport the patients from the area only after you *put on the proper respiratory protection*. This gear will ensure that you don't ingest or inhale any radioactive elements at the scene.

4. **B.** The acronym used to remember the symptoms of cholinergic crisis is *SLUDGE*, which stands for salivation, lacrimation, urinary incontinence, defecation incontinence, generalized weakness, and emesis.

XII. Advanced Airway

This chapter discusses the advanced airway techniques that EMT-Basics may need to employ in the field. It's important to note that not every EMS system allows EMT-Basics to perform these maneuvers. You should consult your supervisor for more information on the types of procedures that EMT-Basics may perform in the field.

For this reason, the NREMT cognitive exam does not include a specific percentage of questions that address advanced airway techniques. However, because you may take an exam that differs from the NREMT cognitive exam, it is important to review the topics in this chapter carefully as you may see questions regarding these techniques on state or municipal examinations.

A. Advanced Airway Management of Adults

In Chapter VI, "Airway," you reviewed the techniques for clearing and managing the airway. This chapter provides an overview of advanced airway techniques for adults, children, and infants. Some of these techniques can look painful to the patient's family members. Ensure them of the importance of these life-saving techniques and ask them to leave the scene if they become too distressed.

Tip: Contact medical direction for the proper protocol before performing any of the following advanced airway management techniques.

1. Orotracheal Intubation

Just as you reviewed in Chapter VI, the EMT-Basic must ensure that the patient's airway remains open and clear at all times. A blocked airway can quickly result in death if left untreated. Without adequate oxygen, brain death can occur in as little as 6 minutes.

The most effective way to maintain the airway is to insert a tube directly into the patient's trachea (windpipe) that allows the EMT-Basic to ventilate the patient using a bag-valve mask (BVM), oxygen-powered breathing device, pocket mask, or other ventilation device. This tube, called an *endotracheal tube,* creates a tight seal between the ventilation device and the trachea. It allows the EMT-Basic to control the amount of air delivered to the patient's lungs and prevents *gastric distention*, a condition that forces air into the stomach during ventilation. The trapped air in the stomach pushes against the diaphragm, making ventilation difficult. If too much air becomes trapped in the stomach, it can force undigested food and gastric juice back up the esophagus in a process called *passive regurgitation*. This is a serious danger to the airway.

EMT-Basics can minimize the risk of gastric distention in adults by using the *Sellick maneuver* when inserting the endotracheal tube during orotracheal intubation. The Sellick maneuver was developed to decrease the risk of passive regurgitation in the operating room. It's used in prehospital settings to reduce gastric distention and prevent regurgitation during ventilation. It should only be used on unresponsive patients who do not have a gag reflex. To perform the Sellick maneuver, place pressure on the cricoid ring to collapse the esophagus. Maintain this pressure until the patient's airway is protected. One disadvantage of this maneuver is the need for an additional EMT-Basic during artificial ventilation. One EMT-Basic must maintain the pressure on the cricoid ring while the other performs ventilation.

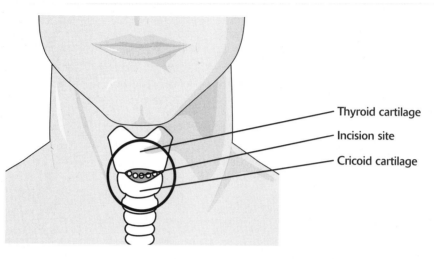

Cricoid ring.

> **Tip:** Do not attempt to perform the Sellick maneuver if you're unsure of the proper location of the cricoid ring. If you apply pressure to another area, you may comprise or damage the airway.

Orotracheal intubation is the most effective way to ventilate a patient who is *apneic* (not breathing) and has no gag reflex. This process helps minimize the risk of aspiration, delivers oxygen to the lungs, provides complete control of the airway, and allows the trachea and bronchi to be suctioned.

While you should always refer to your medical direction physician for the proper protocol, the EMT-Basic should consider using orotracheal intubation in prehospital settings when

- You can't ventilate a patient who is apneic.
- The patient is unresponsive to painful stimuli.
- The patient has no gag reflex.
- The patient can't protect his or her airway.

a. Endotracheal Tube Insertion

Before you begin insertion of the endotracheal tube, you should follow the proper body substance isolation (BSI) precautions. Wear a mask, eyewear, and gloves to protect yourself and the patient.

The endotracheal tube is a hollow, open tube that attaches to a bag-valve mask. The other end, which is placed into the patient's airway, is beveled. There's a small hole on this side of the tube called a *Murphy's eye*, which prevents the tube from becoming obstructed. There's also an inflatable cuff on the tube that creates an airtight seal against the trachea. This seal ensures that air is delivered to the lungs and not the stomach, preventing gastric distention. Before inserting the endotracheal tube, you should ensure that the cuff doesn't have any leaks.

Endotracheal tubes are available in different sizes. You should select the correct size for the patient or use the 7.5 mm tube, which is considered the standard size for most adults. This flexible tube is sometimes difficult to control when inserting it into the airway. Inserting a *stylet*, a pliable piece of metal, inside the tube can assist with insertion.

To insert the endotracheal tube in the trachea, the glottic opening, the space between the vocal cords and the trachea, must be in plain view. You should use a lighted device called a *laryngoscope* to locate the glottic opening. A laryngoscope has two types of blades: a straight blade called a *Miller* and a curved blade called a *MacIntosh*. When inserted into the patient's mouth, the laryngoscope uses these blades to reveal the airway. The Miller blade lifts the epiglottis out of the way to reveal the glottic opening. The MacIntosh blade is inserted into the *vallecula*, a depression at the back of the throat, to reveal the airway. Either blade may be used on an adult, but a Miller blade should always be used on children and infants.

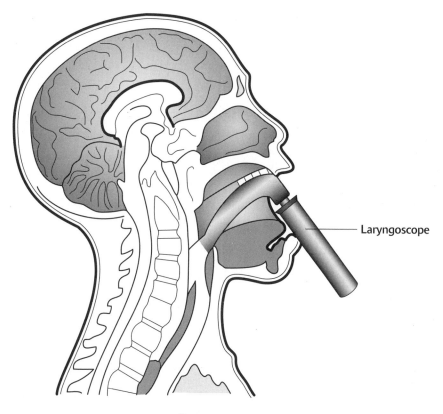

— Laryngoscope

Laryngoscope.

After the laryngoscope is inserted into the patient's throat, select an endotracheal tube and use the stylet to aid with its insertion. After the endotracheal tube is in position, inflate the cuff to create an airtight seal and remove the laryngoscope blade. Secure the tube and place a bite block or oral airway in the patient's mouth to prevent the patient from biting down on the tube.

Tip: Remember, the patient is not receiving oxygen during intubation. Taking more than 30 seconds to intubate puts the patient's life at risk.

After the endotracheal tube is inserted, the EMT-Basic should ventilate the patient and listen for breath sounds over the *epigastrium* (area over the stomach) and the bases of the lungs to ensure that the tube has been inserted properly. If a tube is improperly placed, the patient's lungs will not be ventilated, and the patient will rapidly deteriorate. If you hear gurgling over the epigastrium or cannot hear breath sounds, the tube must be removed. The patient should be ventilated with a BVM and simple airway adjunct prior to any further attempts at intubation. If breath sounds are heard in only one lung, it is likely that the tube has been advanced too far, into one of the mainstem bronchi. If this happens, the tube should be withdrawn in 1-2 cm increments and the tube position should be reassessed.

You may decide to use an end tidal carbon dioxide detector to evaluate tube placement. This device changes color when carbon dioxide is detected. Another method you can use is *pulse oximetry*, which monitors the patient's oxygen levels. However, you should know that neither of these methods is accurate or effective in pulseless patients. Once you establish that the tube is in the correct place, continue to monitor the patient so the tube doesn't move or become extubated, or removed.

Tip: If you are unsure if the endotracheal tube has been placed correctly, remove it immediately and try again after ensuring the patient is reoxygenated.

Sometimes complications can arise while inserting an endotracheal tube. Improper techniques can damage the patient's teeth, lips, tongue, or airway. When inserting an endotracheal tube, it's important to know the distance from the front teeth to the different parts of the airway in an adult:

- 15 cm from front teeth to vocal cords
- 20 cm from front teeth to sternal notch (area between clavicles and sternum)
- 22 cm from front teeth to tip of properly positioned endotracheal tube
- 25 cm from front teeth to carina (point where the trachea divides into two stems)

Taking longer than 30 seconds to intubate deprives your patient of oxygen. Vomiting, hypoxia, and unstable heart rate may occur if intubation and ventilation do not take place quickly. If you're unable to correctly place the endotracheal tube after two tries, you should not make a third attempt. Continue ventilation with an adjunct and transport the patient to the hospital immediately.

2. Esophageal Tracheal Combitubes

In some cases, you won't be able to insert an endotracheal tube. Trauma patients and patients who have bleeding in the airway are often difficult to intubate. In these cases, an *esophageal tracheal Combitube* is another option used to manage the airway. An esophageal tracheal Combitube is used on adults with no gag reflex. This tube is used on patients over 16 years of age who are taller than 5 feet. Smaller Combitubes are available for patients under 5 feet. The Combitube is also used when there is no way to visualize the airway because it's inserted blindly and then advanced into either the trachea or the esophagus. It should not be used on patients who have esophageal conditions, such as cancer, because it can cause bleeding.

An esophageal tracheal Combitube has two ventilation ports—one designed to be inserted into the trachea and one designed to be inserted into the esophagus. When inserting the Combitube into the esophagus, the first port is used and air escapes from the far end through small holes. When inserting the Combitube into the trachea, the second port is used for ventilation and functions in much the same way as the first port. The Combitube has two cuffs to seal the airway.

To insert an esophageal tracheal Combitube, lubricate the tube and insert it into the patient's mouth while lifting the tongue and jaw. Ventilate the patient through the blue tube and listen over the epigastrium while observing the rise and fall of the chest. If you don't hear gurgling but do hear breath sounds, the tube is in the esophagus. Continue to ventilate through the blue tube and inflate the two cuffs. If you hear gurgling and don't hear breath sounds, then ventilate through the white tube while listening over the epigastrium. Note the rise and fall of the chest. If you don't hear gurgling, the tube is in the trachea. Continue to ventilate through the white tube.

Incorrectly identifying tube placement and ventilating through the wrong port can be fatal to the patient. The EMT-Basic should ensure that he or she identifies the correct placement of the Combitube to prevent complications.

Sometimes suctioning may be required to remove liquid and other materials from the airway. Once the patient is intubated, you can suction the trachea using the techniques we reviewed in Chapter VI.

Additional Topics to Review

- Using the Sellick maneuver
- Cricoid ring location
- Operating a laryngoscope
- Suctioning techniques

Practice

Directions (1–10): Select the best answer for each question or incomplete statement.

1. What is the most effective way to ventilate a patient who is apneic and has no gag reflex?

   A. placement of a nasogastric tube
   B. the use of orotracheal intubation
   C. application of a bag-valve-mask device
   D. insertion of a nasopharyngeal airway

2. You're trying to ventilate a 35-year-old male with bleeding in the airway. Which of these devices should you use?

   A. an esophageal tracheal Combitube
   B. an endotracheal tube
   C. a bag-valve mask
   D. a bulb syringe

3. Air trapped in the stomach during ventilation can cause

   A. internal bleeding.
   B. airway damage.
   C. passive regurgitation.
   D. hypovolemic shock.

4. You are trying to intubate a 65-year-old apneic female en route to the hospital. You have improperly placed the endotracheal tube twice and removed it. What should you do next?

    A. Keep trying to insert the endotracheal tube until it's placed correctly.
    B. Apply a nonrebreather mask to allow at least some oxygenation.
    C. Suction the airway before reinserting the endotracheal tube.
    D. Ventilate the patient until you arrive at the hospital.

5. What is the standard size endotracheal tube for most adults?

    A. 7.5 mm
    B. 8.5 mm
    C. 7.0 mm
    D. 9.0 mm

6. When you're performing the Sellick maneuver, you should first locate the

    A. cricoid ring.
    B. trachea.
    C. esophagus.
    D. diaphragm.

7. Your partner intubated an adult male, but she is unsure if she placed the endotracheal tube in the correct spot. She asks you to check it for her, but you are also unsure. What should you do next?

    A. Ventilate the patient.
    B. Remove the tube and insert it again.
    C. Deflate the cuff and reevaluate the patient.
    D. Leave the tube in place until you get to the hospital.

8. Which of these should you use to help make inserting the endotracheal tube easier?

    A. a second hand on the laryngoscope
    B. a laryngoscope
    C. a stylet
    D. a cuff

9. To reveal the airway, you should insert the MacIntosh blade of the laryngoscope into the

    A. larynx.
    B. epiglottis.
    C. glottic opening.
    D. vallecula.

10. You're trying to maintain the airway of a 79-year-old male with a history of esophageal cancer. You should NOT use which of the following?

    A. a Combitube
    B. a laryngoscope
    C. a stylet
    D. a bag-valve mask

Answers

1. **B.** The most effective way to ventilate a patient who is apneic and has no gag reflex is the use of *orotracheal intubation*. This process minimizes the risk of aspiration and delivers oxygen to the lungs while allowing the EMT-Basic to suction the trachea and bronchi.

2. **A.** Because the patient has bleeding in the airway, you should use *an esophageal tracheal Combitube*.

3. **C.** Air trapped in the stomach can cause *passive regurgitation*, a condition that forces gas, partially digested food, and gastric juices up through the esophagus. This puts the airway at great risk.

4. **D.** Because you have already tried to insert the endotracheal tube twice, you should continue to *ventilate the patient until you arrive at the hospital*. If you try to reinsert the endotracheal tube, complications could occur.

5. **A.** The standard size endotracheal tube for most adults is *7.5 mm*.

6. **A.** Before you perform the Sellick maneuver, you should locate the *cricoid ring*, which is located below the patient's Adam's apple.

7. **B.** If you are unsure if the endotracheal tube is placed correctly, you should *remove it and insert it again* only if it is a second attempt. An improperly placed endotracheal tube can be fatal to the patient.

8. **C.** A *stylet* is a flexible piece of metal that is placed in the endotracheal tube to aid with its insertion.

9. **D.** The MacIntosh blade should be inserted into the *vallecula*, a depression at the back of the throat, to reveal the airway.

10. **A.** A *Combitube* should not be used on patients who have esophageal conditions, such as cancer, because it can cause bleeding.

B. Advanced Airway Management of Children and Infants

Managing the airway is crucial in saving any patient's life, but it's especially critical in cases concerning children and infants because so many pediatric emergency situations involve respiratory or airway problems. Understanding the proper techniques for managing the airways of your smallest patients is vital.

Many airway obstruction cases can be solved with the basic techniques we outlined in Chapter VI. However, advanced techniques may be necessary in certain emergency situations. These techniques should only be performed by EMT-Basics who are highly trained in advanced pediatric airway management.

Always contact the medical direction physician before performing any of these interventions.

1. Nasogastric Tubes

Unlike adults, children rely heavily on their diaphragms to assist in breathing. This makes them more prone to developing gastric distention during ventilation. You can release the air trapped in the stomach by using a *nasogastric tube*. Nasogastric tubes are used in hospitals to relieve bowel obstructions, remove toxins or blood from the gastrointestinal tract, and administer medications or nutritional supplements. In emergency settings, this long tube is inserted into the nose, down the esophagus, and into the stomach to decompress air in intubated or unitubated patients.

> **Tip:** An EMT-Basic should insert a nasogastric tube in an unresponsive child or infant who requires ventilation for an extended period of time. It should not be used on patients with facial, head, or spinal trauma.

To insert a nasogastric tube in a child or an infant, first ensure that the patient is in the supine position with his or her head turned to the left. You should place a rolled-up towel under the patient's neck to elevate his or her head. After measuring the tube and selecting the correct size, lubricate the tube for easier insertion. Carefully insert it into the patient's nose. When you're done, you must ensure that you have the correct placement. To check that the tube has been placed correctly, attach a syringe to the end of the tube and withdraw the contents of the stomach. Next, inject air into the tube and listen for gurgling noises over the stomach. After you've ensured the tube is in the correct place, attach the tube to a suction device to aspirate the stomach contents.

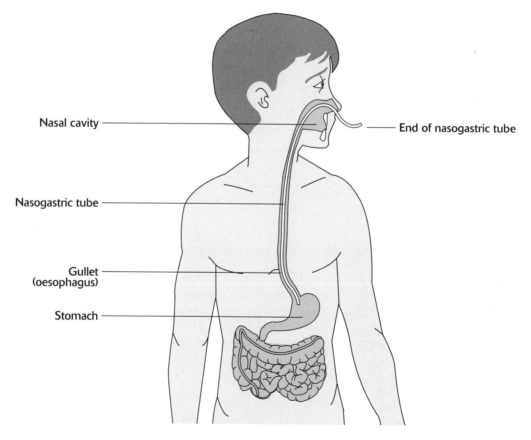

Nasal cavity ——————————— End of nasogastric tube

Nasogastric tube ———

Gullet (oesophagus) ———

Stomach ———

Nasogastric tube.

Complications can occur after the nasogastric tube is placed. Some of these complications can include

- Nasal trauma
- Tracheal insertion
- Vomiting
- Accidental passage of the tube into the patient's cranium in patients with skull fractures
- Obstruction of the patient's airway if the tube curls up in the back of the patient's throat

2. Orotracheal Intubation

The anatomy of a child or an infant differs greatly from the anatomy of an adult. Understanding these differences is vital to performing orotracheal intubation on children or infants. The following lists some of the most important anatomical differences between children/infants and adults that you should consider when performing advanced airway techniques:

- A child's or infant's airway is much smaller than an adult's airway, making it more susceptible to obstruction by fluids, materials, or swelling.
- Children's tongues are proportionally larger and take up more space in the mouth than adults' tongues do. This makes opening the airway and lifting the tongue for airway management slightly more challenging.
- An infant's or child's airway is cone-shaped, which creates a seal at the narrowest point. Because of this, cuffs are not needed to seal the airway when inserting an endotracheal tube. Uncuffed endotracheal tubes are used on children under 8 years of age.
- Infants' and children's heads are proportionally larger than adults' heads. This factor may compromise the airway when the patient is in the supine position.
- A child's trachea and vocal cords lie higher and closer to the front than an adult's. Because of this, a straight blade, or Miller blade, is used when intubating children and infants using a laryngoscope.

While you should always refer to your medical direction physician for the proper protocols, the EMT-Basic should consider using orotracheal intubation for children and infants in the following prehospital situations:

- Prolonged artificial ventilation is required.
- Artificial ventilation is impossible by any other method.
- The patient is apneic or unresponsive.
- The patient doesn't have a gag reflex.

The equipment for intubating a child is the same for intubating an adult—only on a smaller scale. When treating an infant or a child, ensure that you choose the correct size bag-valve mask (BVM). You should also use the straight laryngoscope blade (Miller blade) in younger children because it lifts the epiglottis (which is proportionally larger in children) out of the way for a better view of the glottic opening. A curved laryngoscope blade (MacIntosh blade) should be reserved for older children and adults. Selecting the correct endotracheal tube size is also important. You should use the following guidelines when determining which size to use:

- Newborns/infants: 3.0–3.5 mm
- Up to 1 year of age: 4.0 mm
- 2 years and up: Use the formula (age + 16) ÷ 4 to determine the correct size

You can also use the *Broselow tape device*, which is used to measure the patient from head to toe to calculate the proper tube size.

Broselow tape device.

In emergency situations, you shouldn't focus on recalling charts or figuring out formulas—use clues, such as the size of the child's pinky or the inside diameter of the child's nostril, to determine which size tube to use. Most pediatric endotracheal tubes have black rings near the tip of the tube that help you determine how far the tube should be inserted. For proper insertion, you should know the distance from a child's teeth or gum line to the midtrachea:

- 6 months–1 year: 12 cm
- 2–4 years: 14 cm
- 4–6 years: 16 cm
- 6–10 years: 18 cm
- 10–12 years: 20 cm

a. Endotracheal Tube Insertion

Inserting the endotracheal tube in a child is similar to inserting the tube in an adult. Before inserting the endotracheal tube, put on a mask, eye protection, and gloves to protect yourself and the patient.

Select the appropriate laryngoscope blade and the proper size endotracheal tube. Insert the laryngoscope blade to reveal the airway. Lubricate the tube and use a stylet to aid in insertion. After the endotracheal tube is in position, remove the laryngoscope blade and secure the tube.

After the endotracheal tube is inserted, the EMT-Basic should ventilate the patient and ensure that the tube has been placed in the proper position. A misplaced endotracheal tube may be hard to recognize in children and infants. Monitor the patient's vital signs for any indication of improper insertion. Breath sounds are not a reliable indication of proper insertion in infants and children.

If the tube is placed properly, but the patient's lungs are not expanding normally, there are several possible causes:

- *The tube is too small.* This may create an air leak. Listen above the neck to determine if this is the case. If you can hear air escaping, remove the tube and replace it with a larger one. If the child is over 8 years old, make sure you're using a cuffed tube.
- *The bag-valve mask or tube is leaking or malfunctioning.* Check the bag-valve mask and tube and replace with a new tube if necessary.
- *Inadequate ventilation is being administered.* Ventilate with more volume or use a larger bag-valve mask.
- *The tube is blocked.* Suction the tube to remove fluids or materials. If this doesn't work, replace the tube.

Tip: Be careful not to ventilate a child too forcefully as this can cause the patient's lung to collapse.

Once the tube is placed correctly, continue to monitor the patient to ensure that the tube doesn't move or become extubated. Just as with adults, complications, such as vomiting and self-extubation, can arise even with a correctly placed endotracheal tube. These complications are far more common in children than adults.

Remember, if you're unable to correctly place the endotracheal tube after two attempts, do not attempt to insert it again. Stimulation of the airway can slow the heart rate and complications could arise.

Additional Topics to Review

- Differences between basic airway management techniques in adults and children
- Inserting the nasogastric tube in a child
- Determining endotracheal tube size for children

Practice

Directions (1–10): Select the best answer for each question or incomplete statement.

1. Because children are more prone to gastric distention, the EMT-Basic should use which of the following to release trapped air from a child's stomach?

   A. an endotracheal tube
   B. a bag-valve mask
   C. a nasogastric tube
   D. an esophageal tracheal Combitube

2. The distance from an 8-year-old child's teeth to his or her midtrachea is

    A.   12 cm.
    B.   16 cm.
    C.   18 cm.
    D.   20 cm.

3. Which of the following could occur if a child is ventilated too forcefully?

    A.   The child could lose consciousness.
    B.   The child's lung could collapse.
    C.   The child's heart rate could decrease.
    D.   The child's airway could become blocked.

4. You can use all of the following to determine the proper size endotracheal tube to use for a 5-year-old child EXCEPT

    A.   the (age + 16) ÷ 4 formula.
    B.   the Broselow tape device.
    C.   the size of the child's pinky.
    D.   the child's height.

5. You're treating an unresponsive 6-year-old child at the scene of a car accident who has required several minutes of artificial ventilation. Your partner notices increasing gastric distension, and you decide to place a nasogastric tube. After inserting the tube, you notice much greater resistance to ventilations and the child's chest does not rise and fall with each artificial breath. Which of the following complications could have occurred?

    A.   The nasogastric tube is blocking the child's airway.
    B.   The child has a skull fracture.
    C.   The child has internal bleeding.
    D.   The nasogastric tube is the wrong size.

6. The nasogastric tube has several uses in a hospital setting. Which of the following is NOT a use for the nasogastric tube in a hospital setting?

    A.   to administer medications
    B.   to remove toxins from the blood
    C.   to feed a patient
    D.   to relieve bowel obstructions

7. You've placed an endotracheal tube in a 10-year-old child. As you're listening to the child's neck, you hear air escaping. What should you do next?

    A.   Continue to ventilate the patient until you arrive at the hospital.
    B.   Remove the endotracheal tube and replace it with a larger tube.
    C.   Suction the endotracheal tube and ventilate the patient.
    D.   Use a laryngoscope to check for any airway obstructions.

8. Which of the following factors makes the use of a Miller laryngoscope blade necessary when intubating a child?

    A.   A child's cricoid ring is less developed than an adult's cricoid ring.

    B.   A child's tongue is proportionally larger than an adult's tongue.

    C.   A child's trachea lies higher than an adult's trachea.

    D.   A child's head is proportionally larger than an adult's head.

9. Which of the following devices should be used to administer oxygen to an infant who is in respiratory distress?

    A.   nonrebreather mask

    B.   oxygen-powered ventilation device

    C.   nasal cannula

    D.   oxygen tubing

10. You arrive on the scene to find a 3-year-old male who has difficulty breathing. As you examine him, you notice what looks like a chunk of food lodged in his airway. What should you use to remove the obstruction from the airway?

    A.   bulb syringe

    B.   laryngoscope

    C.   suction catheter

    D.   endotracheal tube

Answers

1. **C.** The EMT-Basic should use *a nasogastric tube* to release trapped air in a child's stomach prior to ventilation.

2. **C.** It is *18 cm* from an 8-year-old child's teeth to his or her midtrachea.

3. **B.** If you ventilate a child too forcefully, *the child's lung could collapse*.

4. **D.** You should not use *the child's height* to determine the proper size endotracheal tube to use on a 5-year-old patient.

5. **A.** In this situation, the most likely answer is that *the nasogastric tube is blocking the child's airway*. The tube could have curled up in the back of the child's throat, causing an obstruction.

6. **B.** In a hospital setting, the nasogastric tube is used to administer medications, feed a patient, and relieve bowel obstructions. It is not used *to remove toxins from the blood*.

7. **B.** In this situation, you would *remove the endotracheal tube and replace it with a larger tube*. Because the patient is 10 years old, you should have used a cuffed endotracheal tube.

8. **C.** *A child's trachea lies higher than an adult's trachea*, so a straight laryngoscope blade, also called a Miller blade, should be used when intubating children and infants.

9. **A.** An infant who is in respiratory distress should receive oxygen via a *nonrebreather mask*. However, it is important that the EMT-Basic ensures that the appropriate sized mask is used.

10. **C.** You should use a *suction catheter* to remove the food from the child's airway.

XIII. Practical Skills Examination

Before you can even qualify to take the EMT-Basic exam, you must first pass a state-approved practical examination. Although the exact protocols for this exam may vary from state to state, most follow the national practical examination process. The exam tests five mandatory skills and one random skill. The mandatory skills include assessing a trauma patient, assessing a medical patient, applying a bag-valve mask device to an apneic patient with a pulse, assessing a cardiac arrest patient, and immobilizing a patient. The random skill may be one of several of the examiner's choosing, such as administering oxygen, controlling bleeding, or applying a traction splint.

Each skill is assessed by an experienced examiner who will provide you with the necessary information to perform the task. These examiners will consult performance checklists as you go through each station. The checklists outline the logical order that most EMT-Basics would follow when performing a particular skill. At some stations, such as the spinal immobilization station, you may be demonstrating your skills on an actual person. Of course, you will not be able to demonstrate some of the more invasive techniques, such as inserting an airway adjunct, on a volunteer. Instead, you may be required to completely verbalize your actions to the examiner or perform your interventions on a dummy.

It is important to remember that missing a single step will not result in automatic failure of a station. The reason that most EMT-Basic candidates fail a skill is because they do something, or fail to do something, that would ultimately result in harm to the patient, themselves, or other EMT-Basics. As long as you focus on the critical criteria for each station, missing a step here or there should not result in failure.

This chapter will review the techniques that you should know before taking the practical skills examination. You'll notice that this chapter differs from other chapters in that there aren't any practice questions. This is because the best way to prepare for the practical skills examination is to practice the skills in class and review each of the following sections carefully.

Remember, a thorough understanding of the concept behind each skill will ensure your success on the exam, so be sure to examine the "Additional Topics to Review" sections in this chapter.

A. Patient Assessment

The patient assessment station of the EMT-Basic practical examination is broken into two sections: trauma assessment and medical assessment. This station is designed to test your ability to think through a situation and verbalize your response. Your "verbal" treatment of a patient should coincide with the actual treatment you provide. Being able to verbalize the care you provide to a trauma or medical patient generally indicates your ability to actually perform the skill safely and efficiently in the field.

For additional information about patient assessment, refer to Chapter VII, "Patient Assessment."

1. Trauma Patient Assessment

The trauma patient portion of the patient assessment station is intended to test your ability to carry out an assessment of a patient who has suffered multiple traumas and verbally treat the patient's condition.

You'll be required to perform the patient assessment just as you would in the event of a real emergency, which includes communicating with the patient. While you assess the patient, you must clearly state your findings. Clinical information that would not be otherwise obtainable through visual or physical examination may be given after you demonstrate how you would gather this information in the field. During this test, you may presume that you are working with two EMT-Basics who are following your commands. This station has a 10-minute time limit. The station's examiner will time you and offer supplementary clinical information. The examiner may also ask for additional information about your assessment and treatment.

When taking this portion of the practical skills examination, the first skill areas you'll be tested in are performing the scene size-up and taking the proper body substance isolation (BSI) precautions. After these two skills are complete, the examiner will assess your ability to perform an initial assessment, a focused physical exam, a patient history, a rapid trauma assessment, and a detailed physical examination.

Tip: Remember to verbalize each step or action you take when assessing the patient.

Although this station covers a broad range of topics, there are some basic concepts to remember that will help you prepare for this portion of the examination:

- Take the proper BSI precautions. This includes wearing gloves, protective eyewear, and a mask. Depending on the situation presented, other protective gear may be necessary.

- Make sure that the scene is safe before approaching the patient. Some scenarios may include dangerous conditions that require special precautions. Remember to ask the examiner about the safety of the scene and state how you would proceed.

- All critical trauma patients require spinal stabilization, so it is important to take the proper spinal precautions while you attend to the patient. You may choose to do this by stating that you will instruct your partner to maintain manual stabilization of the patient's head.

- State your intention to apply immobilization devices such as cervical collars or backboards.

- Provide the patient with oxygen. All critical trauma patients require oxygen treatment. This treatment can be provided through either a nonrebreather mask or a bag-valve mask at 15 L/min. Application of oxygen should occur as soon as you've assessed the adequacy of the patient's respirations.

- Find and treat problems connected to the airway, breathing, hemorrhage, or shock in a timely manner. Problems in any of these areas could threaten your patient's life.

- You must be able to accurately determine whether the patient's condition indicates rapid transport or continued on-scene treatment and assessment. While some scenarios call for detailed physical examination and careful on-scene treatment, others require rapid transport to a medical facility with very little time spent on the scene.

- Remember to perform the initial assessment before the detailed physical examination. Assessing the patient's airway, breathing, and circulation is the most important part of the overall assessment. Once you have determined that the scene is safe, the initial assessment should be the next step. When you perform the detailed physical examination, remember to use the DCAP-BTLS method when checking for injuries.

- Transport the patient within the 10-minute time limit. If you start transport before the end of your time, remember to perform the detailed physical exam while the transport is in progress. Not transporting the patient during the allotted time may result in failure of the station.

2. Medical Patient Assessment

This portion of the patient assessment station is similar to the trauma patient assessment portion. In this case, you are assessing a patient who is suffering from a medical issue, such as an illness. You have 10 minutes to complete the task.

With trauma patients, you can usually see the patient's problem and treat it accordingly. Conversely, with medical patients, the problem is usually not visible and you must rely on your assessment to determine the nature of the patient's condition.

In addition to the standard scene size-up and initial assessment, these types of scenarios require a considerably more detailed physical exam and patient history. You must identify the patient's condition based on his or her signs, symptoms, and history. Possible patient conditions may include respiratory or cardiac distress; altered mental status; allergic reaction; poisoning/overdose; or environmental, obstetrics, or behavioral emergencies.

While this section is similar to the trauma patient assessment, there are also some important concepts that are exclusive to medical patient assessment. It is important to ask questions that are relevant to the patient's complaints. These questions form the basis of your understanding of the patient's condition and will indicate the appropriate treatment. The questions you ask will guide you through the scenario. There are a required number of questions you must ask based on the nature of the patient's condition:

- Respiratory—five or more questions
- Cardiac—five or more questions
- Altered mental status—six or more questions
- Allergic reaction—four or more questions
- Poisoning/overdose—five or more questions
- Environmental emergency—four or more questions
- Obstetrics emergency—five or more questions
- Behavioral emergency—four or more questions

You will not be awarded credit for this step unless you ask at least the minimum number of questions required by the patient's condition.

When treating the patient, you should remember to obtain authorization from the medical direction physician for treatments that require approval. You'll also need to verbalize any standing orders that you choose to incorporate.

Tip: Remember to ask the patient the required minimum number of questions about his or her condition to help you determine the appropriate treatment.

It is also critical to avoid any treatment that may be inappropriate or dangerous. Attempting any form of treatment that is not appropriate for the patient's condition or that may harm the patient could result in failure of the station.

Additional Topics to Review

- Patient assessment (Chapter VII)
- Medical emergencies (Chapter VIII)
- Trauma emergencies (Chapter IX)

B. Applying a Bag-Valve Mask Device to an Apneic Patient with a Pulse

In this station of the practical skills examination, you will be required to properly ventilate an apneic patient with a bag-valve mask device. In this scenario, there are no bystanders and artificial ventilation has not been started. The only treatment you need to be concerned with is management of the patient's airway and ventilatory support. First, you'll ventilate the patient for 30 seconds, after which time the effectiveness of your ventilator volumes will be assessed. The examiner will then inform you that a second EMT-Basic has arrived on the scene and that you must control the airway and maintain the mask seal as your partner provides ventilation. You have 5 minutes to complete the station.

During the test, the examiner will time your progress and observe your ventilations. When you've ventilated the patient for 30 seconds, the examiner will either inform you of your partner's arrival or, in some cases, play the role of the partner.

While you're ventilating the patient, the examiner will be checking that you verbalize the opening of the airway and insertion of an airway adjunct. Remember to select the appropriate size mask and create a proper mask-to-face seal. Next, ventilate the patient at the proper rate with the adequate volume and connect the reservoir and oxygen, adjusting the flow to 15 L/min or greater.

When your partner takes over ventilation, the examiner will check that you verbalize reopening the airway, creating a proper mask-to-face seal, and instructing your partner to resume ventilations at the proper rate with the adequate volume.

Initiation of ventilation should be immediate. When the examiner tells you to begin, you must open the patient's airway and start artificial ventilations with the bag-valve mask. Because you are not required to manually insert an airway adjunct, you can simply verbalize this action. You will be required to ventilate the patient for 30 seconds with room air.

> **Tip: Maintain a secure mask-to-face seal at all times for proper ventilation.**

Ensure that ventilations are not interrupted for more than 20 seconds. Be efficient when connecting supplemental oxygen and the reservoir, as this process may cause an extended interruption if you don't perform the action quickly. You can also save time by noting the location of all your equipment before you begin the test. When you attach supplemental oxygen tubing and the reservoir after ventilating the patient with room air for 30 seconds, remember to state that you've set the oxygen flowmeter to 15 L/min. In some cases, you may have to physically set the flowmeter.

You are allowed one inadequate ventilation during this practical exam. A ventilation is declared inadequate when the patient's chest fails to rise or rises only slightly. The most frequent cause of inadequate ventilation is an improper mask-to-face seal. When this seal is not maintained, inadequate volumes result. If you have trouble with this procedure, you may try firmly holding the mask to the patient's face and pressing the bag against your leg. When you are working with your partner, the mask should be secured to the patient's face using the "E-C-clamp" method.

You should ventilate at a rate of around 12 breaths per minute and wait for the chest to fall completely before you start the next ventilation. Be careful not to ventilate the patient too fast as this can lead to hyperventilation and gastric distention.

Additional Topics to Review

- Respiratory emergencies (Chapter VIII)
- Artificial ventilation (Chapter VI)

C. Cardiac Arrest Management/AED

At this station, you will be asked to manage a prehospital cardiac arrest through the integration of CPR skills, defibrillation, airway adjuncts, and patient and scene management skills. As the scenario begins, you'll find a patient in cardiac arrest. You'll have a first responder and an EMT-Basic to assist you. The first responder will perform one-rescuer CPR—other than this, your assistants will do only what you direct them to do. You must take control of the scene and initiate patient resuscitation with an automated external defibrillator (AED). When it becomes necessary, control the patient's airway and ventilate or direct one of your assistants to ventilate the patient with adjunctive equipment. You have a 15-minute time limit. The examiner will time you and may serve as one of your assistants.

This test has four components: assessment, transition, integration, and transportation. Remember, you must verbalize all of your actions during this station.

In the assessment phase, ask the first responder how long the patient has been in cardiac arrest and how long CPR has been in progress. It is important to do this without interrupting the administration of CPR. Once you understand the event of the cardiac arrest, activate the AED and attach the AED pads to the patient without interrupting CPR. When the AED is activated and fully attached, begin rhythm analysis of the patient. While analysis is in progress, ensure that all rescuers are clear of the patient. Physical contact with the patient at this time may interfere with analysis. When all rescuers are clear of the patient, if indicated by the device, deliver one shock and then ensure CPR is resumed immediately following the shock.

Next is the transition phase, during which you must direct your assistants to resume two-rescuer CPR. During this process, you should assess CPR effectiveness. Feel for a carotid or femoral pulse as your assistants perform chest compressions. At this point, ask any other necessary questions about the patient's cardiac arrest, medical history, and the events that led up to the onset of the cardiac arrest.

During the integration phase, you are required to integrate the proper airway management into the situation without interrupting chest compressions. Don't forget to verbalize the measurement and insertion of an oropharyngeal airway. Next, ventilate or order the ventilation of the patient with either a bag-valve mask device or a pocket mask. Following five cycles of CPR, ensure everyone is clear of the patient and reanalyze the patient's cardiac rhythm. Deliver another shock, if necessary. Keep in mind that CPR should be resumed as soon as the shock is delivered.

In the transportation phase, you'll need to place the patient on a long spine board, continue CPR, and begin transport to a medical facility. Remember to verbalize each of these steps. At this station, you should initiate use of the AED immediately. Ventricular fibrillation is the most frequently occurring initial cardiac dysrhythmia seen during early cardiac arrest in adults, so defibrillation is the most important treatment. Apply the AED pad while chest compressions are in progress. This will help reduce any interruption of CPR.

Tip: Keep in mind that CPR should be actively administered at all times, except during cardiac rhythm analysis and shocks. Don't forget to resume CPR immediately after the analysis and shocks.

Ensure that all rescuers are clear of the patient before administering a shock. Anyone in physical contact with the patient when a shock is delivered may be injured.

Review the steps for operating the AED. Using the AED is a critical component of this scenario and you must know how to use it properly and safely. It is also critical that you don't prevent the AED from delivering a shock in any way. The AED is designed to precisely recognize shockable rhythms. When the AED indicates a shock is required, it should be administered immediately. You should not remove the AED pads from the patient or disconnect the AED cable from the AED at any time.

Additional Topics to Review

- Cardiac emergencies (Chapter VIII)
- Automated external defibrillator (Chapter VIII)
- Ventricular fibrillation (Chapter VIII)

D. Spinal Immobilization

At this station, you will be tested on your ability to properly immobilize a patient who may be in either a seated or a supine position. The position of the patient is predetermined by the examiner or chosen at random as the scenario is prepared. You'll have 10 minutes to complete this station. Remember to verbalize all of your actions.

During this scenario, you'll use a half-spine immobilization device, such as a short spine board or a vest-style device. As the scenario begins, you and an EMT-Basic assistant enter the scene of an automobile accident. You determine that the scene is safe and identify one patient. Your assistant completes the initial assessment and finds that the patient's vital signs are stable and that there are no critical conditions requiring immediate attention. You must treat the patient's unstable spine using a half-spine immobilization device. Remember, your assistant will only follow your instructions during this scenario. Once the initial immobilization is complete, you may transfer the patient to the long spine board verbally.

Along with timing your progress, the examiner will observe your actions and those of your assistant while testing the effectiveness of your attempt at immobilization by trying to manipulate the device.

Remember to place the patient's head in a neutral, in-line position. You can direct your assistant to carry out this manual immobilization. Once the head is manually immobilized, it's important to apply a correctly sized cervical collar before ordering your assistant to release the patient from manual immobilization.

Ensure that your assistant does not release manual stabilization of the patient's head before you have the cervical collar in place and the patient is immobilized to the device. To ensure that manual stabilization is not released before stabilization is maintained mechanically, you should direct your assistant to maintain manual stabilization until you've carefully reassessed the patient's peripheral pulses and neurologic status.

It is also important to avoid excessive or uncoordinated patient movements, as they may compromise the stability of the patient's spine. Because the individual maintaining stabilization of the patient's head is in command of any movements, ensure that your assistant is aware that all movements are at his or her command. All movements must be executed in a uniform fashion, with the patient being moved as a unit at all times.

Remember to apply all immobilization devices gently and carefully. When you're applying the half-spine immobilization device, secure the patient's torso before securing the patient's head. If you secure the patient's head first, you may cause unnecessary movement of the patient's neck while you secure the torso. The head should not be immobilized until full immobilization of the torso is completed.

Do not attempt to position the entire device and then return to tighten the straps. As you position the half-spine immobilization device, check that the device fits the patient snugly under the arms. After positioning is complete, step back and examine the patient to ensure that the device is centered, and then secure the straps.

Tip: Remember to verbalize your actions. Your EMT-Basic assistant will only follow your commands.

Be careful to ensure proper head immobilization in the half-spine immobilization device. When positioning the patient on the half-spine immobilization device, remember that the area between the patient's lower back and the back of the head should always be in an in-line position. In addition, you should remember that the support pad included with the half-spine immobilization device will not be used in most cases, as it is most frequently used with patients who have spinal deformities that don't allow for normal alignment.

When you are securing the patient's torso, do not to affix the straps so tightly that the patient has difficulty breathing. To avoid this problem, you should ask the patient to take and hold a deep breath while you secure the strap, repeating this technique for each strap. This will allow for proper chest expansion. This technique applies only when immobilizing a patient from a seated position.

An improperly positioned head at the completion of immobilization may lead to failure of the station. You should be certain that the patient's cervical collar is correctly sized and that you're not using the support pad unnecessarily.

Remember to assess motor, sensory, and circulatory functions after immobilization is complete and after you've stated that the patient has been moved to the long backboard. During this test, you are required to assess the patient before and after placement of the half-spine immobilization device.

Additional Topics to Review

- Spinal injuries (Chapter IX)
- Head injuries (Chapter IX)
- Immobilization devices (Chapter IX)

E. Random Skills

Along with the five mandatory skills included in the practical skills examination (trauma patient assessment, medical patient assessment, applying a bag-valve mask device to an apneic patient with a pulse, cardiac arrest management/AED, and spinal immobilization), you will need to demonstrate your abilities to perform one additional skill that is chosen at random. You won't know what this skill will be until the day of the exam. The possible skills you may be tested on include the following:

- Oxygen administration
- Airway adjuncts and suctioning
- Mouth-to-mask ventilation with supplemental oxygen
- Traction splint
- Immobilization of a joint injury
- Immobilization of a long bone fracture
- Bleeding control and shock management

1. Oxygen Administration

In this station, you'll be tested on your ability to correctly assemble the required equipment for administering supplemental oxygen in the field. You'll be expected to properly assemble an oxygen tank and regulator and then administer oxygen to the patient with a nonrebreather mask. Once you have accomplished this task, the examiner will instruct you to discontinue use of the nonrebreather mask because the patient is not tolerating this treatment. You'll then administer oxygen with a nasal cannula. When you have successfully initiated oxygen administration with a nasal cannula, the examiner will instruct you to completely discontinue oxygen administration. You have a 5-minute time limit.

When assembling the oxygen tank and regulator, avoid any leaks. Note whether the pin index safety system on the tank is correctly aligned with the corresponding fittings on the regulator. If you hear oxygen leaking when you turn on the tank, turn it off and recheck the fittings.

It is important to ensure the proper flow of oxygen before applying the nonrebreather mask. You must set the flow rate to 12 L/min or higher, so the patient receives the proper oxygen flow.

It is also important to remember to fill the reservoir bag with oxygen before you place the nonrebreather mask on the patient. The nonrebreather mask can't deliver 100 percent oxygen if the reservoir bag isn't filled. When you set the flowmeter, block the outlet port of the mask with your finger until the reservoir is completely filled.

When you're instructed to switch from the nonrebreather mask to the nasal cannula, remember to reset the flowmeter to within a range of 1–6 L/min. Remember, oxygen delivered through a nasal cannula at a rate greater than 6 L/min can be dangerous for the patient.

2. Airway Adjuncts and Suctioning

At this station, you'll be tested on your ability to correctly measure, insert, and remove an oropharyngeal and a nasopharyngeal airway. You'll also be required to perform suction on the patient's upper airway. You have 5 minutes to complete the station.

It is extremely important to select the correct-fitting oropharyngeal airway for the patient. If the airway you choose is too large or too small, it may lead to further complications. It is recommended that you measure the correct size oropharyngeal airway from the corner of the mouth to the angle of the jaw or the earlobe. You can tell if you've placed an oropharyngeal airway correctly if the flange is resting flush with the patient's lips.

It is just as important to select a properly sized nasopharyngeal airway. It is recommended that you use the measurement from the corner of the nose to the angle of the jaw or the earlobe to help you select the correct size nasopharyngeal airway. Always lubricate the nasopharyngeal airway before inserting it. You should never rotate the airway into place as this could harm the patient. Insert the airway with the bevel facing the nasal septum or the base of the nostril. If you encounter any resistance while attempting to insert the airway, don't force it. Remove the nasopharyngeal airway and try inserting it in the other nostril.

When you begin the suctioning portion of the test, you should measure the suction catheter in the same fashion as the oropharyngeal airway. Don't attempt to initiate suction while you're still inserting the catheter. Suctioning should be performed in a circular motion only as the catheter is being removed from the mouth.

Tip: Because oxygen is removed during suctioning, remember to administer oxygen before and after you suction a patient's airway. Also, limit suctioning to 10–15 seconds.

The insertion of any adjunct in a way that could harm the patient may lead to failure of the station. Take your time and do not attempt to force any airway into place.

3. Mouth-to-Mask Ventilation with Supplemental Oxygen

At this station, you'll be required to ventilate a patient with supplemental oxygen via the mouth-to-mask technique. You may start the test with the assumption that mouth-to-barrier ventilation is already in progress and that the patient has a central pulse. The only treatment you'll have to provide is ventilatory support with the mouth-to-mask technique and supplementary oxygen. You'll ventilate the patient for 30 seconds, during which time the examiner will assess the appropriateness of the patient's ventilatory volumes. You have a 5-minute time limit.

Because this scenario requires supplemental oxygen, you'll need to attach the oxygen tank and set the flowmeter. You may do this immediately upon initiating ventilations or after first ventilating the patient with room air.

Pocket masks used without supplemental oxygen can deliver good tidal volume to the patient, but will only provide 16 percent oxygen. If you set the flowmeter at 15 L/min, you can supply the patient with 55 percent oxygen and good tidal volume.

Remember to deliver each breath over 1 second and be sure that the patient's chest rises. You can secure the mask to the patient's face using one of two acceptable methods. The first method involves placing the mask on the face while kneeling at the patient's head, grasping the angles of the jaw, and tilting the patient's head back. When using the second method, execute a head-tilt chin-lift maneuver while kneeling astride the patient and place the mask on his or her face.

It is crucial to ventilate the patient at a rate of 10–12 breaths per minute. You can maintain this rate by ventilating the patient every 5 to 6 seconds.

Tip: You can count out loud or to yourself if you think it will help you maintain the proper rate of ventilation.

It is also critical that you allow the patient time to completely exhale during ventilation. If you're ventilating too quickly, the patient may not be exhaling properly, which can lead to hyperventilation and gastric distention. Ensure that the patient's chest falls completely before starting the next breath.

4. Traction Splint

The traction splint station of the practical skills examination assesses your ability to use a traction splint to stabilize a midshaft femoral fracture. During this scenario, an EMT-Basic assistant will aid you in applying the splint by applying manual traction at your direction. You're only required to treat the isolated femur injury. You'll be instructed to assume that the scene is safe, the initial assessment has already been completed, and that the focused assessment indicated a midshaft femoral deformity. You won't have to monitor the patient's airway, breathing, or central circulation. You have 10 minutes to complete the station.

Proper traction must be maintained at all times. To ensure that traction is always maintained, you should communicate with your assistant to avoid any "surprise" moves and ensure that the traction splint's locking mechanism is fully locked after traction is complete. You can also direct your assistant to place his or her foot against the foot of the patient's uninjured leg before assuming manual traction. This will prevent the patient from sliding when manual traction is pulled and will help your assistant maintain his or her balance.

Evaluate the patient's motor, sensory, and circulatory functions in the injured extremity before and after you apply the splint. Once the extremity has been manually stabilized, check the patient's motor, sensory, and circulatory functions immediately. Assess these functions again after application of the splint. You may also check these functions after the splint is fully secured.

As you prepare to apply the splint, compare the splint to the uninjured leg to ensure that the end of the splint extends no more than 12 inches beyond the injured leg. This will prevent the leg from becoming overextended when mechanical traction is applied. While you or your assistant performs manual stabilization of the leg, ensure that it's as straight as possible and that the patient's foot points upward. This position should be maintained until the splint is fully applied. Using this technique will prevent the leg from rotating unnecessarily.

It is very important that your immobilization attempt fully supports the femur and prevents any leg rotation. To ensure that this happens, ask your assistant to stop you when the degree of mechanical traction either meets or slightly exceeds manual traction. Mechanical traction that fails to meet manual traction may result in a "drop" of the leg. You should also ensure that all straps have been firmly secured to prevent leg movement.

Remember that the leg should not be fully secured to the splint before applying mechanical traction. After you've applied manual stabilization and checked the patient's motor, sensory, and circulatory functions, apply the ankle hitch and manual traction. Next, position the prepared splint beneath the injured leg and lower the leg into the splint. Next, secure the ischial strap and apply mechanical traction. Once mechanical traction is in place, fasten the Velcro straps that will secure the injured leg to the splint.

5. Immobilization of a Joint Injury

This station requires you to correctly immobilize an uncomplicated shoulder injury. You only have to treat the specific, isolated shoulder injury. When you start the scenario, the examiner will instruct you that the scene size-up and initial assessment are complete and that the focused assessment has revealed the shoulder injury. You won't need to monitor the patient's airway, breathing, or central circulation. You have a 5-minute time limit.

When you immobilize the patient's shoulder, it's critical that the joint is supported properly and is not bearing any distal weight. While applying the sling, ensure that the elbow is in flexion and the hand is pointing toward the uninjured shoulder. When the sling is properly applied, the elbow of the injured extremity will rest inside the sling and support the shoulder. You should use caution when applying the sling. Any downward pressure on the injured extremity would force it to bear distal weight.

You must also remember to immobilize the bone above and below the joint. You may have some difficulty identifying which bone is proximal to the injured shoulder. Most shoulder dislocations occur at the glenohumeral joint. This is where the humeral head joins with the glenoid fossa of the scapula. As a result, the scapula would be the proximal bone requiring immobilization. When applied properly and fully secured, the sling will immobilize the scapula.

Throughout the entire process, you should be monitoring the patient's motor, sensory, and circulatory functions in the injured extremity. Make your first check after you have manually stabilized the extremity. Complete your second check after applying the sling and swathe. In this case, circulatory function can be assessed with capillary refill.

6. Immobilization of a Long Bone Fracture

At this station, you'll be asked to correctly immobilize a closed, nonangulated long bone injury. The scene size-up and initial assessment have already been completed. The examiner will inform you that the focused assessment of the patient revealed a closed, nonangulated injury of the radius, ulna, tibia, or fibula. You won't have to monitor the patient's airway, breathing, or central circulation. You have 5 minutes to complete the station.

The most important thing to remember while immobilizing the patient's injured extremity is to avoid any unnecessary or sudden movements. Any movement can result in further injury. You should stabilize the extremity manually and maintain stabilization until the whole extremity is fully immobilized. Exercise caution during application of the splint, being very careful not to move the extremity suddenly.

Don't forget to immobilize the joints adjacent to the injured bone. With radius or ulna injuries, the elbow and wrist should be immobilized. With tibia or fibula injuries, the knee and ankle should be immobilized. In most cases, long bone injures will be immobilized with padded board splints and cravats.

Remember to assess the patient's motor, sensory, and circulatory functions before and after you apply the splint. Your initial check of these functions should take place as soon as you have established manual stabilization of the injured extremity. You will need to assess motor, sensory, and circulatory functions again after the splint has been applied and the extremity is fully immobilized. You may use capillary refill to check the patient's circulatory function.

7. Bleeding Control and Shock Management

This station is scenario-based and is intended to assess your ability to control a hemorrhage. At the beginning of this practical exam, the examiner will read you a scenario and you will have the opportunity to ask questions. The examiner will provide you with updates on the patient's signs and symptoms as you proceed through the scenario. Based on the information you receive from the examiner, you'll determine the necessary treatment. You have a 10-minute time limit.

During the scenario, you can assume that the patient's airway is clear and that he or she is breathing adequately. Keep in mind that the patient will require treatment with high-flow oxygen. All victims of shock must be administered 100 percent oxygen. However, it is important to remember that controlling any bleeding should be your first priority before applying oxygen.

You should initially try to control bleeding with simple techniques, such as direct pressure and elevation. More advanced techniques should only be attempted if simple interventions fail. For example, tourniquets should be used as a last resort because they can sometimes lead to a loss of circulation in the affected extremity. Above all, you must stop or at least control the bleeding as quickly as possible.

Once you have the bleeding under control, don't forget to verbally initiate transport.

Additional Topics to Review

- Oxygen administration (Chapter VI)
- Oxygen equipment (Chapter VI)
- Artificial ventilation (Chapter VI)
- Respiratory care (Chapter VI)
- Immobilization (Chapter IX)
- Musculoskeletal care (Chapter IX)
- Fractures (Chapter IX)
- Joint injuries (Chapter IX)
- Long bone injuries (Chapter IX)
- Soft tissue injuries (Chapter IX)
- Shock (Chapter IX)
- Hemorrhage (Chapter IX)

XIV. Anatomy and Physiology

As you already know, it's important to have an excellent understanding of anatomy and physiology in order to provide your patients with the best care. To review, *anatomy* is the study of the structure of the human body, and *physiology* is the study of the function of the human body.

All EMT-Basics must take an approved course in anatomy and physiology to receive certification. This chapter will help you brush up on medical terminology, anatomical structure, and body systems before taking the EMT-Basic exam. In addition to reading this chapter, you may wish to review your notes from your anatomy and physiology course.

Remember to examine the "Additional Topics to Review" sections in this chapter. They will include supplementary information that you will want to review before taking the exam.

A. Medical Terminology

There are many words and phrases that are unique to both the medical field and, in particular, the field of emergency medical services. The following list will provide an overview of the terms that you may encounter in the field or see on the EMT-Basic exam.

The list includes definitions for common diseases, conditions, and anatomical structures that every EMT-Basic should be familiar with. Some of the definitions will include sentences to improve your understanding of the term. You may have seen some of these terms discussed in earlier chapters. Feel free to refer to those chapters for additional information.

abdomen: The area between the rib margin and the pelvis.

abrasion: An injury to the epidermis or dermis from a shearing force. Abrasions are commonly called *scrapes. The patient suffered abrasions to his face and neck.*

accessory muscle: The additional muscles used to support breathing when a person is in respiratory distress.

airway: The structures of the respiratory system through which air passes.

allergen: Any substance that causes an allergic reaction. Common allergens include certain types of foods and pollen from plants.

allergic reaction: An exaggerated reaction of the immune system to an allergen.

altered mental status: A state of mind that is not normal for the patient. Usually, the patient is unaware of the current situation. An altered mental status may signify the use of drugs or alcohol. It may also be the result of an underlying medical emergency, such as hypothermia.

amputation: The removal of an appendage from the body. *The patient's finger was amputated.*

anaphylaxis: A severe allergic reaction.

aneurysm: An abnormal blood-filled bulge in a blood vessel.

angina: A pain in the chest experienced when the heart does not receive enough oxygen, often felt after exertion.

aorta: The largest blood vessel in the body, which branches into several smaller arteries.

apneic: A term that refers to a patient who is not breathing.

arrest: A term that means *to stop. The patient is suffering from respiratory arrest.*

artery: A blood vessel that carries oxygenated blood.

asphyxia: A term that means *to suffocate. The patient was asphyxiated.*

asthma: A chronic lung condition marked by recurring episodes of airway obstruction.

atrium: An upper chamber of the heart.

avulsion: An injury that occurs when a section of skin or soft tissue is torn partially or fully away from the body.

bases of the lungs: The bottoms of the lungs, located near the sixth rib.

behavioral emergency: A situation in which a person exhibits an altered mental state.

birth canal: The lower part of the uterus and the vagina.

bladder: An organ that serves as a receptacle for urine prior to excretion.

blisters: Bubbles on the skin caused by injury.

blood pressure: The pressure of circulating blood against the walls of the arteries.

bowel: Term used to describe the lower intestine.

brain: The control center of the nervous system.

bruise: *See* contusion.

burn: Damage to the soft tissue caused by heat.

carotid: An artery that branches off the aorta and supplies blood to the brain.

cavity: An anatomical space where organs and other tissues are located.

cervical: A term used to describe a division of the spinal column.

closed injury: An injury in which the skin does not break. These types of injuries can include contusions (bruises), hematomas, and closed crush injuries.

clotting: To coagulate. *Blood clots in the lungs are extremely dangerous.*

constriction: The act or product of tightening. *The constriction of the airway caused the patient to wheeze and cough.*

contraindication: A situation in which medication should not be used.

contusion: A closed injury characterized by damaged skin cells and torn blood vessels in the dermis, commonly called a bruise.

crepitation: A crackling noise and tactile sensation produced when bone ends rub together or when there is air trapped inside the tissue.

crowning: The stage of labor in which the head of a baby is seen at the vaginal opening.

crush injury: An open or closed injury to the soft tissue that results from blunt force trauma.

cyanosis: A blue or purplish discoloration of the skin due to a lack of oxygen.

delirium: An acute and reversible mental disturbance often characterized by confusion. Delirium may be the result of fever, a serious medical condition, an imbalance of electrolytes or other fluids, or the use of prescription medication.

dementia: An irreversible and steady decline in mental status, usually affecting memory, concentration, and the ability to perform tasks. This condition is commonly associated with Alzheimer's disease.

diabetes: A condition that prevents insulin from being produced and/or used properly. Without insulin, the body cannot break down sugar into usable forms of energy. A diabetic emergency can cause a change in mental status.

diaphragm: A dome-shaped muscle that separates the chest and abdominal cavity. The diaphragm assists in breathing.

diastolic blood pressure: The measurement of pressure in the arteries when the ventricles are at rest.

dosage: The amount or rate of administration of a medication. *The EMT-Basic administered a dose of oral glucose.*

drowning: Death from suffocation within 24 hours of being submerged in water.

drug: Any substance that alters the body's normal functions.

dyspnea: Difficulty breathing.

edema: An abnormal collection of fluid that causes swelling.

embolism: A particle such as a piece of fat or bone. Embolisms may break free, causing a stroke or pulmonary artery blockage.

emphysema: A chronic, obstructive pulmonary disease, characterized by decreased lung compliance.

epiglottis: A flaplike piece of elastic cartilage that prevents food and liquid from entering the airway.

epilepsy: A neurological condition that causes recurrent seizures.

epistaxis: Bleeding from the nose.

evisceration: An open wound in the abdomen with protruding organs.

extremities: Limbs. A term usually used to refer to the arms or legs.

febrile: To have a fever.

femur: Long thigh bone.

fetus: An unborn, developing baby.

fracture: A break in a bone. *The patient's femur was fractured.*

frostbite: Also called a *local cold injury*, frostbite occurs when the skin and underlying tissues freeze due to exposure to extreme cold. These injuries are usually confined to the extremities.

full-thickness burn: A burn that affects the epidermis, dermis, and the underlying tissues. These burns may also involve bones and organs.

gag reflex: A reflex that occurs when the back of the throat is stimulated. This response helps patients protect their airways.

geriatric: An elderly patient. *The geriatric patient suffered from dementia.*

glottic opening: Anatomical space between the vocal cords, which leads to the trachea.

glottis: Passageway to the trachea.

hematoma: A closed soft tissue injury resulting from an accumulation of blood underneath the skin.

hemorrhage: Bleeding. *The patient who was involved in the car crash was hemorrhaging.*

hemorrhagic shock: Hypoperfusion that results from blood loss.

hyperthermia: A condition in which the body's core temperature rises above 98.6°F or 37°C.

hyperventilation: Quick breathing. *The stress of the accident caused the patient to hyperventilate.*

hypoglycemia: Low blood sugar.

hypoperfusion: A condition in which the body's cells or organs do not get enough oxygen and there is inadequate removal of wastes. Shock may set in when this condition starts to affect the body's organs.

hypothermia: A condition in which the body's core temperature falls below 98.6°F or 37°C.

hypovolemic shock: Hypoperfusion that results from low blood volume.

infant: A child under 1 year of age.

infarction: Tissue death due to lack of oxygen.

inflammation: Swelling. *The patient experienced inflammation of the airway.*

insulin: A hormone that regulates glucose in the body.

intercostal muscles: Located between the ribs, intercostal muscles help move the chest cavity outward during inhalation and inward during exhalation.

intravenous: Access to the circulatory system through a vein. *The medication was administered intravenously.*

ischemia: A decrease in the blood supply to an organ or tissue due to constriction or obstruction of the blood vessels.

joint: A point where two or more bones are connected.

jugular veins: Veins that bring deoxygenated blood from the head back to the heart.

jugular vein distension: Swelling of the neck veins.

kidney: Organ of the urinary system where blood is filtered and urine is produced.

labor: Childbirth. There are three stages of labor. Labor begins with uterine contractions, followed by the fetus entering the birth canal, and ending when the baby is born and the placenta is delivered.

laceration: A break of the skin caused by a sharp and/or penetrating object.

larynx: The voice box or vocal cords.

ligament: Connective tissue that joins bone to bone.

liver: Organ in the digestive system that is responsible for several vital functions, including detoxification.

meconium: Fetal stool that may be present in the amniotic fluid that protects a fetus.

miscarriage: The spontaneous delivery of a fetus before it is able to live on its own.

myocardial: Term that refers to the heart muscle. *The patient suffered from a myocardial infarction.*

nasal flaring: A symptom that is observed when an infant in distress attempts to increase the size of the airway by expanding the nostrils.

nasopharynx: Part of the pharynx behind the nose.

nature of illness: The description of the patient's major complaint.

near-drowning: An incident in which a person survives beyond 24 hours after being submerged in water.

open injury: An injury that breaks the skin.

oropharynx: Part of the pharynx behind the mouth.

overdose: A situation in which too much medication is taken or administered.

paradoxical motion: Abnormal movement of the chest wall during inhalation and exhalation.

partial-thickness burn: A burn that affects both the epidermis and the dermis, characterized by severe pain and blistering.

penetration or puncture: An open soft-tissue injury caused by an object being pushed into the skin.

perfusion: The process of the circulatory system delivering oxygen to tissues and organs via the blood.

peripheral pulses: Pulse points in the extremities.

petechiae: Pinpoint, non-blanchable round red spots that may indicate bleeding under a patient's skin.

pharynx: Part of the airway behind the nose and mouth. The pharynx is divided into two sections: the nasopharynx and the oropharynx.

placenta: Organ through which a fetus receives oxygen and nutrients and excretes wastes. The placenta is attached to the fetus by the umbilical cord.

psychotic: An altered mental status in which the patient has lost touch with reality.

pulse: A palpable beat felt when the left ventricle of the heart contracts.

pulse oximetry: A process in which the EMT-Basic measures the amount of oxygen in a patient's blood.

radius: One of the two bones in the forearm.

respiratory distress: A condition in which a child or infant begins to increase the rate of breathing.

respiratory failure: A condition in which the patient's rate of breathing increases and his or her condition begins to deteriorate.

resuscitate: To revive, or intervene, to prevent a patient's condition from worsening.

retractions: The use of accessory muscles to increase the work of breathing.

ruptured: Broken. A term usually used to refer to the condition of an organ. *The patient's appendix was ruptured.*

sacral: A spinal column division consisting of five fused vertebrae.

seizure: A condition in which there is a rapid discharge of nerve cells in the brain. This causes rapid muscle contractions that create erratic movements of the body. Altered mental status is often observed in patients who suffer from seizures.

sensation: Feeling or sense. EMT-Basics will often check for sensation in a patient's extremities to rule out a spinal injury.

sepsis: A toxic condition that results from the spread of bacteria throughout the body.

shock: Hypoperfusion of the organs.

stress: Tension in the mind or body caused by physical, emotional, or mental factors.

stridor: A harsh sound during breathing that may indicate an upper airway obstruction.

stroke: A condition caused by an interruption in blood supply to the brain. If the supply is not restored quickly, brain cells begin to die.

subcutaneous: Beneath or under all the other layers of skin.

sublingual: Administration of medication under the tongue.

superficial burn: A burn that affects only the epidermis and results in redness and minor pain. Sunburns are examples of superficial burns.

systolic blood pressure: The measurement of pressure in the arteries when the heart contracts, or beats, to pump blood.

tachycardia: A condition in which a patient exhibits a rapid pulse.

tachypnea: A condition in which a patient exhibits rapid breathing.

tendons: Fibrous connective tissue that joins a muscle to another body part, usually a bone.

thoracic: Referring to the chest cavity.

thorax: Structure made up of the 12 pairs of ribs and the sternum.

tibia: Bone of the lower leg.

trachea: The windpipe.

twisting injury: An injury that is caused by turning a body part in the opposite direction.

umbilical cord: Connecting cord between the fetus and the placenta.

uterus: Female reproductive organ where a fetus grows and develops.

vagina: A canal that leads from the uterus to the vaginal opening in females.

vein: A structure of the vascular system that carries blood to the heart.

vertebrae: Spinal bone.

vomit: The act of disgorging the stomach's contents.

wound: An injury

Additional Topic to Review

- Common terms used by EMS personnel

Practice

Directions (1–8): Select the best answer for each question or incomplete statement.

1. Which organ of the urinary system produces urine?

   A. liver
   B. kidney
   C. vagina
   D. diaphragm

2. A condition in which there is a rapid discharge of nerve cells in the brain is called

   A. epilepsy.
   B. stroke.
   C. seizure.
   D. hypoperfusion.

3. A pain in the chest experienced when the heart does not receive enough oxygen is called

   A. angina.
   B. cyanosis.
   C. sepsis.
   D. ischemia.

4. Which of these is a hormone that regulates glucose in the body?

   A. diabetes
   B. myocardial
   C. insulin
   D. allergen

5. The structure of the female reproductive system in which the fetus grows and develops is called

   A. uterus.
   B. vagina.
   C. placenta.
   D. sacral.

6. Which condition results in the body's core temperature rising above 98.6°F?

   A. hypothermia
   B. hypoglycemia
   C. hyperthermia
   D. hyperventilation

7. An acute mental disturbance often characterized by confusion is called

   A. dementia.
   B. delirium.
   C. psychosis.
   D. stress.

8. An injury to the abdomen that involves protruding organs is called a(n)

   A. hematoma.
   B. contusion.
   C. laceration.
   D. evisceration.

Answers

1. **B.** The *kidney* is an organ the produces urine. The liver is part of the digestive system and the vagina is a part of the female reproductive system.

2. **C.** A rapid discharge of nerve cells in the brain can cause a *seizure*.

3. **A.** *Angina* occurs when the heart does not receive enough oxygen.

4. **C.** *Insulin* is the hormone that regulates glucose in the body. Diabetes is a condition that prevents the body from producing insulin.

5. **A.** The *uterus* is the structure in which the fetus grows and develops. The vagina is the canal that leads from the uterus to the vaginal opening and the placenta provides the fetus with oxygen and nutrients as it grows.

6. **C.** *Hyperthermia* is a condition in which the body's temperature rises above 98.6°F. Hypothermia is when the body's temperature falls below 98.6°F. Hypoglycemia is a condition in which the body's blood sugar levels are low. Hyperventilation is when the patient exhibits quick breathing.

7. **B.** *Delirium* is often characterized by confusion.

8. **D.** An injury to the abdomen involving protruding organs is called an *evisceration*.

B. Anatomy

As an EMT-Basic, you'll be required to speak with both patients and medical professionals. You should speak to patients differently than you speak to medical professionals. When speaking to patients, you should use common terms with which they're familiar. When speaking to medical professionals, however, you should use medical terminology.

Knowing the correct terms for different anatomical positions and lines will help you communicate vital information in a way that all professionals involved in the treatment of the patient will understand.

1. Anatomic Terminology

This section presents an overview of anatomic terminology. All directional and anatomic terms refer to the patient in the *anatomic position*, which is the patient standing upright with his or her face and palms facing forward. Having a starting point enables medical professionals to understand which body parts you're referring to when explaining a medical emergency. The following list contains some of the positional and directional terms you should already know.

Positional terminology:

Fowler's: Patient is seated with knees bent.

prone: Patient is lying on chest, facing down.

semi-Fowler's: Patient is seated with legs straight.

shock: Patient is lying on back with legs raised off ground.

supine: Patient is lying on back, facing up.

Trendelenburg: Patient is lying on back with head lower than legs.

Directional terminology:

abduction: To move away from the body.

adduction: To move toward the body.

anterior: Toward the front of the body.

auxiliary line: Imaginary vertical line running through the body that separates the front and back halves.

bilateral: Both sides of the body.

contralateral: Opposite side of the body.

distal: Away from the trunk.

extension: Act of straightening an extremity.

flexion: Act of bending an extremity.

inferior: Toward the bottom of the body.

ipsilateral: Same side of the body.

lateral: Away from the midline.

medial: Toward the midline.

midline: Imaginary vertical line running through the body that separates the left and right halves.

nipple line: Imaginary horizontal line drawn across the nipple line of the chest.

palmar: Palm of the hand.

plantar: Bottom of the foot.

posterior: Toward the back of the body.

proximal: Toward the trunk of the body.

recovery: Patient is reclined on the left side to maintain a patent airway. The knees are slightly bent, and the arms and legs are crossed to help stabilize the position.

superior: Toward the top of the body.

umbilicus: Imaginary horizontal line drawn across the level of the abdomen.

unilateral: One side of the body.

Additional Topic to Review

- Common prefixes and suffixes used in medical terminology

Practice

Directions (1–5): Select the best answer for each question or incomplete statement.

1. A unilateral injury refers to an injury that is on

    A. one side of the body.
    B. the left side of the body.
    C. the right side of the body.
    D. the front of the body.

2. You find a patient seated with the knees bent. What position is the patient in?

    A. prone
    B. supine
    C. Fowler's
    D. semi-Fowler's

3. During a transport, you call the hospital and tell them that you're transporting a 45-year-old male complaining of "unilateral radius pain" and "an abrasion distal to the left patella." What does this mean?

    A. The patient has pain on the thumb side of his wrist and a laceration on the lower portion of his leg.
    B. The patient has pain on the thumb side of his wrist and a laceration on his upper knee.
    C. The patient has pain on both sides of his hand and a laceration on the upper portion of his leg.
    D. The patient has pain on both sides of his wrist and a laceration on his upper knee.

4. Your patient has a plantar injury. Where is your patient injured?

    A. on the back of the head
    B. on the bottom of the foot
    C. on the palm of the hand
    D. on the left side of the abdomen

5. The line that divides the body into anterior and posterior halves is called the

    A. medial.
    B. midline.
    C. midclavicular line.
    D. midaxillary line.

Answers

1. **A.** A unilateral injury would be on *one side of the body*.

2. **C.** The Fowler's position is when the patient is *seated with the knees bent*. The semi-Fowler's position is when the patient is seated with the legs straight.

3. **A.** The phrases "unilateral radius pain" and "an abrasion distal to the left patella" mean that the patient is experiencing pain on *the thumb side of his wrist*, and the patient has *a laceration on the lower portion of his leg*.

4. **B.** Plantar refers to *the bottom of the foot*.

5. **D.** The *midaxillary line* divides the body into anterior and posterior halves. The midline divides the body into right and left halves. Medial means toward the midline, and the midclavicular lines divide the clavicles in two and extend through the trunk.

C. Body Systems

As an EMT-Basic, you should already be familiar with the physiology and anatomy of the human body and the functions of different body systems. In this section, you'll find a brief review of the different body systems and their functions.

1. The Respiratory System

The respiratory system is made up of the parts of the body through which air passes, including the mouth, nose, lungs, pharynx, trachea, and bronchi. Collectively, these passageways are known as the *airway*. The main function of the respiratory system is to take oxygen into the lungs through either the nose or the mouth and then release carbon dioxide back through the nose or the mouth.

> **Tip: You'll find a diagram and a more detailed explanation of the different parts of the respiratory system in Chapter VI, "Airway."**

The respiratory system further breaks down into the upper respiratory system and the lower respiratory system, which work together to inhale and exhale air. The *upper respiratory system* consists of the nose, nasal cavity, and pharynx (throat). The *lower respiratory system* consists of the larynx (voice box), trachea (windpipe), bronchi, and lung tissues. When you breathe in oxygen, it passes through the upper respiratory system into the lower respiratory system and then to the lungs, where it's exchanged for carbon dioxide, which is released from the body through the mouth or nose when you exhale.

Each lung works independently of the other to ensure that if one lung is damaged, the other lung remains functional. The left lung is smaller than the right lung to accommodate the heart. The lungs are divided into sections called *lobes*. The left lung has two lobes and the right lung has three lobes.

The EMT-Basic should be familiar with how the respiratory system works and be able to recognize the signs of irregular breathing. You must ensure that the patient's airway remains open and clear at all times. A blocked airway can result in death if not properly treated.

2. The Circulatory System

The circulatory system comprises the heart, blood vessels, and blood. The heart is the main organ of the circulatory system. It's also one of the most important muscles in the body. Its main function is to pump blood to other organs throughout the body for survival. The heart has four chambers: two upper chambers, called the *atria*, and two lower chambers, called the *ventricles*. The atria pump blood into the ventricles, and the ventricles pump blood out of the heart. One-way valves pump blood in one direction and prevent blood from pumping back into the heart. The heart contains cells that generate electrical impulses that cause the heart to beat. The number of times the heart beats per minute is called the *heart rate*. A normal resting heart rate for an adult can range from 60–80 beats per minute.

> **Tip:** The heart can pump more than 3,000 gallons of blood per day.

The heart pumps blood through the body's blood vessels, which deliver blood to the organs. *Arteries* are blood vessels that carry blood away from the heart. The largest artery in the human body is the *aorta*, which is connected to the left ventricle of the heart and travels straight down the spine to the abdomen. Arteries expand and contract with each beat of the heart to help push blood through the body. These vessels branch off into smaller vessels called *arterioles*. Arterioles are responsible for regulating blood flow and blood pressure. These small vessels branch off into even smaller blood vessels called *capillaries*. Gas exchange takes place within the thin walls of capillaries. These vessels join together to form a *venule*, which returns blood to the heart. Unlike arteries, which branch into smaller vessels the farther they are from the heart, venules expand as they get closer to the heart and become *veins*. The largest veins in the body are the *inferior vena cava* and the *superior vena cava*. The blood travels directly into the heart from the inferior vena cava and the superior vena cava.

> **Tip:** The aorta has a diameter the size of your thumb.

Blood is an important bodily fluid that serves many functions throughout the body. It's made up of the following components:

- Red blood cells: contain hemoglobin, which transports oxygen and carbon dioxide in the blood
- White blood cells: help the body fight off disease and infection
- Platelets: responsible for blood clot formation
- Plasma: liquid part of the blood that carries the rest of the components through the circulatory system

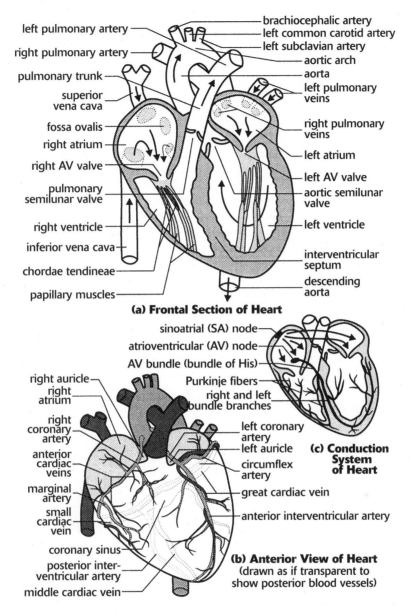

(a) Frontal Section of Heart

left pulmonary artery

right pulmonary artery

pulmonary trunk

superior vena cava

fossa ovalis

right atrium

right AV valve

pulmonary semilunar valve

right ventricle

inferior vena cava

chordae tendineae

papillary muscles

brachiocephalic artery

left common carotid artery

left subclavian artery

aortic arch

aorta

left pulmonary veins

right pulmonary veins

left atrium

left AV valve

aortic semilunar valve

left ventricle

interventricular septum

descending aorta

sinoatrial (SA) node

atrioventricular (AV) node

AV bundle (bundle of His)

Purkinje fibers

right and left bundle branches

(c) Conduction System of Heart

right auricle

right atrium

right coronary artery

anterior cardiac veins

marginal artery

small cardiac vein

coronary sinus

posterior interventricular artery

middle cardiac vein

left coronary artery

left auricle

circumflex artery

great cardiac vein

anterior interventricular artery

(b) Anterior View of Heart
(drawn as if transparent to show posterior blood vessels)

The pathway of blood through the chambers and valves of the heart.

3. The Skeletal System

The skeletal system involves the bones of the body. The skeletal system contains 206 bones that are responsible for the structure, protection, and movement of the body. Bones enable us to stand upright, protect our organs, and allow us to move. The skeletal system further breaks down into the axial skeleton and the appendicular skeleton.

a. Axial Skeleton

The axial skeleton contains the skull, spinal column, and ribs. It's very important for the EMT-Basic to be familiar with the different bones that make up the skull. The skull contains the cranium and the bones of the face. The *cranium*, which consists of eight bones, protects the brain. Bones fit together with joints called *sutures*, which enable the bones to move slightly without breaking. The face consists of 14 bones and includes the *mandible* (lower jaw), *maxilla* (upper jaw), *zygomatic bones* (cheekbones), *nasal bones* (nose), and *orbits* (eye sockets).

The spinal column, rib cage, and sternum form the *thoracic cavity*, which provides the shape for the chest and protects the organs. The spinal column's main functions are to provide structure and support for the body and protect the spinal cord. The bones of the spinal column are called *vertebrae*, and there are 33 vertebrae in the spinal column. The vertebrae stack on top of each other, with soft discs between them for support.

The *rib cage* consists of 12 pairs of ribs. Each rib is attached to the back of the body to one of the thoracic vertebrae. The first 10 ribs are attached to the front of the body to the sternum. The last two ribs are called floating ribs because they extend laterally from the vertebrae. The *sternum* (breastbone) is an important bone of the body because it protects the heart. It is split into three sections of bones: *manubrium* (upper), *body* (middle), and *xyphoid* (lower).

b. Appendicular Skeleton

The appendicular skeleton contains the rest of the bones in the body. It's impossible to cover each bone of the appendicular skeletal system in this section, so we'll give an overview of some of the bones in the lower and upper parts of the skeleton. The EMT-Basic exam asks questions about the many different bones located throughout the body, so be sure that you're familiar with all of the bones in the body.

The lower part of the skeletal system refers to the pelvis, legs, and feet. The *pelvis* is the connecting point between the lower skeleton and the spinal column. It's split into left and right halves, and each side contains the *ilium* (hip bone), *ischium* (lower pelvis), and *pubis bones*. The ischium attaches to the *femur* (thigh bone), which is the largest bone of the body. The lower femur attaches to the *tibia* (shin bone) and *fibula* of the lower leg. The point of connection between the femur and the tibia and fibula is called the *patella* (kneecap). The fibula connects to the ankle bone. The bones of the feet are called *tarsals*, which branch into the *phalanges* (toes).

The upper part of the skeletal system includes the trunk, arms, and hands. The arms connect to the shoulder girdle, which consists of two bones: the *scapula*, which attaches to the rib cage, and the *clavicle* (collarbone). The shoulder bones connect to the *humerus*, the largest bone of the upper skeleton. The humerus attaches to the lower arm bones: the *radius* and the *ulna*. The radius runs along the thumb side of the lower arm and the ulna runs along the pinky finger side of the lower arm. These bones connect to the *carpal bones*, *metacarpal bones*, and *phalanges* (fingers) of the hand.

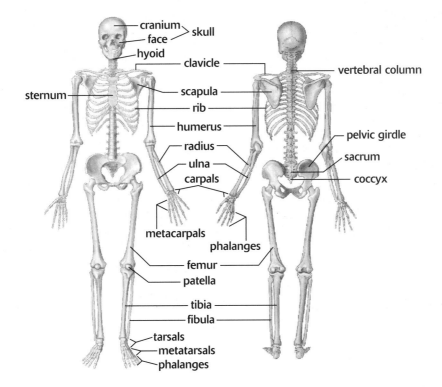

Major bones of the axial and appendicular skeletons.

4. The Muscular System

The muscular system includes the muscles of the body, which attach to the skeletal system. Muscles enable the bones to move. They contract and then relax, which causes the body to move in any direction. If you didn't have any muscles, you wouldn't be able to move. Muscles split into three different types: skeletal, cardiac, and smooth.

Tip: Muscle tissue accounts for half of a person's body weight.

Skeletal muscles attach to the bones of the body. The primary function of the skeletal muscles is to provide movement. These muscles are also called *voluntary muscles* because you use your brain to move these muscles. When you want to move your hand, a signal travels from the brain to your hand to cause it to move. These muscles account for the greatest amount of muscle mass within the body.

The heart is made up of *cardiac muscles*. These muscles keep the heart beating and blood moving throughout the body. These muscles are called *involuntary muscles* because they contract and relax on their own. You don't have to think about the muscles that make your heart beat.

Smooth muscles control the flow through the tubes of the body. They move blood through the blood vessels and food through the digestive system. (The digestive system is explained later in this chapter.) These are also involuntary muscles.

5. The Integumentary System

The skin is not only the largest organ of the human body, but also one of the most important. Skin is part of the integumentary system. It protects the body from environmental factors, such as extreme heat and cold. The skin prevents us from drying out and prevents bacteria and other organisms from entering the body. Skin also plays an important role in regulating body temperature. When your body gets too hot, the blood vessels dilate, and sweat is released. As sweat evaporates, your body cools down. When your body gets too cold, the blood vessels contract to prevent heat loss. Skin is also a sensory organ that contains receptors that can detect heat, cold, touch, pressure, and pain. These receptors transmit information to the central nervous system.

The skin has three layers: *epidermis* (outer layer), *dermis* (middle layer), and *subcutaneous* (innermost layer). The sweat glands, hair follicles, blood vessels, and nerve endings are found in the dermis. The subcutaneous layer connects the skin to the body's tissues and stores fat, which aids the body with insulation and storing energy.

6. The Nervous System

The nervous system is a highly complex system that controls all of the functions of the human body, including voluntary and involuntary activities, thoughts, memory, and emotion. It's split into two components: the central nervous system and the peripheral nervous system.

The brain and spinal cord make up the *central nervous system*, which regulates the body's functions and is responsible for communication and making decisions. The *peripheral nervous system* consists of the sensory and motor nerves in the rest of the body. *Sensory* nerves carry information from the body to the central nervous system. These nerves enable the brain to make decisions using information about the environment, pain, pressure, and body position. *Motor* nerves carry information from the central nervous system to the body. Signals from the motor nerves enable the movement of skeletal muscles.

The brain controls all of the functions of the body. It's one of the largest organs in the body, and it's also one of the most complicated. It sends signals to other body parts, and it controls the movement of muscles and nerves and the functions of the organs. The brain is divided into four different sections or lobes:

- Frontal lobe: controls the body's movement, reasoning skills, language, and cognition
- Parietal lobe: controls the body's senses and sensory information such as pressure, touch, and pain
- Temporal lobe: controls hearing, language, and memories
- Occipital lobe: controls vision

The lobes of the brain further divide into smaller sections:

- Brain stem: controls heart rate, respiratory rate, swallowing, and coughing
- Diencephalon: controls emotions, hunger, thirst, and body temperature
- Cerebrum: controls the senses, including hearing, vision, taste, smell, and touch; also controls personality
- Cerebellum: controls balance and fine motor skills

Because the brain is one of the most important organs of the body, it needs a lot of protection. In addition to the cranial cavity, it's protected by different coverings, or *meninges*, that are split into three layers: *dura mater* (outer later), *arachnoid layer* (middle layer), and *pia layer* (inner layer). It's also surrounded by a cerebrospinal fluid that circulates throughout the brain and spinal cord.

The brain contains 12 pairs of cranial nerves that are responsible for the sensory and motor functions of the body. You should be familiar with the different parts and nerves within the brain and how they work.

Tip: The average brain weighs between 3 and 3.5 pounds.

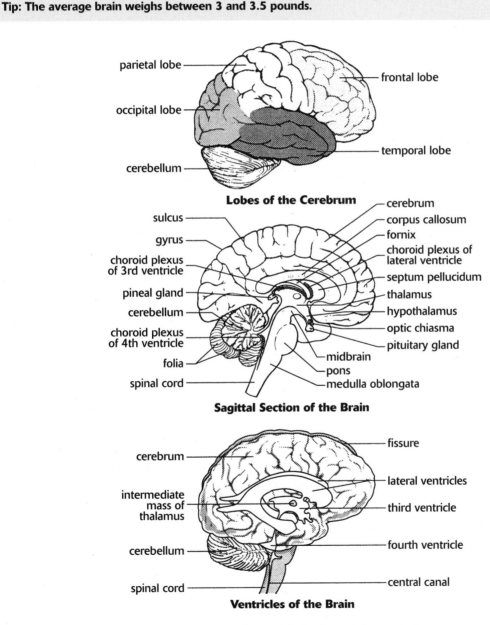

Lobes of the Cerebrum

Sagittal Section of the Brain

Ventricles of the Brain

The four lobes of the adult brain and the cerebellum.

7. The Gastrointestinal System

The gastrointestinal system, also called the digestive system, provides the human body with nourishment and energy through the digestion of food. This system breaks the food we eat into the essential nutrients we need for survival. The process of digestion is divided into two stages. The first state is actual *digestion*, during which food breaks down into molecules that the body can use for energy. The second stage is *absorption*. In the absorption stage, the molecules that result from actual digestion are absorbed into the body for use.

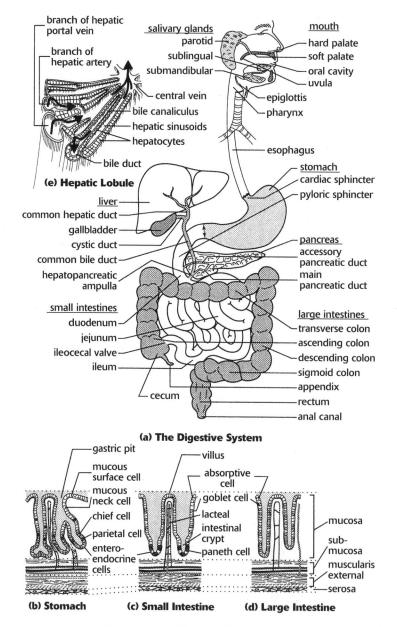

The parts of the digestive system.

Anatomically, the gastrointestinal system is made up of two distinct sections: the gastrointestinal tract and the alimentary canal. The *gastrointestinal tract* includes all of the organs and structures used in digestion. The *alimentary canal* is the long, continuous tube that runs between the mouth and the anal opening. Food travels through the alimentary canal as it's digested.

The process of digestion begins in the mouth as you chew your food. Chewing grinds up food, making it easier to swallow. Saliva produced by the parotid glands contains digestive enzymes that assist in this early stage of digestion. As you swallow food, it passes through the *pharynx* (throat) and into the *esophagus*, which is a muscular tube that secretes mucus and expands and contracts to push food downward into the stomach. No digestion occurs in the esophagus.

The *stomach* serves as a holding tank in the digestive process. The stomach produces digestive enzymes that contribute to the breakdown of food, and this is where protein digestion takes place. When these enzymes are released, the stomach converts the food into *chime*, which is a semi-fluid mass of undigested food that is passed into the small intestine.

The *small intestine* is a long tube that measures 10–12 feet in length. This section of the gastrointestinal system is responsible for the majority of digestion and absorption in the body. The small intestine has three distinct parts: the *duodenum* (first portion), the *jejunum* (middle portion), and the *ileum* (last portion). The small intestine leads into the large intestine. The two connect at the *ileocecal valve*. The *large intestine*, also called the *colon*, is the site of the last steps in the digestive process. The absorption of water stops, thereby solidifying the food. Intestinal bacteria help to convert proteins into various substances that may be absorbed or eliminated.

A substance called *bile* is produced by the liver. Bile assists in the breakdown of fats and metabolizes carbohydrates and proteins. It also serves as a filter for toxic substances and stores glucose and vitamins. The *gallbladder* houses bile made by the liver. When necessary, the gallbladder excretes this bile into the large intestine. The *pancreas* is responsible for the secretion of some digestive enzymes and hormones that regulate blood sugar. Finally, the colon pushes the remaining indigestible food into the *rectum*. The rectum forces these waste products out of the body through the *anus*. Liquid waste is eliminated by the *urinary system*.

8. The Urinary System

The urinary system produces, stores, and eliminates urine. It's composed of two kidneys, two ureters, a bladder, and a urethra. The *kidneys* filter blood and remove toxins and then send these toxins to the bladder for elimination. The kidneys also regulate blood volume and the body's pH level. The kidneys need a constant supply of blood. An EMT-Basic should keep this in mind when treating patients in a state of *hypoperfusion*, a condition that causes the flow of blood from the kidneys to stop and redirect to the heart, lungs, and brain. If blood flow to the kidneys stops, kidney failure could result. If the kidneys fail, toxins can build up in the body and lead to infection or death.

The *ureters* are muscular tubes that move urine from the kidneys to the bladder. The bladder stores the urine until it's ready to be eliminated by way of the *urethra*, a tube that connects the bladder to the genitals.

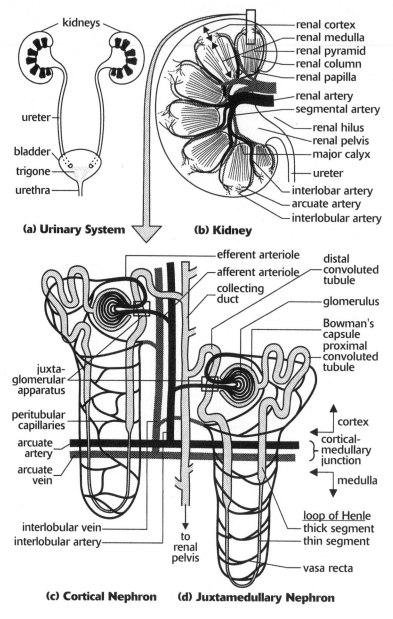

(a) Urinary System   **(b) Kidney**

(c) Cortical Nephron   **(d) Juxtamedullary Nephron**

The urinary system.

9. The Endocrine System

The endocrine system is a highly complex system composed of a series of glands located throughout the body. These glands produce chemicals known as *hormones*. Hormones help regulate the activities and functions of many other body systems. The structures that make up the endocrine system include the pituitary, pineal, parathyroid, thyroid, and adrenal glands.

The *pituitary gland* is the primary gland of the endocrine system. Often called the "master gland," this tiny gland, which is located at the base of the brain, is responsible for the secretion of hormones that move throughout the body and stimulate the production of various hormones in other glands. Among the most important hormones released by the pituitary gland is growth hormone, which is responsible for normal growth and development during childhood.

The *pineal gland* produces melatonin, which is thought to inhibit the production of gonadotropin. It's also thought to play a role in the control of sleep patterns. The *parathyroid glands* produce hormones that regulate the body's levels of calcium and phosphorus. The *thyroid gland* secretes hormones that regulate metabolism, which plays a vital role in digestion.

The *adrenal glands* are composed of two separate endocrine organs: adrenal cortex and adrenal medulla. The *adrenal cortex* secretes hormones that help control blood sugar and burn proteins and fats. It also plays an important role in the body's response to fever, illness, and injury. The *adrenal medulla* is responsible for the production of epinephrine, which can elevate heart rate, open airways to increase respiration, and increase muscular blood flow. The release of epinephrine is often a reaction to a sudden, intense emotion.

Some body parts are not actually part of the endocrine system but contain endocrine tissue. The pancreas, for example, produces insulin and glucagon. These two hormones are vital to the regulation of blood sugar.

The endocrine system also plays an important role in sexual development. The testicles and ovaries are both endocrine organs that produce testosterone and estrogen and progesterone, respectively.

10. The Reproductive System

The reproductive system consists of sexual organs, gonads, and genitalia. Males and females have different reproductive organs. The female *gonads* are the ovaries and the male gonads are the *testes* (testicles). Gonads secrete hormones such as testosterone in males and estrogen and progesterone in females. They also produce eggs in females and sperm in males. These are necessary to create another life.

The male's reproductive organs are located outside the body. These organs include the testes (testicles), the duct system, the accessory glands, and the penis. In a mature male, the testes produce and store sperm. The male's duct system includes the epididymis and the vas deferens. The *epididymis* is a set of coiled tubes that connects to the *vas deferens,* which is a muscular tube used to transport semen, the fluid that contains sperm. The epididymis and testes are located in a sac called the *scrotum.* This sac helps regulate the temperature of the testes so they can produce sperm. The accessory glands include the seminal vesicles and prostate gland. These provide fluids to lubricate the duct system and nourish the sperm. The seminal vesicles are attached to the vas deferens and the prostate gland is situated near the base of the urethra, which eliminates urine and transports semen outside the body through the penis.

The penis is made up of a shaft and glans. The *shaft* is the main part of the penis and the *glans* is the tip or head. Semen and urine pass through a small opening at the end of the glans. The male sexual organs work together to produce and release semen into the reproductive system of the female during sexual intercourse.

Unlike the male's reproductive organs, the female's reproductive organs are located inside the body. These organs include the vulva, labia, vagina, uterus, fallopian tubes, and ovaries. The *vulva* is the external part of the reproductive organs, which covers the vaginal opening. The *labia* are two flaps of skin surrounding the vaginal opening. The labia open up to the *vagina*, which is a long, muscular tube that extends to the uterus. The vaginal walls can stretch and contract to accommodate a penis during intercourse and a fetus during childbirth.

The *uterus* is the organ responsible for contracting and expelling the fetus during childbirth. The two *fallopian tubes* connect the uterus to the *ovaries*, which produce, store, and release eggs into the fallopian tubes in a process called *ovulation*. Ovulation is the point in a woman's cycle when a mature egg is released from the ovary. A woman can get pregnant during ovulation.

Tip: The female reproductive system is covered in greater detail in Chapter VIII, "Medical Emergencies."

Additional Topics to Review

- Functions of the different parts of the respiratory system
- Blood circulation
- Bones of the skeletal system
- Vertebrae of the spinal column
- Muscles of the muscular system
- Tissues of the body
- Divisions and functions of the brain
- Nerves of the brain
- Differences between an adult's brain and a child's brain
- Diet and nutrition
- Hyperglycemia and hypoglycemia
- Endocrine disorders
- Sexual intercourse and reproduction
- Other systems of the body, such as the lymphatic and immune systems

Practice

Directions (1–10): Select the best answer for each question or incomplete statement.

1. What is the largest organ of the human body?

   A. brain
   B. heart
   C. skin
   D. femur

2. Cortisol, which helps control blood sugar, is produced by the

   A. pituitary gland.
   B. adrenal glands.
   C. thyroid gland.
   D. pineal gland.

3. Which of the following structures is part of the alimentary canal?

    A. gallbladder
    B. parotid glands
    C. pharynx
    D. tongue

4. Which of the following are responsible for regulating blood flow and blood pressure?

    A. arterioles
    B. capillaries
    C. venules
    D. vas deferens

5. A 30-year-old man has fallen off his roof and hit his head. You arrive at the scene and he is sitting up, coherent, and talking. He says he has a headache and can't smell anything. This can be an indication of an injury to the

    A. parietal lobe.
    B. frontal lobe.
    C. occipital lobe.
    D. temporal lobe.

6. A large amount of which of the following can lead to thrombosis?

    A. bile
    B. white blood cells
    C. platelets
    D. insulin

7. Which of these are responsible for protecting the brain?

    A. meninges
    B. brain stem
    C. cranial nerves
    D. cerebrum

8. When the body gets overheated, blood vessels in the dermis layer of the skin

    A. contract and release sweat.
    B. dilate and release sweat.
    C. contract to prevent heat loss.
    D. dilate to prevent heat loss.

9. The part of the body where protein digestion takes place is called the

   A. stomach.
   B. colon.
   C. small intestine.
   D. large intestine.

10. The purpose of the esophagus is to

    A. digest food.
    B. move food through the digestive tract.
    C. produce enzymes to break down food.
    D. covert food to chime.

Answers

1. **C.** While the brain is one of the largest organs in the body, *skin* is actually the largest organ of the human body. The heart is the main organ of the circulatory system, and the femur is the largest bone in the human body.

2. **B.** The *adrenal glands* are responsible for producing cortisol.

3. **C.** Because the alimentary canal runs from the mouth to the anus, the *pharynx*, or throat, is one of its components.

4. **A.** The *arterioles* are responsible for regulating blood flow and blood pressure.

5. **B.** A *frontal lobe* injury is often associated with damage to the olfactory bulbs, so patients may complain of a reduced or an altered sense of smell.

6. **C.** If the blood contains a large amount of *platelets*, blood clots can lead to the formation of thrombosis.

7. **A.** The brain is protected by the cranial cavity, cerebrospinal fluid, and *meninges*.

8. **B.** When the body gets too hot, the blood vessels *dilate,* or open up, *and release sweat*. When the sweat evaporates from the skin, the body cools down.

9. **A.** The *stomach* serves as a holding tank in the digestive process where protein digestion takes place.

10. **B.** The esophagus is a muscular tube that *moves food through the digestive tract*.

XV. Full-Length Practice Test with Answer Explanations

The Practice Test is designed to assess how far you've come in your studies and help you identify topics that still require attention. Candidates taking the NREMT cognitive exam have two hours to complete the test. Remember, you may take a test that differs from the NREMT in terms of the number and types of questions you'll be required to answer and the length of time you will have to complete the exam. This Practice Test includes 100 questions that cover everything from airway obstructions to ambulance operations. The questions on this test are grouped by subject. This will help you identify targeted areas that you should continue studying.

You should only spend 2½ hours on the Practice Test. When you're done, note all of the questions that you answered incorrectly and read the answer explanations carefully. You should review the topics that presented difficulties in your next study session.

Answer Sheet

1 Ⓐ Ⓑ Ⓒ Ⓓ	36 Ⓐ Ⓑ Ⓒ Ⓓ	71 Ⓐ Ⓑ Ⓒ Ⓓ
2 Ⓐ Ⓑ Ⓒ Ⓓ	37 Ⓐ Ⓑ Ⓒ Ⓓ	72 Ⓐ Ⓑ Ⓒ Ⓓ
3 Ⓐ Ⓑ Ⓒ Ⓓ	38 Ⓐ Ⓑ Ⓒ Ⓓ	73 Ⓐ Ⓑ Ⓒ Ⓓ
4 Ⓐ Ⓑ Ⓒ Ⓓ	39 Ⓐ Ⓑ Ⓒ Ⓓ	74 Ⓐ Ⓑ Ⓒ Ⓓ
5 Ⓐ Ⓑ Ⓒ Ⓓ	40 Ⓐ Ⓑ Ⓒ Ⓓ	75 Ⓐ Ⓑ Ⓒ Ⓓ
6 Ⓐ Ⓑ Ⓒ Ⓓ	41 Ⓐ Ⓑ Ⓒ Ⓓ	76 Ⓐ Ⓑ Ⓒ Ⓓ
7 Ⓐ Ⓑ Ⓒ Ⓓ	42 Ⓐ Ⓑ Ⓒ Ⓓ	77 Ⓐ Ⓑ Ⓒ Ⓓ
8 Ⓐ Ⓑ Ⓒ Ⓓ	43 Ⓐ Ⓑ Ⓒ Ⓓ	78 Ⓐ Ⓑ Ⓒ Ⓓ
9 Ⓐ Ⓑ Ⓒ Ⓓ	44 Ⓐ Ⓑ Ⓒ Ⓓ	79 Ⓐ Ⓑ Ⓒ Ⓓ
10 Ⓐ Ⓑ Ⓒ Ⓓ	45 Ⓐ Ⓑ Ⓒ Ⓓ	80 Ⓐ Ⓑ Ⓒ Ⓓ
11 Ⓐ Ⓑ Ⓒ Ⓓ	46 Ⓐ Ⓑ Ⓒ Ⓓ	81 Ⓐ Ⓑ Ⓒ Ⓓ
12 Ⓐ Ⓑ Ⓒ Ⓓ	47 Ⓐ Ⓑ Ⓒ Ⓓ	82 Ⓐ Ⓑ Ⓒ Ⓓ
13 Ⓐ Ⓑ Ⓒ Ⓓ	48 Ⓐ Ⓑ Ⓒ Ⓓ	83 Ⓐ Ⓑ Ⓒ Ⓓ
14 Ⓐ Ⓑ Ⓒ Ⓓ	49 Ⓐ Ⓑ Ⓒ Ⓓ	84 Ⓐ Ⓑ Ⓒ Ⓓ
15 Ⓐ Ⓑ Ⓒ Ⓓ	50 Ⓐ Ⓑ Ⓒ Ⓓ	85 Ⓐ Ⓑ Ⓒ Ⓓ
16 Ⓐ Ⓑ Ⓒ Ⓓ	51 Ⓐ Ⓑ Ⓒ Ⓓ	86 Ⓐ Ⓑ Ⓒ Ⓓ
17 Ⓐ Ⓑ Ⓒ Ⓓ	52 Ⓐ Ⓑ Ⓒ Ⓓ	87 Ⓐ Ⓑ Ⓒ Ⓓ
18 Ⓐ Ⓑ Ⓒ Ⓓ	53 Ⓐ Ⓑ Ⓒ Ⓓ	88 Ⓐ Ⓑ Ⓒ Ⓓ
19 Ⓐ Ⓑ Ⓒ Ⓓ	54 Ⓐ Ⓑ Ⓒ Ⓓ	89 Ⓐ Ⓑ Ⓒ Ⓓ
20 Ⓐ Ⓑ Ⓒ Ⓓ	55 Ⓐ Ⓑ Ⓒ Ⓓ	90 Ⓐ Ⓑ Ⓒ Ⓓ
21 Ⓐ Ⓑ Ⓒ Ⓓ	56 Ⓐ Ⓑ Ⓒ Ⓓ	91 Ⓐ Ⓑ Ⓒ Ⓓ
22 Ⓐ Ⓑ Ⓒ Ⓓ	57 Ⓐ Ⓑ Ⓒ Ⓓ	92 Ⓐ Ⓑ Ⓒ Ⓓ
23 Ⓐ Ⓑ Ⓒ Ⓓ	58 Ⓐ Ⓑ Ⓒ Ⓓ	93 Ⓐ Ⓑ Ⓒ Ⓓ
24 Ⓐ Ⓑ Ⓒ Ⓓ	59 Ⓐ Ⓑ Ⓒ Ⓓ	94 Ⓐ Ⓑ Ⓒ Ⓓ
25 Ⓐ Ⓑ Ⓒ Ⓓ	60 Ⓐ Ⓑ Ⓒ Ⓓ	95 Ⓐ Ⓑ Ⓒ Ⓓ
26 Ⓐ Ⓑ Ⓒ Ⓓ	61 Ⓐ Ⓑ Ⓒ Ⓓ	96 Ⓐ Ⓑ Ⓒ Ⓓ
27 Ⓐ Ⓑ Ⓒ Ⓓ	62 Ⓐ Ⓑ Ⓒ Ⓓ	97 Ⓐ Ⓑ Ⓒ Ⓓ
28 Ⓐ Ⓑ Ⓒ Ⓓ	63 Ⓐ Ⓑ Ⓒ Ⓓ	98 Ⓐ Ⓑ Ⓒ Ⓓ
29 Ⓐ Ⓑ Ⓒ Ⓓ	64 Ⓐ Ⓑ Ⓒ Ⓓ	99 Ⓐ Ⓑ Ⓒ Ⓓ
30 Ⓐ Ⓑ Ⓒ Ⓓ	65 Ⓐ Ⓑ Ⓒ Ⓓ	100 Ⓐ Ⓑ Ⓒ Ⓓ
31 Ⓐ Ⓑ Ⓒ Ⓓ	66 Ⓐ Ⓑ Ⓒ Ⓓ	
32 Ⓐ Ⓑ Ⓒ Ⓓ	67 Ⓐ Ⓑ Ⓒ Ⓓ	
33 Ⓐ Ⓑ Ⓒ Ⓓ	68 Ⓐ Ⓑ Ⓒ Ⓓ	
34 Ⓐ Ⓑ Ⓒ Ⓓ	69 Ⓐ Ⓑ Ⓒ Ⓓ	
35 Ⓐ Ⓑ Ⓒ Ⓓ	70 Ⓐ Ⓑ Ⓒ Ⓓ	

CUT HERE

Directions (1–100): Select the best answer for each question or incomplete statement.

1. The EMT-Basic is responsible for the safety of all persons present on the scene. What is the proper order of priority for scene safety?

    A. the EMT-Basic, his partner, the patient, bystanders
    B. the patient, the EMT-Basic, his partner, bystanders
    C. the patient, bystanders, the EMT-Basic, his partner
    D. bystanders, the patient, the EMT-Basic, his partner

2. Many significant advances in prehospital medicine have come during

    A. accidents.
    B. economic recessions.
    C. wars.
    D. political turmoil.

3. Patients who have a valid Do Not Resuscitate Order (DNR) should

    A. not be transported to the hospital.
    B. not be treated with oxygen.
    C. be treated only with oxygen.
    D. none of the above

4. You respond to the scene of a reported domestic disturbance. The police arrive before you and secure the scene. Upon your arrival, you find a teenage female sitting on the couch and vomiting into a trash can. The patient tells you that she is 17. She is frightened and unable to describe what has happened. The police suspect that the patient's aunt hit her with a baseball. The aunt is being restrained by the police, yelling that she will "sue you" if you touch the patient. You are unable to contact the patient's parents. You should

    A. transport the patient under minor consent.
    B. transport the patient under implied consent.
    C. remain on scene and monitor the patient until her parents arrive.
    D. allow the police to decide whether the patient should be transported.

5. Your crew enters a large apartment building to respond to a report of a person bleeding. As you enter, you realize that you have recently responded to two shooting incidents at this complex. You hear several loud voices as you approach the apartment. After discussing the issue with your partner, you decide to wait around the corner of the hallway and use a _____ radio to request law enforcement backup.

    A. mobile
    B. base station
    C. portable
    D. citizens' band (CB)

6. Indications for high-flow oxygen via a non-rebreather mask include all of the following EXCEPT

   A. cyanosis.
   B. rales.
   C. stridor.
   D. apnea.

7. Common mistakes when performing artificial ventilations with a bag-valve mask include all of the following EXCEPT

   A. failure to maintain manual maneuvers.
   B. failure to use a properly sized mask.
   C. failure to inflate the reservoir bag prior to applying the device.
   D. failure to maintain a proper mask seal.

8. Nasal cannulas supplied with proper oxygen flow can deliver up to

   A. 44% oxygen.
   B. 66% oxygen.
   C. 80% oxygen.
   D. 100% oxygen.

9. Your patient falls unconscious and within seconds you notice gurgling sounds and vomitus in his airway. After calling for help, your first action is to

   A. apply oxygen.
   B. suction the patient's oropharynx.
   C. perform the Heimlich maneuver.
   D. move the patient to the lateral recumbent position.

10. Complications of the flow-restricted, oxygen-powered ventilation device include all of the following EXCEPT

    A. risk of pneumothorax.
    B. risk of oxygen toxicity.
    C. inability to gauge compliance.
    D. gastric insufflations.

11. In order to reduce the pressure of compressed oxygen to a usable and comfortable level, a _____ is necessary.

    A. flowmeter
    B. regulator
    C. nonrebreather mask
    D. reservoir

12. When providing artificial respiration to patients of different ages, it is important to select

    A. the appropriate size mask.
    B. the appropriate size bag.
    C. the appropriate ventilation rate.
    D. all of the above

13. A portion of each breath occupies space known as the anatomical dead space. The remaining portion is available for

    A. alveolar ventilation.
    B. minute ventilation.
    C. artificial ventilation.
    D. lung ventilation.

14. You respond to a call at a home where you find an elderly man who is severely cyanotic and not breathing. His wife says that he hasn't taken a breath for several minutes. You find a weak carotid pulse at 60 beats per minute. You should ventilate this patient at a rate of

    A. 20 breaths per minute, regardless of exam findings.
    B. 20 breaths per minute until his heart rate improves.
    C. 24 breaths per minute until his skin color improves.
    D. 12 breaths per minute, regardless of exam findings.

15. You are the first person on the scene of a medical emergency at a private residence. As you enter the residence with your equipment, a man frantically tells you that his wife fell while trying to walk from the bed to the bathroom and hasn't spoken or taken a breath since. You assess the patient and find she is apneic and pulseless. The best way to ventilate this patient is with the

   A. bag-valve mask.
   B. flow-restricted, oxygen-powered ventilation device.
   C. pocket mask.
   D. nonrebreather mask.

16. Your patient is experiencing crushing chest pain and tells you that it feels "just like my last heart attack." He is restless, anxious, and will not allow you to place a mask over his face to provide him with oxygen. You should

   A. have the patient sign a signature of refusal (SOR) and tell his wife to drive him to the hospital.
   B. tell the patient that his condition will deteriorate if he doesn't allow you to give him oxygen.
   C. hold the mask near the patient's face to deliver at least some oxygen.
   D. deliver oxygen via a nasal cannula.

17. Important history findings when interviewing the respiratory patient include

   A. history of alcohol abuse.
   B. history of prior intubation.
   C. history of bleeding disorders.
   D. all of the above

18. You are treating a 19-year-old male who thinks he is having a panic attack. The patient is breathing approximately 45 times per minute. He complains that his hands and wrists are cramping and have started to spasm into a flexed position. He has no cyanosis, no accessory muscle use, no retractions, no wheezing, and no history of pulmonary or cardiac problems. The correct management of this patient includes

   A. telling the patient to breathe into a paper bag.
   B. applying a nonrebreather mask that is not attached to oxygen.
   C. applying a nasal cannula at 2 liters per minute.
   D. none of the above

19. Airway obstructions may be indicated by the presence of

   A. wheezing.
   B. stridor.
   C. gurgling.
   D. all of the above

20. When artificially ventilating a patient with a stoma, the EMT-Basic may need to

   A. seal the BVM mask over the patient's stoma and occlude the nose and mouth.
   B. seal the BVM mask over the nose and mouth and occlude the stoma.
   C. A or B
   D. none of the above

21. In the conscious patient, a majority of the initial assessment can be accomplished by

   A. looking, listening, and feeling for breathing.
   B. identifying yourself and asking the patient a simple question.
   C. performing a scene size-up.
   D. assessing the patient's capillary refill.

22. Obtaining information verbally from the patient, family, and bystanders is a process known as

    A. primary assessment.
    B. physical examination.
    C. scene size-up.
    D. history taking.

23. The pulse oximeter may give false readings in cases involving all of the following EXCEPT

    A. carbon monoxide poisoning.
    B. warm temperatures.
    C. direct sunlight.
    D. peripheral artery disease.

24. When assessing the patient with a significant mechanism of injury (MOI), the EMT-Basic should expose

    A. only the areas of the body where the patient complains of pain.
    B. only the areas of the body where there is suspected injury.
    C. the entire body.
    D. the lower portion of the body.

25. Your patient is a 62-year-old male who has a history of coronary artery disease and COPD. He calls 911 complaining of difficulty breathing. You decide a focused examination is appropriate. You should

    A. perform a detailed assessment of the entire body.
    B. assess the chest and cardiovascular system.
    C. assess the cardiovascular and respiratory systems.
    D. perform only the initial assessment because the patient requires rapid transport.

26. During the scene size-up, EMT-Basics must be able to recognize signs of impending violence. Of the choices below, the LEAST likely sign of violence is

    A. loud voices.
    B. unusual silence.
    C. overturned furnishings.
    D. people crying.

27. Your patient is a 72-year-old male who passed out at a family function. Although the patient denies any injury from the resulting fall, you examine him and find that several minutes after he regained consciousness his skin is abnormally pale. This finding is known as _____ and usually indicates a problem with _____.

    A. cyanosis; breathing
    B. cyanosis; perfusion
    C. pallor; perfusion
    D. jaundice; kidney function

28. You are called to the scene of a motor vehicle collision. As you progress through your assessments, you begin to compile multiple pieces of information that lead you to believe the patient is likely to be suffering from shock. This consideration of all factors leading you to suspect an injury is called your

    A. mechanism of injury.
    B. index of suspicion.
    C. index of reflection.
    D. field impression.

29. While performing an interfacility transfer, you use your service's automatic non-invasive blood pressure (NIBP) device. Your patient is an alert 73-year-old woman who is being transferred from one hospital to another for specialty surgery. En route, you are conversing with the patient, who is cheerful and telling stories, when the machine alarms and displays a reading of 60/10. Your first action should be to

   A. take a manual blood pressure.
   B. repeat the initial assessment.
   C. ask the patient if she has always had low blood pressure.
   D. begin CPR with the help of your partner.

30. Vital signs should always be taken as a complete set. A set of vital signs should include all of the following EXCEPT

   A. pulse strength.
   B. respiratory rate.
   C. allergies.
   D. pupil size and reaction.

31. Specialized resources that may need to be called to a trauma scene include

   A. extrication teams.
   B. hazardous materials teams.
   C. law enforcement.
   D. all of the above

32. When comparing the two numbers obtained when taking a patient's blood pressure, the

   A. systolic is always less than the diastolic.
   B. diastolic is usually one-fourth the systolic.
   C. diastolic is usually one-half the systolic.
   D. systolic is always greater than the diastolic.

33. You are assessing a dark-skinned patient's circulation. To examine the patient's skin color, you should

   A. assess the patients palms or fingernail beds.
   B. skip this step, as it is impossible to assess in the dark-skinned patient.
   C. assess the inside of the patient's cheeks or lip.
   D. A or C

34. Bradycardia can be caused by

   A. hypoxia.
   B. medications.
   C. heart attack.
   D. all of the above

35. You respond to the scene of a high-speed motor vehicle collision (MVC). Your patient was the driver of a small pickup truck that struck the rear of a stopped tractor-trailer. The patient is awake but trapped underneath the rear of the semi, and the extrication team is setting up hydraulic extrication tools to free him. Because of the numerous engines and tools running nearby, the best way to obtain this patient's blood pressure is most likely via

   A. auscultation.
   B. palpation.
   C. estimation.
   D. respiration.

36. All patients who show signs of respiratory distress should be treated with

   A. prescribed inhalers.
   B. positive-pressure ventilation.
   C. high-flow oxygen via nasal cannula.
   D. high-flow oxygen via a nonrebreather mask.

37. While transporting a patient complaining of chest pain, you observe him stop talking and fall unconscious in the middle of a sentence. You quickly assess his ABCs and find him to be apneic and pulseless. This patient should have an AED applied and a shock should be delivered

    A. after 2 minutes of chest compressions.
    B. after two rounds of ventilations and compressions.
    C. immediately following intubation by a paramedic.
    D. immediately if indicated by the AED.

38. The primary goal of nitroglycerin administration for a patient experiencing chest pain is to reduce

    A. pain and anxiety.
    B. cardiac workload.
    C. blood pressure.
    D. cardiac output.

39. Patients experiencing tearing pain in the chest radiating to the back should be suspected of experiencing

    A. exacerbation of COPD.
    B. pulmonary embolus.
    C. angina pectoris.
    D. aortic aneurysm.

40. All patients suspected of having _____ should be treated with _____.

    A. heart attack; defibrillation
    B. cardiac arrest; nitroglycerin
    C. heart attack; nitroglycerin
    D. heart attack; oxygen

41. An automated external defibrillator (AED) should only be applied to patients who are

    A. unresponsive and pulseless.
    B. complaining of chest pain.
    C. unresponsive and apneic.
    D. apneic and hypotensive.

42. Rescuers treating a patient in cardiac arrest should

    A. retain roles throughout the call to minimize confusion.
    B. rotate chest compressions to avoid rescuer fatigue.
    C. assign roles based on seniority.
    D. none of the above

43. All of the following are side effects of nitroglycerin EXCEPT

    A. low blood pressure.
    B. shortness of breath.
    C. headache.
    D. dizziness.

44. You arrive on the scene of a medical emergency in which bystanders have been performing CPR on a patient in cardiac arrest. Your first action is to

    A. find out the patient's medical history.
    B. begin CPR with your own crew.
    C. confirm that the patient is pulseless.
    D. apply the AED to the patient.

45. The patient should NOT be touched while the AED is

    A. analyzing the rhythm.
    B. between shocks.
    C. delivering a shock.
    D. A and C

46. Patients complaining of chest pain and without contraindications should be given aspirin in order to

    A. reduce pain levels.
    B. increase cardiac workload.
    C. break up the blockage causing the infarction.
    D. prevent additional damage from worsening of the blockage.

47. The cardiac rhythm that is most common in sudden cardiac arrest and is characterized by chaotic, rapid "twitching" of the heart muscle instead of regular, efficient contractions is known as

   A. atrial fibrillation.
   B. ventricular tachycardia.
   C. ventricular fibrillation.
   D. asystole.

48. Not all patients experiencing a cardiac event will present with classic symptoms. The groups of people who are prone to atypical presentation include all of the following EXCEPT

   A. the elderly.
   B. females.
   C. African Americans.
   D. diabetics.

49. You respond to the home of a patient whose wife tells you he isn't acting right. You find the patient to be alert but somewhat agitated, saying that he doesn't understand why you are interrupting his work. The wife tells you he took all his normal medication, including his morning insulin, but he has been working on a physically demanding home improvement project and has not eaten yet today. You suspect _____ and treat the patient with _____.

   A. hyperglycemia; oral glucose
   B. hypoglycemia; oral glucose
   C. overdose; activated charcoal
   D. transient ischemic attack; high-flow oxygen

50. When assessing a patient suspected of suffering from a behavioral emergency, EMS providers should

   A. tell the patient to calm down until he can be trusted to behave rationally.
   B. surround the patient to show support and establish control of the situation.
   C. allow only one provider to interact with the patient and limit visual and audible stimuli.
   D. tell the patient he must be transported to the hospital, so it will be easier if he goes willingly.

51. Patients suffering from hypothermia should be handled gently to prevent

   A. bradycardia.
   B. ventricular fibrillation.
   C. frostbite.
   D. apnea.

52. You respond to a call at a local tavern about a patron who fell while trying to leave after several hours of heavy drinking. You find the patient responsive only to loud verbal stimuli but without obvious injury. While treating this patient, you should have _____ available and ready at all times.

   A. activated charcoal
   B. intubation equipment
   C. a Combitube
   D. large bore suction

53. An obstetrical condition that may cause painless, bright red bleeding is

   A. placenta abruptio.
   B. placenta previa.
   C. meconium staining.
   D. preeclampsia.

54. When preparing for multiple-birth deliveries, the EMT-Basic should

    A. anticipate a higher likelihood of low birth weight.
    B. anticipate the presence of more than one placenta.
    C. anticipate each of the neonates requiring ventilatory support.
    D. all of the above

55. Patients who experience severe vaginal bleeding should be treated similar to patients suffering from

    A. major trauma.
    B. respiratory arrest.
    C. premature childbirth.
    D. pulmonary embolism.

56. When securing a patient to a long spine board, the _____ should always be secured before the _____.

    A. legs; arms
    B. torso; head
    C. head; torso
    D. head; extremities

57. You respond to the scene of a motorcycle MVC in which the driver lost control of his motorcycle, hit a parked car, flew over the handlebars, and then slid more than 25 feet across the pavement wearing only khaki shorts, a T-shirt, and sandals. You expect this patient to show signs of hypovolemic shock due to all of the following EXCEPT

    A. internal bleeding.
    B. fluid loss from large abrasions.
    C. traumatic brain injury.
    D. lacerations due to open fractures.

58. Of the following, the burns most likely to be associated with a life threat are

    A. 18% chemical burns to the patient's anterior legs.
    B. 24% thermal burns to the patient's back and posterior arms.
    C. 4% thermal burns to the patient's face and upper chest.
    D. 12% superficial burns to the patient's entire anterior surface.

59. Traction splints may be used for

    A. open upper-leg fractures.
    B. closed upper-leg fractures.
    C. closed upper- or lower-leg fractures.
    D. A and B

60. Your patient is a 26-year-old male who was involved in an altercation. He has a severe laceration to the upper arm after being pushed through a large storefront window. Bystanders reported bright red blood spurting from the patient's wounds. A bystander applied direct pressure to the wound with a towel prior to your arrival, but the patient continues to bleed and appears pale. This patient likely suffered a laceration of the _____, and your first priority should be to _____.

    A. brachial artery; initiate rapid transport
    B. radial artery; apply pressure to the proximal arterial site
    C. subclavian artery; place the patient in Trendelenburg position
    D. brachial artery; immediately place a tourniquet on the patient's arm

61. Penetrating wounds to the neck are particularly worrisome to the EMT-Basic because of the potential for

    A. serious hemorrhage.
    B. spinal cord trauma.
    C. air embolism.
    D. all of the above

62. All suspected fractures should be splinted

   A. in the position found.
   B. prior to transport.
   C. after the initial assessment.
   D. prior to arrival at the emergency department.

63. You respond to a call in a residential neighborhood. Upon your arrival, you find a male who appears to be in his 50s lying in the grass next to a two-story house. He does not respond to your questions. You notice an extension ladder extended to the roofline and a toolbox on the roof. As you begin your initial assessment, you find the patient has noisy, shallow respirations at 8 breaths per minute and obvious bleeding from both legs. His pulse is 120 beats per minute and difficult to palpate at the radius. Your first priority in treating this patient is to

   A. secure tourniquets to both legs.
   B. ventilate with a BVM and 100% oxygen.
   C. apply a jaw thrust and manual, in-line stabilization of the neck.
   D. apply a cervical collar in case the patient's spine is injured.

64. Your patient is a 17-year-old high school baseball player who was struck in the forehead by a batted ball. When you assess the injury site, you are likely to find

   A. a contusion.
   B. a laceration.
   C. subcutaneous emphysema.
   D. A and B

65. Trauma patients should be treated for internal bleeding if

   A. the mechanism of injury suggests internal bleeding is likely.
   B. shock is present without obvious cause.
   C. the systolic blood pressure is less than 100.
   D. A or B

66. When performing a rapid trauma assessment, the EMT-Basic should begin with

   A. the area of the body where the worst injury is located.
   B. the head.
   C. the area of the body where the patient feels the most pain.
   D. the chest.

67. You are treating a motorcyclist involved in a high-speed MVC. Your partner asks if you are going to remove the patient's helmet to examine his ears. Appropriately sized helmets that fit snugly should only be removed if

   A. the patient does not complain of neck pain.
   B. the patient has motor and sensory function in all extremities.
   C. they interfere with your ability to manage the airway or the patient's breathing.
   D. A and B

68. A vital step when assessing the trauma patient is to carefully consider the amount, location, and direction of forces applied to the patient's body during the traumatic event. This drives further assessment and is called considering the

   A. nature of illness.
   B. patient history.
   C. mechanism of injury.
   D. chief complaint.

69. While performing a rapid trauma assessment on the unresponsive victim of a high-speed motorcycle collision, you note a deformity to the patient's left lower leg. You should

    A. immediately splint the leg then continue the assessment.

    B. apply an ice pack and transport immediately.

    C. complete your assessment and splint the leg when time allows.

    D. splint the leg and repeat the initial assessment.

70. Scene clues that will help the EMT-Basic assess the mechanism of injury at motor vehicle collision scenes include

    A. size and type of vehicles involved.

    B. distance of intrusion to the outside of the vehicle.

    C. distance of intrusion into the patient compartment.

    D. all of the above

71. You respond to an emergency call involving a toddler. Upon entering the house, the child's frantic mother states that the child had a fever and she put him to bed earlier in the evening. Later, she found him awake but unable to talk. You find the child sitting upright on his bed, looking frightened and refusing to speak. You also note that he does not present any signs of labored breathing, but he is drooling without making attempts to swallow. Recognizing the child's condition, you know the best course of treatment is to

    A. transport the child in the supine position and assist ventilations with a bag-valve mask.

    B. apply high-flow oxygen and transport immediately.

    C. attempt to suction the mouth and oropharynx.

    D. allow the patient to sit in a comfortable position and transport him with as little stimulation as possible.

72. Potential signs of child abuse include all of the following EXCEPT

    A. injuries that have no rational explanation.

    B. cigarette burns on the child's skin.

    C. foreign airway obstructions.

    D. bruises to the posterior thighs.

73. In the infant patient, a critical finding distinguishing respiratory failure from respiratory distress is

    A. loss of muscle tone.

    B. a respiratory rate that is greater than 30.

    C. inconsolable crying.

    D. a capillary refill time that is greater than 3 seconds.

74. You respond to a call for an adolescent who is having difficulty breathing at school. You find the patient in the nurse's office, unable to speak and clearly in distress. The nurse reports that the patient brought her albuterol inhaler and attempted to use it, but found it was empty. The patient has audible wheezes and a prolonged expiratory phase. The most likely cause of this patient's distress is

    A. cardiac disease.

    B. airway obstruction.

    C. asthma.

    D. bronchitis.

75. Because obtaining an accurate blood pressure in very young children is difficult and often inaccurate, EMT-Basics should assess _____ as a measure of perfusion.

    A. respiratory rate

    B. capillary refill

    C. skin turgor

    D. patient irritability

76. Immobilizing the infant trauma patient may be accomplished by

    A. placing the patient on a short spine board.

    B. leaving the patient in his own car seat and padding voids.

    C. using a Kendrick Traction Device (KTD).

    D. positioning the infant securely in the rescuer's arms.

77. Toddlers who fall more than a few feet commonly land on their

    A. feet.

    B. hands.

    C. head.

    D. buttocks.

78. Young pediatric patients who are unable to tolerate receiving oxygen via mask should

    A. be transported without oxygen.

    B. have oxygen supplied via nasal cannula.

    C. have oxygen supplied via blow-by.

    D. be intubated to ensure proper oxygenation.

79. While treating an 11-year-old female who fell off her bicycle and injured her arm, you note several bruises to her inner thighs, some of which appear to be several days old. Her stepfather becomes agitated by your line of questioning and insists that the bruises are from the bicycle accident. You should

    A. assess and treat the arm injury because it is the current injury.

    B. stop the ambulance and call the police for further assistance.

    C. ask the stepfather to exit the ambulance and perform a thorough physical exam.

    D. continue treating the patient and communicate your findings and concerns to the ER staff.

80. When assessing and treating a pediatric patient with special needs, the most knowledgeable expert as to what is abnormal for the child is the

    A. patient's personal physician.

    B. patient's parent or primary caregiver.

    C. EMS medical director.

    D. patient's visiting nurse.

81. After completing a patient care encounter, the highest priority should be placed on

    A. documenting the call.

    B. preparing your unit for the next call.

    C. returning to your station.

    D. contacting the station for your next assignment.

82. On most extrication scenes, the role of the EMT-Basic assigned to the ambulance is to provide

    A. initial treatment and lifesaving care only.

    B. advanced extrication tools and techniques.

    C. leadership and scene management.

    D. none of the above

83. EMT-Basics in a supervisor or group leader role should be assigned no more than _____ responders to manage or supervise.

    A. 2

    B. 1–3

    C. 3–5

    D. 5–10

84. When documenting a patient encounter, it is important to list the presence or absence of certain symptoms that are commonly related to the patient's chief complaint. If these symptoms are present, they are known as _____. If they are absent, they are known as _____.

    A. pertinent positives; pertinent negatives
    B. pertinent negatives; absent findings
    C. associated complaints; pertinent negatives
    D. associated complaints; absent findings

85. Your crew has requested helicopter evacuation for a trauma patient in a rural area. Which of these would be the best landing zone?

    A. a straight, flat stretch of two-lane highway between two curves
    B. a school playground that has been cleared of children
    C. a livestock pasture with cattle at one end
    D. a field of freshly cut grass

86. Most collisions involving EMS units responding to emergency calls happen

    A. at night.
    B. in poor weather conditions.
    C. at intersections.
    D. in heavy traffic.

87. Equipment that should be brought to every patient's side includes personal protective equipment (PPE) and

    A. oxygen, AED, and long spine board.
    B. suction, airway adjuncts, and the ambulance stretcher.
    C. oxygen, suction, airway adjuncts, bandages, and the AED.
    D. suction, oxygen, and an OB kit.

88. When performing triage, the EMT-Basic should treat a single patient with

    A. CPR or mechanical ventilation only.
    B. bleeding control or manual airway maneuvers only.
    C. bandaging and splinting only.
    D. oxygen and spinal immobilization only.

89. You are called to respond to a motor vehicle collision involving a tanker truck with possible hazardous materials release. You should attempt to identify hazards

    A. before treating the patient.
    B. by questioning the driver as you begin treatment.
    C. by retrieving shipping papers from the truck's cab.
    D. as you approach the scene with binoculars.

90. When transmitting priority traffic to your dispatch center, the first step is to

    A. confirm that you have the dispatcher's attention.
    B. ensure the channel is clear by listening for several seconds.
    C. talk loudly and get your point across quickly.
    D. transmit emergency tones.

91. When treating a multiple-trauma patient, the patient compartment of the ambulance should be kept

    A. at a comfortable temperature for technicians.
    B. at a comfortable temperature for the patient.
    C. warmer than room temperature.
    D. cooler than room temperature.

92. When two emergency vehicles are responding to the same scene from the same direction, they should

    A. stay close together so the lead vehicle can clear the way for the following vehicle.
    B. attempt to take different routes to the scene.
    C. allow the lead vehicle to travel at least 500 feet or more in front of the following vehicle.
    D. travel side by side to alert other motorists of their presence.

93. Which of the following is NOT routinely transmitted during the radio patient report?

    A. the patient's age
    B. the patient's chief complaint
    C. the patient's medical history
    D. the patient's name

94. Which statement regarding the movement of a patient to the ambulance is true?

    A. You must always transport a patient to the ambulance on a wheeled stretcher.
    B. Patients should only be moved to the ambulance after all treatment is complete.
    C. Some patients may be allowed to walk to the ambulance.
    D. Patients may be left unattended in the ambulance for short periods of time.

95. In most states, the operator of an ambulance may disobey certain specific traffic laws only when responding to an emergency and when

    A. at least one emergency light is flashing or illuminated.
    B. at least two emergency lights are illuminated and the siren is sounded.
    C. all emergency lights and scene lighting are flashing or illuminated.
    D. all emergency lights are flashing or illuminated and the siren is sounded.

96. Ideally, the endotracheal tube should be advanced until the tip lies just

    A. superior to the carina.
    B. inferior to the carina.
    C. medial to the epiglottis.
    D. anterior to the epiglottis.

97. You have just placed an endotracheal tube in a patient with multiple traumas. After inflating the bulb and ensuring that your partner is delivering adequate breaths, your first action should be to

    A. secure the endotracheal tube.
    B. auscultate for proper placement.
    C. assess for accessory muscle use.
    D. position a nasogastric tube.

98. You are assessing a 28-year-old male patient. His roommates tell you that he was despondent over a recent breakup and took a handful of pills at an unknown time. The roommates found the patient asleep an hour ago and have been unable to wake him since. After assessing the patient, you find him to be snoring loudly and unresponsive to painful stimuli. He is breathing at a rate of approximately 12 breaths per minute with adequate chest rise and fall. Your paramedic partner asks you to intubate the patient. The indication for intubation in this case is

   A. inadequate oxygenation.
   B. airway obstruction.
   C. airway protection.
   D. inadequate tidal volume.

99. Landmarks that may be visualized while performing endotracheal intubation include all of the following EXCEPT

   A. alveoli.
   B. arytenoids.
   C. glottis.
   D. vallecula.

100. The first sign of a dislodged endotracheal tube is often

   A. decreasing oxygen saturation.
   B. change in skin color.
   C. increasing heart rate.
   D. change in chest excursion.

Answer Key

1. A	26. D	51. B	76. B
2. C	27. C	52. D	77. C
3. D	28. B	53. B	78. C
4. A	29. B	54. D	79. D
5. C	30. C	55. A	80. B
6. D	31. D	56. B	81. B
7. C	32. D	57. C	82. A
8. A	33. D	58. C	83. C
9. D	34. D	59. B	84. C
10. B	35. B	60. D	85. B
11. B	36. D	61. D	86. C
12. D	37. D	62. C	87. C
13. A	38. B	63. C	88. B
14. D	39. D	64. D	89. D
15. C	40. D	65. D	90. B
16. D	41. A	66. B	91. C
17. B	42. B	67. C	92. C
18. D	43. B	68. C	93. D
19. D	44. C	69. C	94. C
20. C	45. D	70. D	95. D
21. B	46. D	71. D	96. A
22. D	47. C	72. C	97. B
23. B	48. C	73. A	98. C
24. C	49. B	74. C	99. A
25. C	50. C	75. B	100. D

Answer Explanations

1. **A.** The EMT-Basic must always ensure his own safety first. Following that, his partner is the most valuable person on the scene in terms of lifesaving skills. Only after ensuring his own safety and the safety of his partner can the EMT-Basic direct his attention to the safety of the patient and bystanders. Therefore, Choice A is the best answer. *(Chapter VII: Section A.2)*

2. **C.** Some of the first ambulance transports were developed during the Crusades and the Napoleonic Wars. Although EMS has slowly evolved in times of peace, many great innovations occurred during times of *war* when responders were forced to find creative ways to save soldiers and citizens. *(Chapter V)*

3. **D.** The language of Do Not Resuscitate orders varies from state to state and often from patient to patient. Patients with DNR orders have refused in advance lifesaving procedures, such as invasive airway procedures, artificial ventilation, chest compressions, and/or defibrillation. However, they may still benefit from other treatments or comfort measures, including the administration of oxygen or simple medications. These patients should be treated to the fullest extent allowable without disregarding the DNR order. Therefore, Choice D is the best answer. *(Chapter V: Section C.4)*

4. **A.** This patient obviously has sustained trauma and her vomiting is an ominous sign of a possible head injury. Because the patient is not yet 18, you can *transport the patient under minor consent* for evaluation and possibly lifesaving treatment. It is not acceptable to wait for the patient's parents or guardians as there is no telling how long it would take for them to arrive. *(Chapter V: Section C.1)*

5. **C.** The citizens' band radio should only be used as a last resort. Radios issued to EMS personnel should have specific frequencies assigned by the Federal Communications Commission (FCC), which are monitored at all times by a dispatch center. A base station radio is secured to a fixed site, while a mobile radio is mounted in a vehicle. *Portable* radios are small and light enough that one person may carry them while on duty. Although they are less powerful than other radios, *portable* radios are key pieces of safety equipment. *(Chapter VII: Section E.1)*

6. **D.** While *apnea* is certainly an indication for oxygen administration, apneic patients will not benefit from the passive supply of oxygen provided by a nonrebreather mask. They must have their ventilations assisted by a bag-valve mask for the oxygen to be useful. *(Chapter VI: Section C.5)*

7. **C.** The reservoir does not need to be filled prior to ventilating a patient with a bag-valve mask because the device will deliver a mix of ambient air until the reservoir is filled with oxygen. This is an important distinction as the nonrebreather mask may not be applied until the reservoir has been filled. This prevents the patient from breathing outside air and, for this reason, may actually prevent the patient from breathing at all. Therefore, Choice C is the best answer. *(Chapter VI: Section C.3)*

8. **A.** The nasal cannula is a low-flow device, useful for patients with little or no distress but also for those who require carefully controlled amounts. However, at liter flows above 6 liters per minute, the reservoir created by the nasopharynx and posterior pharynx is overfilled, and surplus oxygen is simply wasted. Therefore, the maximum delivery concentration is *44%*. *(Chapter VI: Section C.5)*

9. **D.** Although suction is a desirable intervention and should be performed, it may take several seconds to apply suction and will require repeated attempts to remove a large amount of liquid obstruction. *Moving the patient to the lateral recumbent position*, however, will immediately allow vomitus to drain from the mouth. Suction may be used to remove the rest of the obstruction and oxygen may be applied after the airway is cleared. *(Chapter VI: Section B.3)*

10. **B.** The flow-restricted, oxygen-powered ventilation device was once a mainstay of resuscitation, but in recent years has fallen out of favor. Its high pressure, rapid delivery of oxygen places the patient at risk for pneumothorax or other barotraumas. The use of this device often results in significant amounts of air being pushed into the stomach, which can lead to vomiting and compromise the airway. Another disadvantage of the flow-restricted, oxygen-powered ventilation device is that it does not allow the rescuer to gauge the compliance, or ease of ventilation, of each breath delivered to the patient. For this reason, many services and providers prefer a manual ventilator such as the bag-valve mask. The only answer choice that is not a complication of using the flow-restricted, oxygen-powered ventilation device is *risk of oxygen toxicity. (Chapter VI: Section C.4)*

11. **B.** Oxygen *regulators* reduce pressure and create constant, adjustable flow. This allows the EMT-Basic to administer the proper dose and makes the experience more comfortable for the patient. *(Chapter VI)*

12. **D.** Selecting the proper size equipment ensures that the EMT-Basic will be able to maintain a proper mask seal and appropriate tidal volumes when ventilating the patient. The selection of an appropriate ventilation rate is also important because under- and over-ventilating can be dangerous to the patient. Therefore, Choice D is the best answer. *(Chapter VI: Section C)*

13. **A.** The anatomical dead space is the volume of air required to fill the pharynx, trachea, bronchi, and smaller airways before air can be delivered to the alveoli for gas exchange. *Alveolar ventilation* describes the passage of air into and out of the alveoli. *(Chapter VI)*

14. **D.** All adult patients should be ventilated at a rate of *12 breaths per minute, regardless of exam findings.* Ventilating at a rate higher than this will not necessarily improve oxygenation or ventilation, and it could have a negative effect on cardiac output, which this patient is already struggling to maintain. *(Chapter VI: Section A.2)*

15. **C.** Although the bag-valve mask allows delivery of higher oxygen concentrations, the *pocket mask* is advantageous in this instance because it allows the lone rescuer to more quickly move from ventilations to compressions and back again. Until someone arrives to help, the pocket mask is the device of choice. *(Chapter VI: Section C.2)*

16. **D.** While the nasal cannula cannot deliver high-flow oxygen at concentrations as high as the nonrebreather mask, it will deliver up to 44% oxygen, and that amount is better than none. This patient's anxiety will only be worsened by being bullied or by having the mask anywhere near his face, but almost all patients will find the *nasal cannula* tolerable. *(Chapter VI: Section C.5)*

17. **B.** While the other findings may be helpful in isolated cases, all respiratory patients should be assessed for *history of prior intubation.* You should discover when the last intubation occurred, the length of time ventilation was required, and other such details. The more frequently and more recently a patient has been intubated, the more significant this history can be considered. *(Chapter XII: Section 1)*

18. **D.** Although the likely suspicion is that this patient is experiencing an episode of hyperventilation resulting from acute anxiety, it is dangerous to assume that this is the case. Asking the patient to breathe into a paper bag or a nonrebreather mask without an oxygen supply will cause the patient to rebreathe carbon dioxide. While this may help the suspected anxiety attack, it could have disastrous consequences if the symptoms are actually the result of another condition. The best course is to apply high-flow oxygen via nonrebreather mask. If the patient is truly just anxious, this may have a calming effect on the patient's anxiety. If, however, there is an underlying case, then oxygen therapy is medically appropriate. Therefore, Choice D is the best answer. *(Chapter VI: Section C.5)*

19. **D.** Wheezing, stridor, and gurgling are all sounds associated with airway obstructions. Wheezing and stridor are common in solid obstructions or partial obstructions caused by inflammation. Gurgling is a common sound in patients who have liquid obstructions such as emesis, blood, or excess airway secretions. Therefore, Choice D is the best answer. *(Chapter VII: Section B.3)*

20. **C.** Some patients with stomas have no passageway between the trachea and the pharynx. In these patients, ventilations delivered to the mouth and nose are ineffective and will produce no chest rise. In other patients, the stoma, trachea, and pharynx are all connected by the same passageway. In those circumstances, it will most likely be necessary to occlude whichever orifice is not being ventilated to ensure proper volumes are directed into the lungs. Therefore, Choice C is the best answer. *(Chapter VI: Section C.3)*

21. **B.** If the patient appears conscious, the EMT-Basic can gauge several factors with a simple verbal exchange. EMT-Basics can accomplish the majority of the initial assessment by *identifying themselves and asking the patient a simple question*. If the patient is able to answer the question with a coherent response, the EMT-Basic may find that the patient has a patent airway, can breathe at least well enough to form a sentence, and has a mental status that allows for an appropriate response. *(Chapter VII: Section B)*

22. **D.** Medical providers across all specialties and professions are expected to *take a history* when evaluating a patient. This involves finding out about the patient's past medical history, current complaints, and other factors that may relate to his or her illness. *(Chapter VII: Section C)*

23. **B.** The accuracy of pulse oximeters depends heavily on the conditions under which they are used. Carbon monoxide poisoning, direct sunlight, and decreased peripheral perfusion can all result in poor readings. Cold temperatures often have an adverse effect on the accuracy of pulse oximetry readings, but *warm temperatures* should not have such an effect. *(Chapter VII)*

24. **C.** In patients with a significant mechanism of injury, a rapid trauma exam or full body scan is indicated. Because you can't treat what you can't see, these patients should be exposed head to toe so that no significant injuries are missed. Efforts should be made to preserve the patient's modesty and body heat, but *the entire body* must be inspected. *(Chapter VII: C.1)*

25. **C.** Shortness of breath may be a result of an exacerbation of this patient's lung disease or a symptom of the patient's cardiac problems. Because the patient's complaint may likely originate from either the cardiovascular or respiratory system, they *both should be assessed*. While rapid transport to ALS intercept or an emergency department is important, an examination of the body regions or systems involved is necessary. *(Chapter VII: Section C.1)*

26. **D.** EMT-Basics respond to many types of calls and, in many cases, will encounter a patient, family member, or bystander who is *crying* or worried about a loved one. This does not necessarily indicate that violence is imminent. However, signs of a struggle or disagreement (such as overturned furniture, a broken door, or loud voices) should clearly place the EMT-Basic on high alert for potential violence. Similarly, unusually silent groups may indicate that bystanders are concealing illegal activity or the true story behind the patient's illness or injury. *(Chapter VII: Section A.2)*

27. **C.** When patients appear abnormally pale and complain of illness, this is known as *pallor*. The most common cause is an insufficient circulation, which leads to decreased *perfusion* of the skin and results in pallor. Patients with breathing disorders normally appear cyanotic, not pale. *(Chapter IX: Section A.1)*

28. **B.** The *index of suspicion* is a tool used by EMS providers to decide on treatment and transport priorities. The higher the index of suspicion, the more vigilant EMT-Basics must be when assessing for and treating potential injuries. *(Chapter VII: Section B.6; Chapter XI: Section C.3)*

29. **B.** Although it will be important to obtain an accurate manual blood pressure, the immediate concern is to *repeat the initial assessment* to ensure the patient has not had a sudden change in cardiac output. This can quickly and easily be assessed by evaluating the patient's ABCs. When you are satisfied that no life threat exists, you should obtain a manual blood pressure. *(Chapter VII: Section D.2)*

30. **C.** *Allergies* are obtained as a part of the SAMPLE history. All other answers should be obtained in each set of vital signs and can be trended to gauge a patient's improvement or deterioration. *(Chapter VII: Section C.1)*

31. **D.** Extrication teams are often needed to free trauma victims from machinery or vehicles. Hazardous materials teams are often present at motor vehicle accidents or industrial accidents. Law enforcement teams may be necessary in the case of trauma resulting from violence. These are only three examples of the specialized resources available to the EMT-Basic. It is important to know which resources are available in your area and how to request or contact them. Therefore, Choice D is the best answer. *(Chapter VII: Section A; Chapter XI)*

32. **D.** The diastolic blood pressure measures the pressure in the circulatory system when the heart is at rest, a phase known as diastole. When the heart is contracting, blood is pushed out into the system, creating a higher pressure. This phase is called systole. Therefore, *the systolic blood pressure should always be greater than the diastolic pressure. (Chapter XIV: Section A)*

33. **D.** Any of the mucous membranes may be assessed—the most readily available and accurate are those around the eyes and mouth. The palms of the hands or fingernail beds are also reliable ways to assess for peripheral perfusion. Therefore, Choice D is the best answer. *(Chapter VII)*

34. **D.** Bradycardia is a common response to hypoxia and, therefore, oxygen is an important first step in treatment of patients with low heart rate. Many common medications can also cause this result, as can a heart attack involving the portions of the heart responsible for controlling heart rate. Other common causes of bradycardia include stroke, metabolic syndromes, or vagal responses. Therefore, Choice D is the best answer. *(Chapter VIII)*

35. **B.** The amount of ambient noise at an extrication scene makes auscultation of a blood pressure nearly impossible. Although it is theoretically possible to estimate a patient's blood pressure based on the most distal site a pulse can be felt, the amount of blood pressure necessary to create a pulse at a distal point varies from patient to patient, making this method inaccurate. Therefore, the best way to obtain the blood pressure is to combine the distal pulse site with a sphygmomanometer and obtain the blood pressure by *palpation. (Chapter VII)*

36. **D.** Providing *high-flow oxygen via a nonrebreather mask* is the first step in treating patients with respiratory distress. The preferred device to use is the nonrebreather mask because it delivers the highest concentrations. While prescribed inhalers and positive-pressure ventilation may be necessary for some patients, oxygen is the only intervention given to all patients with this complaint. *(Chapter VII: Section B.4)*

37. **D.** This patient has experienced a witnessed cardiac arrest and should be defibrillated *immediately if indicated by the AED.* Any additional delay will decrease the patient's chance of survival. Unobserved arrests or those with long intervals without CPR should be treated with 2 minutes of chest compressions prior to defibrillation. *(Chapter VIII: Section C.5)*

38. **B.** Nitroglycerin is a vasodilator that reduces *cardiac workload* by reducing preload and afterload. While it does, in fact, reduce pain, blood pressure, and cardiac output, the primary purpose is to reduce the heart's workload to decrease the chance and/or severity of ischemia. *(Chapter VIII: Section C.7)*

39. **D.** The aorta is the only organ in the chest capable of sensing tearing pain. Often, this pain is a result of a dissecting aneurysm, in which the layers of the aorta separate as they are split apart by the high pressures created by the left ventricle. Therefore, Choice D is the best answer. *(Chapter XIV: Section A)*

40. **D.** All patients suspected of having any type of cardiac event or symptom should be treated with oxygen to minimize the chance of ischemia. Not all heart attack victims will require defibrillation or are good candidates for the administration of nitroglycerin (as in the case of a patient who has recently taken Viagra or similar medications). Lastly, patients in cardiac arrest should never receive nitroglycerin. Therefore, Choice D is correct. *(Chapter VIII: Section C.2)*

41. **A.** Defibrillation is not helpful and may be harmful to patients who are not suffering from ventricular fibrillation or ventricular tachycardia. Because of this, the AED should not be applied to any patient until it is confirmed that the patient is *unresponsive and pulseless. (Chapter VIII: Section C.4)*

42. **B.** Chest compressions are a physically demanding task and rescuers can become fatigued after only a few minutes. This can quickly lead to ineffective compressions, which will drastically reduce the patient's chance of survival. Therefore, rescuers should *rotate chest compressions* to ensure quality compressions throughout the process. *(Chapter XIII: Section C)*

43. **B.** Nitroglycerin works by dilating blood vessels in the body, decreasing the amount of circulating blood volume to reduce the workload of the heart. However, this can also reduce blood pressure significantly and, therefore, can also cause dizziness. Headache is also often reported by patients after taking nitroglycerin. *Shortness of breath* is often present before and after nitroglycerin use as part of the patient's complaint but is not caused by the drug. *(Chapter VIII: Section C.7)*

44. **C.** CPR and AED use can be harmful to patients who have a spontaneous pulse. Laypersons and inexperienced rescuers sometimes fail to find a pulse that is actually present or fail to notice when a patient's pulse returns. Therefore, it is important to *confirm that the patient is pulseless*, apneic, and unresponsive prior to resuming CPR or applying the AED. *(Chapter VIII: Section C.5)*

45. **D.** Touching a patient while the AED is analyzing the patient's heart rhythm may result in an inappropriate shock being given. Touching the patient while a shock is delivered may result in an injury to the rescuer. However, the patient should be touched between shocks to deliver chest compressions and other appropriate treatments. Therefore, Choice D is correct. *(Chapter VIII: Section C.5)*

46. **D.** Aspirin is ineffective at clearing blockages and reducing pain level. Its use is not intended to increase cardiac workload. The primary purpose of aspirin is to prevent platelet aggregation. This *prevents additional worsening of the blockage. (Chapter VIII)*

47. **C.** In *ventricular fibrillation*, the heart's electrical system becomes erratic and is unable to coordinate the contraction of the numerous muscle fibers of the myocardium. Because all heart cells have the ability to depolarize on their own, the cells fire independently of each other in the absence of a coordinated rhythm. The result is a chaotic, random firing of heart cells that is incapable of producing any meaningful cardiac output. This condition could become lethal within minutes. *(Chapter XIII: Section C)*

48. **C.** Patients who present with atypical symptoms may complain of shortness of breath, nausea or vomiting, diaphoresis, or even simple fatigue. The elderly, females, and diabetics are all more likely to have such presentations, especially when the patient is a member of more than one of these groups.

African American patients have a higher overall risk of heart disease, but they are not especially prone to such atypical presentations. *(Chapter VIII)*

49. **B.** This patient has two potential causes of hypoglycemia: insulin use without adequate oral intake and an increased level of physical activity. Although a transient ischemic attack is also a potential cause of the patient's altered level of consciousness, it is wise to treat the most likely cause first since the EMT-Basic will not be able to definitively diagnose either in the field. Therefore, Choice B is the best answer. *(Chapter VIII: Section D.1)*

50. **C.** Patients with behavioral problems often fear losing the ability to control their lives. Therefore, taking choices away from an agitated patient will surely create conflict. In addition, these patients often feel overwhelmed and anxious when dealing with too many stimuli at once. Limiting noises and allowing patients to work with *only one provider* allows them to feel more in control and will decrease their anxiety significantly. *(Chapter VIII: Section H; Chapter XIV: Section A)*

51. **B.** Hypothermia causes irritability of the myocardium. Even the slightest trauma can cause spontaneous *ventricular fibrillation*. While gentle handling is also beneficial in cases of frostbite, it is will not prevent such an injury, and the threat of VF is the most important reason to be vigilant when handling hypothermic patients. *(Chapter VIII: Section C)*

52. **D.** The level of consciousness of this patient is concerning but does not yet seem to support the use of an invasive airway. While patients experiencing alcohol emergencies may occasionally require ventilatory support, it is much more likely that they will require assistance clearing their airway of vomitus whether or not they require an invasive airway. Therefore, *large bore suction* would be appropriate. *(Chapter VIII)*

53. **B.** *Placenta previa* is a condition in which the placenta attaches close to or over the opening of the cervix. This can cause painless, bright red bleeding when the cervix dilates in preparation for birth. This is important for the EMT-Basic to recognize, as the condition will not allow for a routine vaginal delivery. *(Chapter VIII: Section I.3)*

54. **D.** When preparing for multiple births, it is important for the EMT-Basic to remember that multiples may be significantly premature and suffer all the same complications that other premature neonates do. It is also important not to underestimate how quickly the scene can become chaotic. You'll want to ensure that you have ample resources available before the first neonate is delivered. Therefore, Choice D is the best answer. *(Chapter VIII: Section I.5)*

55. **A.** Vaginal bleeding can result in a life-threatening hemorrhage. This type of emergency is difficult to treat because you cannot treat the source of the bleeding with direct compression. Severe vaginal bleeding must be treated very similar to other common causes of internal hemorrhage, such as *major trauma*. *(Chapter VIII: Section I.3)*

56. **B.** It is important to minimize the likelihood of manipulation of the cervical spine while the patient is being secured. Securing the *torso* first reduces this risk because the patient can be properly positioned on the board first and immobilization devices can then be applied around the *head*. *(Chapter IX: Section D.2)*

57. **C.** The patient is likely to have all of these injuries. Internal bleeding may result from impact with the handlebars, the parked car, or the second impact with the pavement. The patient is likely to have large areas of abraded skin, which can quickly lead to fluid loss. *Traumatic brain injury* is highly possible because the patient was not wearing a helmet. Lacerations may also result from open fractures caused by the impact of the crash. However, *traumatic brain injury* is unlikely to cause hypovolemic shock because the cranium is an enclosed space that does not allow for the loss of large amounts of blood or fluid. *(Chapter IX: Section D.4)*

58. **C.** Although Choice C describes a small burn, the concern is based on the location. Burns to the face and upper chest are frequently associated with airway or inhalation burns. While Answers A and B describe burns with significant consequences, the threat of an airway burn is the most likely life threat. *(Chapter IX: Section B.5)*

59. **B.** The traction splint is useful in the field for counteracting and relieving spasm of large muscle masses as a result of femur fracture. It is not indicated in any other fracture, such as those of the lower leg. In addition, it should not be used in open fractures, as it may contribute to contamination of these injuries when bone ends are pulled back into the wound. Therefore, Choice B is the best answer. *(Chapter IX: Section C.3)*

60. **D.** The location of the injury and the bystanders' description of the bleeding should lead you to suspect a laceration of the *brachial artery*. Because the bleeding cannot be controlled with direct pressure and the patient is already showing signs of shock, *a tourniquet should be applied immediately* and will likely save the patient's life. *(Chapter IX: Section A.3)*

61. **D.** Serious hemorrhage is possible because of the large vessels present in the neck, the carotid arteries and jugular veins. Because laceration of these vessels may allow air to pass into the circulatory system, air embolism is also possible. Lastly, penetrating injuries to the neck are also associated with spinal injuries in many cases. Therefore, Choice D is the best answer. *(Chapter IX: Section A.3)*

62. **C.** Suspected fractures should be splinted only if time and resources allow after life threats are controlled. For some severely injured patients, there may not be sufficient time or resources to perform this task before arriving at the emergency department. In this case, treatment of life threats and rapid transport must take precedence. It is also untrue that all fractures should be splinted in the position found, because some will require repositioning to ensure adequate circulation. Therefore, Choice C is the best answer. *(Chapter IX: Section C)*

63. **C.** Although this patient has many possible life threats, the airway must take precedence. Therefore, you must first perform *a jaw thrust and provide manual, in-line stabilization of the neck* because the suspicion of trauma is high. *(Chapter IX)*

64. **D.** Although lacerations are usually thought of as the result of contact with a sharp object or a penetrating injury, they are also a likely result of blunt trauma. This occurs when the force exerted is stronger than the skin it impacts. This is especially true of skin stretched over bony areas with little adipose tissue to help absorb the forces of impact, such as the forehead. Therefore, Choice D is the best answer. *(Chapter IX: Section A.3)*

65. **D.** It is important to treat internal bleeding quickly, so the EMT-Basic should be alert to patients who are at a great risk for this condition. The mechanism of injury will be one of the earliest indications of internal bleeding. You may also assume that internal bleeding is a factor if you find a patient who is in shock without obvious external hemorrhage or injury. Low systolic blood pressures may be associated with these patients as well, but can also be a normal, nonpathologic finding in many patients. Therefore, the best answer is Choice D. *(Chapter IX, Section A.4)*

66. **B.** The rapid trauma assessment is always performed in a *head-to-toe* fashion. Obvious threats to airway, breathing, or circulation should already have been treated in the initial assessment, and other injuries should be treated as they are encountered. In a focused exam, the EMT-Basic may examine only the body part or body system from which the patient's chief complaint seems to originate. *(Chapter VII)*

67. **C.** Removing most helmets is difficult to accomplish without manipulating the cervical spine. For this reason, it is often better to immobilize the patient with the helmet in place, being careful to pad under the shoulders to ensure the helmet does not cause flexion of the neck on the long spine board. However, helmets should be removed if *they interfere with your ability to manage the airway or the patient's breathing*. Removing the helmet before the patient requires intervention allows rapid response if the patient's condition deteriorates. *(Chapter IX: Section D.4)*

68. **C.** Consideration of the *mechanism of injury* determines the EMT-Basic's index of suspicion when assessing for various injuries. For example, a patient who is struck in the arm by a batted baseball would most likely benefit from a focused exam to the affected arm, searching for contusions, deformities, or tenderness. However, a patient who is struck in the arm by a large vehicle traveling 30 mph and is then thrown to the pavement warrants a much more thorough rapid trauma assessment. *(Chapter VII: Section A.3)*

69. **C.** While the injury is notable and will benefit from the application of a specific splint, this patient's mechanism of injury and level of consciousness dictate that only life threats be addressed prior to transporting the patient. Therefore, the EMT-Basic should concentrate her efforts on correction of life threats and rapid transport. The leg and other non-life-threatening injuries may be treated en route to the hospital if time and manpower allow. Therefore, Choice C is the best answer. *(Chapter VII: Section A.3)*

70. **D.** When arriving at the scene, it is important for the EMT-Basic to understand the mechanism of injury before beginning the search for injuries. Witness accounts, skid marks, location and severity of damage including external and internal damage, and information regarding safety devices in use can all add to your understanding of the type and amount of force applied to the patient's body. Therefore, Choice D is the best answer. *(Chapter VII: Section A.3)*

71. **D.** This child has classic symptoms of epiglottitis, an infection that causes swelling of the epiglottis and painful speech or swallowing. Any stimulation of this patient can cause a worsening of the swelling and may result in total airway obstruction. For this reason, the best course of treatment would be to *allow the patient to sit in a comfortable position and transport him with as little stimulation as possible.* *(Chapter X)*

72. **C.** Although small children are more prone to airway obstructions, they are commonly an accidental occurrence, even in children who receive the best care and oversight. Therefore, *foreign airway obstructions* are not considered a potential sign of child abuse. *(Chapter X: Section C.1)*

73. **A.** Respiratory failure is defined as the inability of the respiratory system to sustain life. Altered mental status is one of the earliest and most reliable signs of this progression. In infants, this can be most easily seen in the *loss of muscle tone*. Respiratory rates up to 60 per minute may be normal for some infants. Inconsolable crying and extended capillary refill times may indicate the presence of illness, but are not associated with respiratory problems. *(Chapter X: Section C.2)*

74. **C.** *Asthma* commonly affects adolescent patients and is the most common reason for a patient of this age being prescribed an inhaler. *(Chapter VIII: Section B.1)*

75. **B.** *Capillary refill* has been shown to be an inaccurate and unreliable predictor of perfusion in adults. In children, however, it is considered more useful, and in cases where a blood pressure cannot be accurately obtained, is often considered the measure of choice, along with assessment of other indicators such as level of consciousness, fontanelles, and others. *(Chapter X: Section B)*

76. **B.** If undamaged, *the patient's own car seat* can serve as an effective immobilization device and minimizes manipulation of the spine that may result from attempting other immobilization methods.

However, the EMT-Basic should be careful to securely pad voids to ensure that the patient's head, neck, and torso are secure. *(Chapter IX: Section D.4)*

77. **C.** In this age group, children's heads are proportionally larger than the heads of adults. This accounts for a significant amount of their weight. Therefore, in many falls the *head* often becomes the leading body part. *(Chapter XII: Section B.2)*

78. **C.** Children of this age who are unable to tolerate a mask are even less likely to tolerate a nasal cannula. In these cases, delivering oxygen *via the blow-by method* may be the best course of action to avoid further irritation to the patient. *(Chapter X: Section C.2)*

79. **D.** While this patient's injuries are certainly suspicious, the EMT-Basic must be careful not to arouse suspicion, judge the stepfather prematurely, or create a confrontation that may lead to violence. The best course of action in this situation is to transport the patient to the ER for treatment and evaluation of all injuries. Be sure to communicate your concerns to the ER staff. Therefore, Choice D is the best answer. *(Chapter VIII: Section H.2)*

80. **B.** Although all of these choices can be useful sources of information during an emergency, *the parents or primary caregivers* of a special needs child will know what is abnormal for the child. They have likely spent countless hours monitoring and caring for the child as well as troubleshooting any home medical equipment the child may rely on. The EMT-Basic should not overlook the opinions or assessments of these people. *(Chapter X: Section D)*

81. **B.** Documenting the call and returning to your station promptly are both of great importance, but the EMT-Basic should place the highest priority on *preparing the unit for the next call*. This ensures that the unit and crew are ready for their next assignment. *(Chapter XI: Section A)*

82. **A.** Although EMT-Basics may be trained in basic extrication techniques, they are only required to provide *initial treatment and lifesaving care*, if necessary. On most extrication scenes, it is important for the EMT-Basic to stay out of the extrication team's way. In addition to preventing overlap and confusion, this allows the EMT-Basic to focus solely on the patient's medical needs. When not needed to provide patient care, the EMT-Basic should stay well clear of the scene. *(Chapter XI)*

83. **C.** Correct span of control states that a single person can effectively and efficiently manage no more than *3–5* other responders on an emergency scene. *(Chapter XI)*

84. **C.** While documenting all of the patient's complaints is clearly important, the EMT-Basic should also remember that the absence of a suspected or expected symptom may be just as significant. Therefore, the EMT-Basic should be careful to document all findings whether the symptoms are present or not. *(Chapter VII: Section C)*

85. **B.** The straight stretch of highway may seem like the best choice, but the curves on either end present a safety risk. Similarly, the freshly cut grass poses a hazard as it may create a visibility problem for the helicopter's pilot. Lastly, livestock cannot be trusted to remain still when the aircraft approaches. Therefore, *a school playground that has been cleared of children* may offer the best landing zone. *(Chapter XI: Section A.2)*

86. **C.** Although the other choices may sometimes be contributing factors, most collisions involving EMS units responding to emergency calls happen during daytime hours in clear weather with light traffic. However, data shows that *intersections* are the most frequent locations for collisions to occur. *(Chapter XI: Section A.1)*

87. **C.** Although each piece of equipment mentioned may be helpful for different patients, the equipment listed in Choice C is the most complete list of equipment needed to treat the most immediate life threats. Bringing this equipment to the patient's side initially minimizes the risk of having to delay care while you or your partner retrieves something from the unit. *(Chapter VII: Chapter XI)*

88. **B.** On multiple-casualty scenes, the EMT-Basic must resist the urge to dive headlong into treating patients. The goal of triage is to identify the number and severity of injuries. Therefore, performing extra interventions in the triage phase is unwise. However, the EMT-Basic should make every effort to *open each patient's airway manually and/or control any bleeding that may be present*, as these possibly lifesaving interventions take little time. *(Chapter XI: Section C.3)*

89. **D.** If the presence of hazardous materials is known or suspected, the EMT-Basic must take care to identify hazards from as great a distance as possible. Being close enough to the incident to speak to the driver, access the cab, or treat the patient would all indicate that the EMT-Basic is in danger. Ideally, the EMT-Basic should approach from the uphill, upwind side and *identify the threat through binoculars* by looking for placards, container shapes, and other visual clues. *(Chapter XI: Section C.1)*

90. **B.** If the operator attempts to transmit while the channel is already in use, he may not be able to transmit at all or his message may be garbled and unintelligible. Therefore, the first step is to *ensure that the channel is clear by listening for several seconds*. Speaking loudly into the microphone will often decrease the clarity of the transmission, and emergency tones are usually transmitted only by the dispatch center. *(Chapter VII: Section E.1)*

91. **C.** Although you may be tempted to keep the ambulance as cool as possible on a hot summer day, it is important to keep trauma patients warm. Trauma patients are especially susceptible to shock, which causes patients to lose some of their ability to maintain a stable body temperature. Therefore, the ambulance should be kept *warmer than room temperature* to maintain the trauma patient's core temperature. *(Chapter XI: Section A.1)*

92. **C.** While it is acceptable and good practice for both responding units to take the same route to an emergency, care must be taken not to confuse other drivers. *Separating vehicles with at least 500 feet* should allow both units to arrive at the scene safely and without incident. *(Chapter XI: Section A.1)*

93. **D.** The purpose of the radio patient report is to alert the emergency department of an incoming patient. This gives them time to prepare space, staff, and equipment to treat the patient promptly. Except in rare cases, such as a patient who has just left the emergency department, it is not necessary to transmit *the patient's name* and may be considered a breach of patient confidentiality. *(Chapter VII: Section E.1; Chapter XI: Section A.1)*

94. **C.** As in the cases of a patient with an upper extremity injury or a patient who requests transport for a behavioral emergency, there are several categories of patients who *may be allowed to walk to the ambulance*. The EMT-Basic should never to allow patients with a lower extremity or spinal injury or those who may have or may develop a decreased level of consciousness to walk to the ambulance. *(Chapter XI: Section A.1)*

95. **D.** When responding to an emergency, it is imperative to ensure that *all emergency lights are flashing or illuminated and the siren is sounded* to alert other drivers of your presence. Therefore, states require that all devices present must be in operation. While exceptions are usually made for police vehicles that may need to approach a scene without alerting a suspect of their arrival, it is unusual to use the ambulance for such functions. *(Chapter XI: Section A.1)*

96. **A.** The tip of the endotracheal tube must be advanced until the tip is slightly *superior to the carina*. This minimizes the risk of dislodgement while still preventing hypoventilation that may be caused by unintentional intubation of the mainstem bronchi. *(Chapter XII: Section A.1)*

97. **B.** The EMT-Basic should *auscultate for proper placement* immediately after placing the tube and inflating the cuff. This is important because improper tube placement could create serious complications for the patient. *(Chapter XII: Section A.1)*

98. **C.** According to the assessment, this patient seems to be breathing well on his own. However, the patient displays a severely decreased level of consciousness and his snoring indicates an inability to maintain an airway. Therefore, even though the patient may be oxygenating and ventilating well enough to breathe on his own, *airway protection* is indicated. *(Chapter XII)*

99. **A.** The glottic opening is the entrance to the trachea through which the endotracheal tube should be passed. The arytenoids cartilages are located on the posterior border of the glottic opening. The vallecula is the space anterior to the epiglottis into which the curved blade is placed. All of these structures can be visualized in most patients. However, the *alveoli* are the terminal units of the smaller airways, located deep in the lungs, where gas exchange takes place. These are not visible while performing endotracheal intubation. *(Chapter XII: Section A.1)*

100. **D.** Although changes in skin color, heart rate, and oxygen saturation are easy parameters to monitor, it may take up to 2 minutes after dislodgement occurs for any of these signs to present. A provider who closely and vigilantly assesses the rise and fall of the chest will quickly spot the problem on the first assisted breath after the tube is dislodged. Therefore, Choice D is the best answer. *(Chapter VI: Chapter XII)*

Appendix: Resources for EMT Candidates

Many resources are available to EMT candidates who are interested in learning more about training programs and opportunities for employment. The following appendix provides a list of the EMS services available in each state and includes contact information for professional EMS organizations and publications.

State Agencies

Each state has specific guidelines for training and certification in emergency medicine. Many states offer training programs that you can access to start your journey on the road to becoming an EMT-Basic. You will need to contact these agencies for more information on training and testing facilities in your area.

Each state has an emergency medical services division, usually within the Department of Health, the Department of Public Safety, or the Department of Homeland Security. The following provides a list of addresses, phone numbers, and Web sites for the EMS offices in every state as well as the District of Columbia:

Alabama
Department of Public Health
Emergency Medical Services and Trauma
RSA Tower
201 Monroe Street, Suite 750
Montgomery, AL 36104
Phone: (334) 206-5383
Fax: (334) 206-5260
Web site: www.adph.org/ems/

Alaska
Department of Health and Social Services
Emergency Programs
410 Willoughby Avenue, Room 103
PO Box 110616
Juneau, AK 99811
Phone: (907) 465-2274
Fax: (907) 465-1733
Web site: www.hss.state.ak.us/dph/ipems/

Arizona
Department of Health Services
Bureau of Emergency Medical Services and
Trauma System
150 N. 18th Avenue, Suite 540
Phoenix, AZ 85007
Phone: (602) 364-3150
Fax: (602) 364-3568
Web site: www.azdhs.gov/bems/index.htm

Arkansas
Department of Health
Emergency Medical Services
5800 W. 10th Street, Suite 800
Little Rock, AR 72204
Phone: (501) 661-2262
Fax: (501) 280-4901
Web site: www.healthy.arkansas.gov

California
Emergency Medical Services Authority
1930 9th Street
Sacramento, CA 95811
Phone: (916) 322-4336
Web site: www.emsa.ca.gov

Colorado
Department of Public Health and Environment
Emergency Medical and Trauma Services
4300 Cherry Creek Drive S.
Denver, CO 80246
Phone: (303) 692-2980
Fax: (303) 691-7720
Web site: www.cdphe.state.co.us/em/index.html

Connecticut
Department of Health
Office of Emergency Medical Services
410 Capitol Avenue
PO Box 340308
Hartford, CT 06134
Phone: (860) 509-7975
Fax: (860) 509-7987
Web site: www.ct.gov/dph/

Delaware
Division of Public Health
Emergency Medical Services
Jesse Cooper Building
417 Federal Street
Dover, DE 19901
Phone: (302) 223-1350
Fax: (302) 223-1330
Web site: www.dhss.delaware.gov/dph/ems/
ems.html

District of Columbia
Fire and Emergency Medical Services
1923 Vermont Avenue, NW, Suite 102
Washington, DC 20001
Phone: (202) 673-3331
Fax: (202) 673-3188
Web site: fems.dc.gov

Florida
Department of Health
Bureau of Emergency Medical Services
4052 Bald Cypress Way, Bin #C18
Tallahassee, FL 32311
Phone: (850) 245-4440
Fax: (850) 488-9408
Web site: www.doh.state.fl.us/demo/ems/
index.html

Georgia
Division of Public Health
Emergency Medical Services
2600 Skyland Drive, Lower Level
Atlanta, GA 30319
Phone: (404) 679-0547
Fax: (404) 679-0526
Web site: ems.ga.gov

Hawaii
Department of Health
Emergency Medical Services and Injury
Prevention System
Trotter Building, Basement Level
3675 Kilauea Avenue
Honolulu, HI 96816
Phone: (808) 733-9210
Fax: (808) 733-9216
Web site: hawaii.gov/health/family-child-health/
ems/index.html

Idaho
Department of Health and Welfare
Emergency Medical Services
PO Box 83720
Boise, ID 83720
Toll free: (877) 554-3367
Fax: (208) 334-4015
Web site: www.healthandwelfare.idaho.gov

Illinois
Department of Public Health
Emergency Medical Systems and Highway
Safety
535 W. Jefferson Street
Springfield, IL 62761
Phone: (217) 782-4977
Fax: (217) 782-3987
Web site: www.idph.state.il.us/ems/index.htm

Indiana
Department of Homeland Security
Emergency Medical Services Commission
302 W. Washington Street, Room E239
Indianapolis, IN 46204
Phone: (317) 233-0208
Web site: www.in.gov/dhs

Iowa
Department of Health
Bureau of Emergency Medical Services
Lucas State Office Building
321 E. 12th Street
Des Moines, IA 50319
Toll free: (800) 728-3367
Web site: www.idph.state.ia.us/ems/

Kansas
Board of Emergency Medical Services
Landon State Office Building
900 SW Jackson Street, Suite 1031
Topeka, KS 66612
Phone: (785) 296-7296
Fax: (785) 296-6212
Web site: www.ksbems.org/ems/

Kentucky
Board of Emergency Medical Services
300 N. Main Street
Versailles, KY 40383
Phone: (859) 256-3565
Toll free: (866) 97KBEMS
Fax: (859) 256-3128
Web site: kbems.kctcs.edu

Louisiana
Department of Health and Hospitals
Emergency Medical Services
11224 Boardwalk Drive, Suite A-1
Baton Rouge, LA 70816
Phone: (225) 275-1764
Web site: www.dhh.louisiana.gov/
offices/?ID=220

Maine
Department of Public Safety
Emergency Medical Services
45 Commerce Drive, Suite 1
152 State House Station
Augusta, ME 04333
Phone: (207) 626-3860
Fax: (207) 287-6251
Web site: www.maine.gov/dps/ems

Maryland
Institute for Emergency Medical Services
Systems
653 W. Pratt Street
Baltimore, MD 21201
Toll free: (800) 762-7157
Fax: (410) 706-0853
Web site: miemss.org/home

Massachusetts
Department of Health and Human Services
Office of Emergency Medical Services
99 Chauncy Street, 11th Floor
Boston, MA 02111
Phone: (617) 753-7300
Fax: (617) 752-7320
Web site: www.mass.gov/dph/oems/

Michigan
Department of Community Health
Emergency Medical Services
Capitol View Building
201 Townsend Street
Lansing, MI 48913
Phone: (517) 373-3740
Web site: www.michigan.gov/mdch/

Minnesota
Emergency Medical Services Regulatory Board
2829 University Avenue, SE, Suite 310
Minneapolis, MN 55414
Phone: (651) 201-2800
Toll free: (800) 747-2011
Fax: (651) 201-2812
Web site: www.emsrb.state.mn.us

Mississippi
Department of Health
Emergency Medical Services/Trauma
PO Box 1700
Jackson, MS 39215
Phone: (601) 576-7400
Web site: www.msdh.state.ms.us/index.htm

Missouri

Department of Health and Senior Services
Emergency Medical Services
PO Box 570
Jefferson City, MO 65102
Phone: (573) 751-6356
Fax: (573) 751-6348
Web site: www.dhss.mo.gov/ems/

Montana

Department of Health and Human Services
Emergency Medical Services and Trauma
PO Box 202951
Helena, MT 59620
Phone: (406) 444-3895
Fax: (406) 444-1814
Web site: www.dphhs.mt.gov/ems/

Nebraska

Department of Health and Human Services
Emergency Medical Services
PO Box 95026
Lincoln, NE 68509
Phone: (402) 471-3578
Web site: www.hhs.state.ne.us/ems/emsindex.htm

Nevada

State Health Division
Emergency Medical Systems
4150 Technology Way, Suite 101
Carson City, NV 89706
Phone: (775) 687-7590
Fax: (775) 687-7595
Web site: health.nv.gov/EMS_EmergencyMedical.htm

New Hampshire

Department of Safety
Bureau of Emergency Medical Services
33 Hazen Drive
Concord, NH 03305
Phone: (603) 223-4200
Fax: (603) 271-4567
Web site: www.nh.gov/safety/divisions/fstems/ems/index.html

New Jersey

Department of Health and Senior Services
Office of Emergency Medical Services
PO Box 360
Trenton, NJ 08625
Phone: (609) 633-7777
Fax: (609) 633-7954
Web site: www.nj.gov/health/ems/index.shtml

New Mexico

Department of Health
Emergency Medical Systems
1301 Siler Road, Building F
Santa Fe, NM 87507
Phone: (505) 476-8200
Fax: (505) 471-2122
Web site: www.nmems.org/index.shtml

New York

Department of Health
Bureau of Emergency Medical Services
Hedley Park Place
433 River Street, Suite 303
Troy, NY
Phone: (518) 402-0996
Fax: (518) 402-0985
Web site: www.health.state.ny.us/nysdoh/ems/main.htm

North Carolina

Division of Health Service Regulation
Office of Emergency Medical Services
2707 Mail Service Center
Raleigh, NC 27699
Phone: (919) 855-3935
Fax: (919) 733-7021
Web site: www.ncems.org

North Dakota

Department of Health
Division of Emergency Medical Services and Trauma
600 E. Boulevard Avenue, Dept. 301
Bismarck, ND 58505
Phone: (701) 328-2388
Fax: (701) 328-1702
Web site: www.ndhealth.gov/EMS/

Ohio
PO Box 182073
1970 W. Broad Street
Columbus, OH 43218
Phone: (614) 466-9447
Fax: (614) 466-9461
Web site: ems.ohio.gov

Oklahoma
Department of Health
Emergency Medical Services Division
1000 NE 10th, Room 1104
Oklahoma City, OK 73117
Phone: (405) 271-4027
Web site: www.ok.gov/health/Protective_Health/
Emergency_Medical_Services/

Oregon
Department of Health
Emergency Medical Services and Trauma
Systems
800 NE Oregon Street, Suite 465
Portland, OR 97232
Phone: (971) 673-0520
Fax: (971) 673-0555
Web site: oregon.gov/DHS/ph/ems/

Pennsylvania
Department of Health
Bureau of Emergency Medical Services
625 Forster Street, Room 606
Harrisburg, PA 17120
Phone: (717) 787-8740
Fax: (717) 772-0910
Web site: www.portal.state.pa.us/portal/server.pt/
community/emergency_medical_services/14138

Rhode Island
Department of Health
Office of Health Professionals Regulation
Division of Emergency Medical Services
3 Capitol Hill, Room 105
Providence, RI 02908
Phone: (401) 222-2401
Fax: (401) 222-3352
Web site: www.health.ri.gov/hsr/professions/
ems/index.php

South Carolina
Department of Health and Environmental
Control
Division of Emergency Medical Services and
Trauma
2600 Bull Street
Columbia, SC 29201
Phone: (803) 545-4204
Fax: (803) 545-4989
Web site: www.scdhec.gov/health/ems/

South Dakota
Department of Public Safety
Emergency Medical Services
118 W. Capitol Avenue
Pierre, SD 57501
Phone: (605) 773-4031
Fax: (605) 773-6631
Web site: dps.sd.gov/emergency_services/
emergency_medical_services/

Tennessee
Department of Health
Emergency Medical Services
Heritage Place, Metro Center
227 French Landing, Suite 303
Nashville, TN 37243
Phone: (615) 741-2584
Fax: (615) 741-4217
Web site: health.state.tn.us/ems/

Texas
Department of Health
Emergency Medical Services and Trauma
Systems
PO Box 149347
Austin, TX 78714
Phone: (512) 834-6700
Fax: (512) 834-6714
Web site: www.dshs.state.tx.us/
emstraumasystems/

Utah

Department of Health
Bureau of Emergency Medical Services
PO Box 142004
Salt Lake City, UT 84114
Phone: (801) 273-6666
Toll free: (800) 284-1131
Fax: (801) 273-4149
Web site: health.utah.gov/ems/

Vermont

Department of Health
Office of Emergency Medical Services and Injury
Prevention
108 Cherry Street
Burlington, VT 05402
Phone: (802) 863-7310
Fax: (802) 865-7577
Web site: healthvermont.gov/hc/ems/ems_index.
aspx

Virginia

Department of Health
Office of Emergency Medical Services
1041 Technology Park Drive
Glen Allen, VA 23059
Phone: (804) 888-7507
Fax: (804) 371-3108
Web site: www.vdh.state.va.us/oems/

West Virginia

Department of Health and Human Resources
Trauma and Emergency Medical System
350 Capitol Street, Room 425
Charleston, WV 25301
Phone: (304) 558-3956
Fax: (304) 558-3856
Web site: www.wvoems.org/

Washington

Department of Health
Office of Emergency Medical Services and
Trauma Systems
PO Box 47853
Olympia, WA 98504
Phone: (360) 236-2800
Fax: (360) 236-2830
Web site: www.doh.wa.gov/hsqa/emstrauma/

Wisconsin

Department of Health Services
Emergency Medical Services
PO Box 2659
Madison, WI 53701
Phone: (608) 261-6870
Web site: www.dhs.wisconsin.gov/ems/

Wyoming

Department of Health
Emergency Medical Services
Hathaway Building, 4th Floor
Cheyenne, WY 82002
Phone: (307) 777-7955
Fax: (307) 777-5639
Web site: wdh.state.wy.us/sho/ems/index.html

Professional EMS Organizations and Publications

There are many professional EMS organizations and publications that represent EMS personnel and work for the promotion of educational standards. These organizations also provide exclusive member services such as job listings, training scholarships, and the opportunity to connect with other EMS providers from across the country. Take the time to investigate each organization and decide which ones would best suit your needs.

The following provides a list of contact information for several notable EMS organizations and publications:

National Association of Emergency Medical Technicians
PO Box 1400
Clinton, MS 39060
Phone: (601) 924-7744
Toll free: (800) 34-NAEMT
Fax: (601) 924-7325
Web site: www.naemt.org

National Association of EMS Educators
250 Mount Lebanon Boulevard, Suite 209
Pittsburgh, PA 15234
Phone: (412) 343-4775
Fax: (412) 343-4770
Web site: www.naemse.org

National Association of EMS Physicians
PO Box 19570
Lenexa, KS 66285
Phone: (913) 895-4611
Toll free: (800) 228-3677
Fax: (913) 895-4652
Web site: www.naemsp.org

National Registry of Emergency Medical Technicians
Rocco V. Morando Building
6610 Busch Boulevard
PO Box 29233
Columbus, OH 43229
Phone: (614) 888-4484
Fax: (614) 888-8920
Web site: www.nremt.org

Annals of Emergency Medicine
American College of Emergency Physicians
1125 Executive Circle
Irving, TX 75038
Phone: (972) 550-0911
Toll free: (800) 798-1822
Fax: (972) 580-2816
Web site: www.annemergmed.com

EMS Magazine
7626 Densmore Avenue
Van Nuys, CA 91406
Toll free: (800) 547-7377
Fax: (818) 786-9246
Web site: www.emsresponder.com

Journal of Emergency Medical Services (JEMS)
525 B Street, Suite 1800
San Diego, CA 92101
Toll free: (800) 266-5367
Fax: (619) 699-6396
Web site: www.jems.com